QUALITY IN AMERICA

How To Implement A Competitive Quality Program

QUALITY IN AMERICA

How To Implement A Competitive Quality Program

V. DANIEL HUNT

President
Technology Research Corporation

BUSINESS ONE IRWIN
Homewood, Illinois 60430

© V. Daniel Hunt, Technology Research Corporation, 1992

The views, opinions and conclusions in this book are those of the author and do not represent those of the United States Government.

Public domain information and those documents abstracted or used in full, edited or otherwise used are noted in the acknowledgements or on specific pages or illustrations.

This publication is designed to provide accurate and authoritative information in regard to the subject matter covered. It is sold with the understanding that neither the author nor the publisher is engaged in rendering legal, accounting, or other professional service. If legal advice or other expert assistance is required, the services of a competent professional person should be sought.

From a Declaration of Principles jointly adopted by a Committee of the American Bar Association and a Committee of Publishers.

Sponsoring editor: Jeffrey A. Krames
Project editor: Jean Roberts
Production manager: Irene H. Sotiroff
Designer: Larry J. Cope
Jacket designer: Tim Kaage
Compositor: Carlisle Communications, Ltd.
Typeface: 11/13 Palatino
Printer: R. R. Donnelley & Sons Company

Library of Congress Cataloging-in-Publication Data

Hunt, V. Daniel.
    Quality in America : how to implement a competitive quality
program / V. Daniel Hunt.
        p.   cm.
    Includes bibliographical references.
    ISBN 1-55623-536-4
    1. Total quality management—United States.   2. Quality control—
United States.   I. Title.
    HD62.15.H86   1992
    658.5′62′0973—dc20   91–25971

Printed in the United States of America
1 2 3 4 5 6 7 8 9 0 DOC 8 7 6 5 4 3 2 1

To my wife, Janet Claire Hunt

Preface

Producing quality goods and services is crucial not only to the continued economic growth of the United States, but also to our national security and the well-being and the standard of living of each American family. America has been recognized for its leadership in producing quality products. However, in recent years, the position of America as quality leader has been challenged by foreign competition in domestic and overseas markets.

Reasserting our leadership position will require a firm commitment to quality and the "Quality First"[1] principle of continuous quality improvement. America can, and must, excel in this area, setting new standards for world-class quality and competing vigorously in international markets.

Improving quality takes time and resources and can only be achieved through a combination of factors. It takes a long-term commitment by top management that involves working with suppliers to improve performance; educating, training, and motivating workers; developing accurate and responsive management systems; and establishing targets for quality improvement.

Quality improvement principles apply to small companies as well as large corporations, to service industries as well as manufacturing, and to the public sector as well as private enterprise. Improving the quality of goods and services goes hand in hand with improving productivity and lowering costs. It is also essential to enhancing worker fulfillment and customer satisfaction.

Private sector organizations and government institutions across the country are joining forces to promote a national commitment to "Quality First." Business executives are working again together to develop the skills and techniques needed to produce quality goods and services in America.

V. DANIEL HUNT
Fairfax Station, Virginia

---

[1]"Quality First" is a trademark of Technology Research Corporation.

Acknowledgements

Quality in America has been developed based on information from a wide variety of authorities who are specialists in their respective fields.

The following publications were used as the basic resources for this book. Portions of these publications may have been used in the book. Those definitions or artwork that have been used are reproduced with the permission to reprint of the respective publisher.

AT&T Quality Improvement Process Guidebook, AT&T, Baskin Ridge, New Jersey, 1988.

Deming Management at Work, Mary Walton, G.P. Putnam, New York, 1990.

The Deming Route to Quality and Productivity, William W. Scherkenbach, CEE Press, Washington, D.C., 1988.

Diffusion of Innovations, Everett M. Rogers, Free Press, New York, 1983.

Excellence in Government: Total Quality Mangement in the 1990s, David K. Carr, and Ian D. Littman, Coopers and Lybrand, Washington, D.C., 1990.

Federal Total Quality Management Handbook, U.S. Government Printing Office, Washington, D.C., 1990.

A Guide to Benchmarking in Xerox, NTIS Publication PB91-780106, Washington, D.C., 1990.

State-of-the-art report, *A Guide for Implementing Total Quality Management*, Reliability Analysis Center, Rome, New York, Report SOAR-7, 1990.

In Search of Excellence, Thomas J. Peters and Robert H. Waterman, Jr., Harper and Row, 1982.

An Introduction to the Continuous Improvement Process, Principles and Practices, Brian E. Mansir and Nicholas R. Schacht, Logistics Management Institute, Bethesda, MD, August, 1989.

Juran on Planning for Quality, J.M. Juran, The Free Press, New York, 1988.

Juran's Quality Control Handbook, J.M. Juran, Editor in Chief and Frank M. Gryna, Associate Editor, McGraw-Hill, New York, 1988, 4th Edition.

Made in America: Regaining the Productive Edge, Michael L. Dertouzos, Richard K. Lester, Robert M. Solow, The MIT Commission on Industrial Productivity, The MIT Press, 1989.

Out of the Crisis, W. Edwards Deming, MIT Center for Advanced Engineering Study, Boston, MA, 1986.

A Passion for Excellence, Tom Peters and Nancy Austin, Random House, New York, 1985.

Quality is Free, Philip B. Crosby, McGraw-Hill, New York, 1979.

Quality and Productivity Self-Assessment Guide for Defense Organizations, Department of Defense, Washington, D.C., 1990.

Quality Without Tears, Philip B. Crosby, New American Library, New York, 1985.

Total Quality Management Guide, Volumes 1 and 2, Office of the Deputy Assistant Secretary of Defense for Total Quality Management, DoD 5000.51-G, February 15, 1990. Washington, D.C.

USMG Partnership: The Way We Work, Xerox, USMG Printing Office, Rochester, New York, 1988.

This book was conceived during a series of discussions with Mr. G. Raymond Fox of Andersen Consulting and the author. I appreciate Ray's interest in seeing this book come to fruition.

The preparation of a book of this type is dependent upon an excellent staff, and I have been fortunate in this regard. Special thanks to Donald Keehan, Ronald Fraser, Charles Wolfgang Zschock, and Chuck Doe, for research assistance of the material for this book. I appreciate the careful and conscientious editing of Lori Ackerman. The technical graphic art was prepared by Karl J. Samuels.

I appreciate the careful and accurate preparation of the manuscript by Anne Pond.

Many individuals provided material, interview comments, and their insights regarding how to improve quality in America. I appreciate their input and help in defining this book. Special recognition is noted for: Peter Angiola, TQM Manager, Office of the Under Secretary of Defense for Acquisition, Total Quality Management; Dr. Laurie A. Broedling, Deputy Under Secretary of Defense for Total Quality Management; Richard Bueton, Senior Vice President and Director of Quality, Motorola Inc.; David K. Carr, Partner, Coopers & Lybrand; Jeffrey M. Clark, Cadillac Motor Car Division; James C. Cline, Corporate Quality Manager, Globe Metallurgical Inc.; Karen A. Collard, Xerox Corporation; John F. Cooney, Manager, National Quality Award Office, Xerox Business Products and Systems; Dr. Robert Costello, Hudson Institute; Dr. Mary A. Hartz, Total Quality Management Section Leader, IIT Research Institute; Robert H. Hayes, Professor of Management of Technology, Harvard Business School; Newt Hardie, Vice President, Quality, Milliken & Company; Sandi

Janssen, International Business Machines Corporation; Bob King, GOAL;
Ian D. Littman, Director, Total Quality Management, Coopers & Lybrand;
Paul A. Noakes, Vice President and Director, External Quality Programs,
Motorola, Inc.; William Smith, Vice President and Senior Quality
Assurance Manager, Communications Sector, Motorola Inc.; Mike Spiess,
Executive Vice President, Wallace Co., Inc; Frank Voehl, Vice President of
QualTec; Chuck Vogel, Manager-Total Quality, Westinghouse Electric
Corporation, Commercial Nuclear Fuel Division; John R. West, Manager,
Corporate Quality Improvement, Federal Express.

Table of Contents

Chapter One

Quality in America Today

"The improvement of quality in products and the improvement of quality in service—these are national priorities as never before."

George Bush

QUALITY IS GOOD BUSINESS

Quality pays. Quality gets results. Quality sells. Quality increases profit. The first question CEOs ask when they evaluate whether they need to improve their quality program is, "What's in it for the company?"

All too often, companies ask this question in times of crisis. Their markets are changing, global competitors have sneaked up on them, and then they are forced to change the way they do business to survive.

Listen to why American quality leaders improved their quality, and what they got in return.

William Smith, Vice President and Senior Quality Assurance Manager at Motorola, Inc., tells us: "We put Motorola's quality process in place to satisfy customers. The real payoff from our quality improvement program is that it has certainly been instrumental in helping us to increase market share, to increase sales, to increase profitability. The corporate goal that we stated was to improve quality 10 times by 1989, and 100 times by 1991. Our sales per employee in 1985 was $60,500; by 1990 it has increased to $113,200."

Globe Metallurgical, Inc., also demonstrates that any firm, large or small, can develop an excellent quality program, and one that pays off. James C. Cline, Corporate Quality Manager for Globe Metallurgical Inc., gives this account of his company's renewed commitment to quality begun in 1984. "That was our turning point from what we call the detection mode to the prevention mode. The benefits, we found, are both measurable and unmeasurable, and in many ways the unmeasurable ones are the most significant. We have been able to increase our market share tremendously. . . . Before 1984 we shipped virtually no products overseas, less than a truckload a year. Today one of our biggest customers is in Europe, and we also ship to Australia, Korea, and Taiwan.

"We have a much more stable work force because of employee satisfaction and have not laid off a single employee in seven years. Absenteeism has been virtually eliminated, and workers leaving Globe to go to work somewhere else are virtually unheard of. The climate in our company is no longer 'us and them.' It's not workers and management. It's just us."

Chuck Vogel, quality manager for Westinghouse, CNFD Division, reiterated that "total quality is people." You should not look at quality improvement as a marketing tool, but as a management tool. Lots of American companies are shortsighted. They concentrate too much on near-term profits and fail to see the long-term impact of quality improvement on their global markets. Westinghouse recognized the changing global market and made quality a priority in its business.

If you don't care where American industry and your firm are headed in the 1990s, if you think your quality performance can not be improved, or if you're still in a state of "global marketplace denial," this book won't help you.

On the other hand, if you are not so sure business as usual is the wave of the future, read on. This book can help you. Because the 1990s are shaping up as a change-filled period full of opportunities—and risks—this book is designed to help make sure you and your firm are well positioned not only to cope in the increasingly competitive global marketplace of the 1990s, but to prosper in it.

Unlike the overly optimistic quality rhetoric of the 1980s, this down-to-earth book seeks a middle ground. It recognizes that in the 1990s American business leaders must strike a balance between the quick-fix approach of the past and the fact that widespread ignorance concerning the real level of quality performance in American business is still found in many parts of the manufacturing and service sectors. Improved quality is not a cure-all for all American business ills, but it is an essential first step in the right direction.

A very few American companies are counted among the world-class leaders in quality improvement. But, thousands upon thousands of other companies have yet to take that all-important first step to ensure their products and services deliver to each customer a dependable high level of quality. Drawing in part on the lessons learned by the early quality leaders in America, this book is a no nonsense guide for the next wave of American firms—some large, some small—that must adopt quality management practices in the next 5 to 10 years if they are to survive.

QUALITY DRIVEN BY GLOBAL COMPETITION

Since World War II, the world has been "shrinking." Advances in telecommunications have linked all parts of the world electronically and, to a lesser extent, politically. Over the years a new economic infrastructure has also replaced the old one. As national companies serving primarily domestic markets expanded into the international marketplace, a "global web," as Robert Reich calls it, of economic interconnectedness formed and is today a dominant economic force shaping the American economic scene.

That the coming decade will see a further extension of these trends and become an economic turning point for America and the rest of the world is beyond question. During the 1980s, two

significant events—in addition to the coming of age of the global economy—have set the stage for the 1990s. First, under
growing pressure from foreign competition, American corporations rediscovered "quality." After decades of indifference to,
and neglect of, what was happening in Japan and elsewhere in
the world, the American business community began its turnaround in the mid-1980s when a few large corporations became
convinced that quality products and services were their ticket
to the future. By the late-1980s, talk about quality became the
"in" topic.

The end of the 40-year Cold War and the collapse of the So-
viet economy in 1990-1991 is the second fundamental sea
change that will make the coming decade unique. With the
"evil empire" preoccupied with its own internal economic tur-
moil, both America and Europe could redirect their energies
from military confrontation to worldwide commercial competition. A new Germany serving as the economic core of a unified
European Community will soon become the world's third regional economic super-force. In addition to the United States
and the Pacific Rim, including Japan, these three regions will
dominate the international economy of the 1990s.

American manufacturing and service companies cannot afford to remain passive in the coming years. The American
economy will either fully integrate itself into new and evolving
global markets, or large parts of it are likely to be left behind as
foreign competitors absorb greater and greater shares of the
only market that really matters anymore: the global market.
Economic isolationism means stagnation and slow economic
death. The time is ripe for virtually all American businesses to
adopt a new world view built on proven quality improvement
practices.

A better understanding of the nature of global competition,
and what it means for American companies, is found in the
work of Robert Reich of Harvard University. Reich is very
much interested in the changing independent national economies that dominated the world economic order prior to World
War II, and in the rise of the interconnected global economy.
The old American national economy was characterized by the
popular "Built by Americans for Americans" slogan often

heard in the 1950s. Now it is very difficult to tell what "Made in America" means. The new global economy is described by Reich, in his new book entitled *The Work of Nations*, in the following terms: "When an American buys a Pontiac Le Mans from General Motors, for example, he or she engages unwittingly in an international transaction. Of the $20,000 paid to GM, about $6,000 goes to South Korea for routine labor and assembly operations, $3,500 to Japan for advanced components (engines, transaxles, and electronics), $1,500 to West Germany for styling and design engineering, $800 to Taiwan, Singapore, and Japan for small components, $500 to Britain for advertising and marketing services, and about $100 to Ireland and Barbados for data processing. The rest—less than $8,000—goes to strategists in Detroit, lawyers and bankers in New York, lobbyists in Washington, insurance and healthcare workers all over the country, and General Motors shareholders.

"The proud new owner of the Pontiac is not aware of having bought so much from overseas, of course. General Motors did the trading, within its global web. This is typical. By the 1990s, most 'trade' no longer occurred in arm's-length transactions between buyers in one nation and sellers in another, but between people within the same web who are likely to deal repeatedly with each other across borders."

Reich paints an entirely new picture of how American companies go about building a car. The very same picture, however, is equally valid for thousands of other products and services. It is becoming more and more difficult for an American company to isolate itself from what is going on in other nations. Consequently, when the rest of the world, or important parts of it, shifts to a new method for organizing work, it is almost impossible for American firms to ignore this change.

Figure 1–1 captures the scope of this remarkable shift described by Reich. The message it delivers loud and clear is this: Because of these intricate global webs in which American companies are now full-fledged partners, they have little or no choice but to keep up with the other global competitors in the web if they want to remain competitive. Whether or not to adopt improved quality practices is no longer a real option for most American companies. The only option, really, is when to

FIGURE 1–1
Shift to Global Integration

Pre-World
War II

- Isolated national economies
- Companies within each national economy trade among themselves
- Focus on quantity

1945 — — — —

- Period of change from quantity to quality

1990 — — — —

- Global web of economic interconnectedness
- Multinational firms blur national boundaries
- Focus on quality

shift and whether your company will do it soon enough to remain competitive.

But still, the United States has been slow to accept and adapt to the realities of a highly competitive global marketplace, and slow to regard the industrial development of competing countries as a challenge to, as well as an opportunity for, our own economic growth. Consequences of this national failure to adapt are measured in terms of loss of market share, unnecessary plant closings, high unemployment, and noticeable deterioration in the quality of jobs available to American workers. Most observers of this condition have long since concluded that

FIGURE 1–2
Level of Quality Adoption in Japan and America

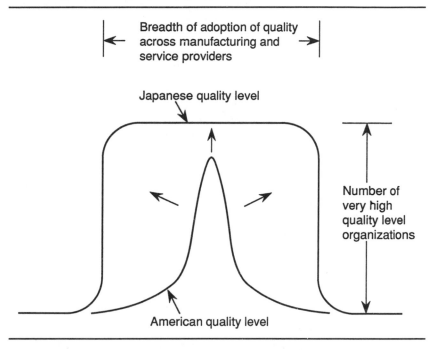

any successful challenge to these problems entails the need for the United States to acknowledge the erosion of the comparative advantage of many of its manufacturing and service industries in such important activities as quality, technology, innovation, investment, and productivity, and to take the needed corrective actions.

Figure 1–2 graphically shows that the number of companies in America that have aggressively adopted quality management practices lags far behind their global competitors, such as Japan. Japanese firms, on average, have also attained a higher level of quality in their products and services. As quality improvement spreads throughout America in the 1990s, the U.S. spike shown in Figure 1–2 should swell both outward and upward.

It is important that business executives fully appreciate that Washington cannot solve the global competition problems facing American firms in the years ahead. The role traditionally played by the federal government with regard to international trade is largely obsolete in the emerging global market economy. Congress can try to protect American firms from their competitors but, as this passage from a study prepared by the House Republican Research Committee Task Force for members of Congress will highlight, protection is not a workable answer in the 1990s. "For the U.S. to remain strong, to grow and to regain lost markets, we must recognize where we are weak and seek solutions to those weaknesses. It is important that we recognize a significant portion of our trade deficit is due to the ability of foreign competitors to deliver higher-quality products that are either novel, less costly to produce, promise better service, or some combination of the above. Our competitors, most notably the Japanese, are challenging us, not so much with better science and technology, but in the way they organize their work . . . in the way their firms and factories are organized and managed. The United States, in short, is being challenged through a commitment to quality.

"What makes quality different from other competitiveness solutions is its emphasis on actually improving our ability to compete. Most competitiveness solutions seek to relieve competitive pressures rather than working to strengthen the competitor. While streamlining regulations, ensuring foreign market access, providing market information, and other such efforts are laudable, they will all be for naught if 'Made in America' is viewed as a euphemism for costly, inferior products and services. No amount of playing field 'leveling' will obtain U.S. market share in fields that are on the technological cutting edge without a commitment to quality. That goes for computers, cars, machinery, chemicals or whatever."

Experts all have a slightly different view of the global business in the 1990s. The common thread, however, is strong. Nearly every American manufacturing and service sector will be increasingly vulnerable to imports in the foreseeable future. Automation isn't the answer, for it would only quicken the production of poor-quality products. Import barriers and protection are not the answer, either. Americans can no longer hide from foreign competition or survive by selling only to

Americans. The only way out is through the door marked "Quality."

HOW ARE WE DOING?

America's global competitors create and produce items of high quality because it pays! Continual improvement in quality leads to reduced costs because of less rework, fewer mistakes, fewer delays, and better use of time and materials. In America, 20 to 25 percent of production costs is spent in finding and correcting mistakes. Add the additional costs incurred in repairing or replacing faulty products in the field and the total cost of poor quality may approach 30 percent. In Japan it is about 3 percent. The cost of ignoring quality is enormous. American companies all too often achieve quality by setting acceptable quality levels and using "tailgate" inspection to measure compliance. With this passive-reactive approach, improving quality results in increased scrap and rework, and in increased costs. Our competitors do not do it that way. First, they do not subscribe to the notion of an acceptable quality level because it assumes that some defects are acceptable. Their goal is one of no defects, that is, through a process of continuous improvement. Second, they have adopted a proactive or preventive approach to quality. They consider quality to be an integral part of product and process design, not something that is achieved through management oversight or inspection. To achieve designed-in quality, global competitors use systematic product and process techniques based on statistical analyses to identify sources of process or material variation, to decide when it is economical to reduce these sources of variation, and to ensure the product is robust in light of remaining variability. They then closely monitor process performance.

World-class, quality-focused companies declare that quality is the concern and responsibility of every employee, "from the president to the janitor," and that quality concerns are pervasive from product inception through customer support. Top management is directly involved in quality, as contrasted with just supporting quality or committing the company to it. Managers in quality-focused companies accept responsibility for quality, direct and participate in quality education, establish quality goals, and take management action required to help realize these goals. Managers direct and participate in quality policy, self-assessments, direct allocation of resources for quality efforts, and spend substantial time with workers on the projects. Quality teams provide the principal mechanism for workers to meet frequently with their colleagues on improvement projects and for periodic and frequent meetings with management, so that management can find concrete ways to help.

While global competitors believe that quality is a design and process issue, they still recognize the need for inspection as part of an overall process control strategy. The responsibility for in-process inspection and analysis is primarily assigned to individual production workers, not to quality assurance personnel. There are quality assurance personnel in the competitors' companies, but their role generally is limited to participating in the concurrent design teams and carrying out quality planning and higher level analyses. The workers carry out the elementary statistical analyses to detect unacceptable process variability and in most cases are authorized to take corrective action when indicated by the analyses. Only if the worker can not solve the problem does it get referred to a higher level.

By placing so much quality emphasis on the individual worker, our competitors generate individual pride in workmanship and quality with a resulting major gain in employee motivation. They have also achieved a closed-loop operation in which variations in process quality are determined very early and corrected at the lowest level of the organization at which such a correction can be made.

Coopers and Lybrand have developed a set of "World-Class Metrics" for manufacturing companies, as shown in Table 1–1. In terms of quality, you can see the disparity between the quality performance of American companies and of our competitors.

Closing the Competitive Gaps: The International Report of the Manufacturing Futures Project, published by Boston University, states, "Each part of the world (Europe, Japan, and America) believes that it has an advantage over its competitors in a different dimension. The Europeans believe they are ahead in

TABLE 1–1
World-Class Metrics

Attribute	World-Class Standard	US Average
Setup time	System < 30 minutes	2-4 hrs
Quality	Cell < 1 minute	
	1500 PPM captured	3-5% captured
	300 PPM escapes	2-5% in warranty
	cost of quality 3-5%	15-25% cost of quality
Ratio of manufacturing space to total space	> 50%	25-35%
Work as a function of time	20%	1.75-5%
Material velocity	> 100 turns	2-4 turns
Material residence time	3 days	3 months
Flexibility	270 parts/machine tool	25 parts/machine tool
Distance	300 ft	> 1 mile
Uptime	95%	65-75%

Source: Ronald R. Barris, National Director of Industrial Automation, Coopers and Lybrand.

product performance, the Japanese in flexibility, and the Americans (to their surprise) in price." As these competitors approach parity on the fundamentals of quality in the 1990s, performance, price, and especially flexibility, will become more important elements of business strategies.

Global competitors have made significant changes in their strategic plans over the past decade. European and American manufacturers have improved their manufacturing capabilities in order to hold or attempt to regain a viable market share position depending on type of products. Their strategy often has been based on a return to the fundamentals of effective product and process development integration, with a special focus on quality improvement and organizational restructuring. In contrast, the Japanese, feeling confident that they produce the best quality products in the world, have emphasized flexibility through the use of automation (CAD—computer added design, robots, CIM—computer integrated manufacturing) and price reduction of their products.

Figure 1–3 shows the relative importance of the generic strat-

FIGURE 1–3
Importance of World-Class Competitive Strategies

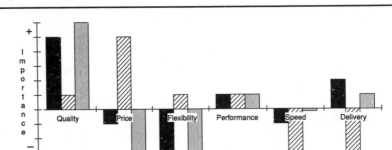

Source: Reproduced with permission of Manufacturing Roundtable, Boston University.

egies used in American, European, and Japanese companies. These generic strategic elements help distinguish the direction of international competitive strategies for the 1990s. The strategic elements are:

- Quality manufacturing—The ability to provide consistent high-quality products.
- Flexible manufacturing—The ability to make rapid design changes and/or introduce new products very quickly.
- Competitive pricing—The ability to compete worldwide on price.
- Product performance—The ability to design and produce high-performance products.
- Speed of product introduction—The ability to deliver products quickly.
- Reliable delivery—On-time delivery (as promised).

Figure 1–3 illustrates the differences between American, Japanese, and European manufacturing strategic priorities. Compared with Japan, the Americans and Europeans still place the least emphasis on quality; the Japanese are emphasizing price. Next most important for the Americans and Europeans is on-time delivery, but to the Japanese the critical strategic issue is flexible manufacturing. The Japanese emphasis on flexibility allows them to introduce new products and incorporate changes quickly.

Global competitive strategies in the typical European approach are to exploit a perceived lead in delivering quality products while avoiding head-on price competition. The Japanese strategy seeks to gain advantage by offering a wide variety of new products while redressing their price disadvantage. The American strategy focuses on improving quality, maintaining on-time delivery capability, and enhancing product performance.

Table 1–2 lists, in rank order, the importance of programs that companies in America, Japan, and Europe stress as their near-term priorities. The Americans and Europeans are focused on quality improvement programs such as statistical process control, zero defects, and supplier quality enhancement efforts. The Japanese appear to be aggressively advancing their lead in flexible production by their emphasis on computer-aided flexible systems (CAD, Computer Automated Manufacturing, CIM), and creating new production processes for new products.

NO QUICK FIX

What to do? The key to American competitiveness in the 1990s is to avoid emulating the German or Japanese companies, and to keep an honest set of American priorities firmly fixed in our corporate minds to guide our actions. We should not be drawn into playing another nation's game. We will be far better off if we follow an American-made blueprint to our quality future.

Perhaps the most daunting part of the challenge facing the American business community is the nature of the change that is required in the years ahead. If the problem was just slow pro-

TABLE 1–2
Enhancement Priorities in America, Japan, and Europe

America	Japan	Europe
Supplier quality	Lead time reduction	Zero defects
Statistical process control	Computer-aided design	New product introduction
Systems integration	Value analysis	Supplier quality
Lead time reduction	New process/product development	Systems integration
Worker safety	Systems integration	Team motivation
Zero defects	New product introduction	Lead time reduction
Defining strategy	Job enlargement	Supervisor training
Supervisor training	Supplier lead time reductions	Just-in-time
New product introduction	FMS/CIM/EIS*	Statistical quality control

*Flexible Manufacturing Systems, Computer Integrated Manufacturing, Enterprise Integration Systems

Source: Reproduced with permission of Manufacturing Roundtable, Boston University.

duction, we could design faster machines. If the problem was simply one of poorly trained workers, we could redesign the education system to accommodate the needs of the modern worker. As we will see in the pages that follow, American organizations are facing the prospect of massive changes in the basic culture that underlies how we do business.

Unlike mechanical fixes, cultural change takes time and is hard work. When it comes to building quality into a company where it does not now exist, there is simply no quick fix. Interviews with business leaders have repeatedly confirmed how difficult it is for a company to shift from a culture that condones poor quality to one that insists on high-quality processes, products, and services. Many firms simply don't have sufficient energy and leadership to make the change, and for them the future is bleak. Change may be difficult, but what's the alternative? In the 1990s, as you shall see repeatedly in this book, the *quick fix* mentality is the problem, not the cure.

When confronting a new crisis or problem, individuals and organizations characteristically react in a similar way: They deny that a problem exists. The denial period may last a brief moment or it may never end. Nonetheless, until the individual or organization overcomes this initial stage in the problem-solving process and faces reality, the crisis will remain unsolved. Those firms entering the 1990s with a business-as-usual attitude are unwilling to acknowledge reality and are stuck—for a moment or forever—in denial. Until they get over or go around this barrier, they are setting themselves up for failure in the coming years.

"QUALITY FIRST"

The concept of "Quality First" is used in this book as a shorthand way of stressing two fundamental tenets:

- Quality must become the company's *number one* business strategy priority. Quality is not a sprint; it is a long-distance event that takes top management attention and persistence, and lots of it. If you have world-class quality products, services, and people, you will also generate world-class profits.

- A company's quality program must address its own unique needs. Off-the-shelf, "just add water" canned quality solutions cannot generate the level of human commitment within the organization needed to succeed. In fact, you may substitute your company's quality initiative name in place of the term "Quality First" when thinking about the concepts presented in this book.

"Quality First" is both a philosophy and a set of guiding concepts, principles, and practices that represent the foundation of a continuously improving organization. It applies human resources and quantitative methods to improve the materials and services supplied to your company; to improve all of the processes within the company; and to improve the company's ability to meet the needs of the customer now and in the future. It integrates fundamental management techniques, existing improvement efforts, and technical tools in a disciplined, focused, and continuous improvement process.

"Quality First" addresses the quality of management as well as the management of quality. It involves everyone in an organization in a systematic, long-term endeavor to develop processes that are customer oriented, flexible and responsive, and constantly improving in quality. Quality includes all aspects of every product or service of value to a customer. Ultimately, "Quality First" is a means through which an organization creates and sustains a culture committed to continuous improvement.

Thousands of American firms are still employing the tools, management techniques, and paradigms of the Machine Age as we begin to deal with the problems and complexities of the 21st century. The management methods that still predominate are based on the theories of Taylor, Skinner, and other pioneers of scientific management. Those approaches were reductionist in nature and were patterned on the very machines that shaped the age. They were appropriate for their time, but they are excess baggage today.

Russell Ackoff illustrates the point with the following example: Suppose you were to acquire all the makes of automobiles produced in the world and then systematically select from the set the best carburetor, transmission, brakes, and so forth. When you attempt to assemble the world's best possible automobile from the collection of the best parts, you would not even be able to produce an automobile, because the parts would not fit together. The performance of the whole—its quality—is not the sum of the performance of the parts; it is a consequence of the relationship between the performance of the parts.

Under "Quality First," your organization will deliberately seek to create a positive and dynamic working environment, foster teamwork, apply quantitative methods and analytical techniques, and tap the creativity and ingenuity of all of your people. You will focus on collective efforts to better understand and meet internal and external customer needs and to continuously increase customer satisfaction.

The "Quality First" philosophy provides a comprehensive way to improve total organization performance and quality by examining each process through which work gets done in a systematic, integrated, consistent, organization-wide manner. It includes understanding the concept of variation and its implications for process improvement. "Quality First" addresses all forms of work and applies equally to every person in the organization, including top management, marketeers, service providers, designers, production workers, white-collar workers, and laborers.

Whoever you are, it is often easy to fall into the trap of thinking that your company is too big to be affected by individual actions. That perception is common and frustrating, and fortunately, it is a false one. Only through the collective efforts of their individual members do companies change; companies are incapable of changing themselves.

Whatever your position in your company, your efforts to perform a job and to improve your performance directly affect the influence you will have in the company, the control you will have over your personal situation, and your ability to manage and lead. Combined with the efforts of others, your effectiveness directly influences the company's overall ability to meet its mission and ultimately affects the performance of the United States as a nation. Furthermore, how you perform today will also affect future generations.

"Quality First" is a means for improving personal effectiveness and performance and for aligning and focusing all individual efforts throughout an organization. It provides a framework within which you may continuously improve everything you do and affect. It is a way of leveraging your individual effort and extending its effect and its importance throughout an organization and beyond.

"Quality First" is not a destination but a journey toward improvement. The rest of this book will help you get started on that journey. It will help you understand the benefits of continuous improvement and your role and responsibilities in leading the improvement effort in your company. In it, you will explore why continuous improvement is important to each of us. This book will serve as a frame of reference for the ongoing dialogue about "Quality First," and it will help you set the direction for your own journey of improvement. As you read these words, your journey has begun.

If you care about where American industry in general, and your company in particular, are headed in the 1990s, now is the time to act. Companies that procrastinate and delay taking the first step toward the "Quality First" concept, or stay in a state of denial too long, risk failure in the competitive years ahead.

The choice is yours. You can pick a smooth, planned transition to your competitive future, or you can wait for the coming crisis to force your company into the quality arena. The choice is yours. Read on!

Chapter Two
An Executive's Guide to Quality

"Neither a wise man nor a brave man lies down on the tracks of history to wait for the train of the future to run over him."

Dwight D. Eisenhower, 1952

WHAT IS QUALITY?

Why All the Fuss about Quality?

During the 1980s, America rediscovered quality. Suddenly, the word seemed to appear everywhere, here as an adjective, there as a noun. Parents were expected to spend quality time with their children, kids were going to receive quality educations, and everyone was concerned about the declining quality of life in America. In the business community, management by objective was out. Total Quality Control and Total Quality Management were suddenly in. Even President Bush got into the act, declaring that if American business was to be a world-class player it would have to "look at quality first."

The purpose of this chapter is threefold. First, it will acquaint you with the language and key concepts of "Quality First" management. Second, it will serve as a primer, raising your awareness of quality to a level sufficient to ensure you will benefit fully from the book. Finally, it is hoped this chapter will develop in you a personal desire to assume a leadership role in your company's "Quality First" efforts.

Definitions Galore

Table 2–1 is a good place to start your search for the meaning of quality. Notice that businessmen do not have a monopoly on the term. The quotes from Robert Pirsig, a novelist, and Barbara Tuchman, a historian, indicate how far the quality idea has infiltrated other parts of society. The so-called quality movement in America has become a society-wide issue.

The table also shows how broadly and subtly the term is being defined within the business community. Quality is not just a product-based term or a service-based term or a manufacturing-based term. As you read over this array of definitions, ask yourself this question:

> Is quality resident only in a firm's product or service, or is quality also found in the process that produces the product or service?

The answer to this question will bring you to a new level of awareness concerning the real meaning of quality, and a realization that quality *is* actually present in, or missing from, every aspect of a firm's operation from top to bottom and side to side. And remember, there is no one "right" definition of quality. The definition adopted by your firm will be "right" only if it fits the firm's unique managerial conditions and competitive requirements.

For the "Quality First" concept we define quality as the extent to which products and services produced conform to customer requirements. Customers can be internal as well as external to the organizational system (e.g., products or services may flow to the person at the next desk or work area rather than to people outside of the immediate organization).

The days of limiting the definition of quality to the "soundness" of the product—its hardness or durability, for example—

TABLE 2–1
Definitions of Quality

1. **Customer-based**
   "Quality is fitness for use."

   J. M. Juran

   "Total Quality is performance leadership in meeting customer requirements by doing the right things right the first time."

   Westinghouse

   "Quality is meeting customer expectations. The Quality Improvement Process is a set of principles, policies, support structures, and practices designed to continually improve the efficiency and effectiveness of our way of life."

   AT&T

2. **Manufacturing-based**
   "Quality [means] conformance to requirements."

   Philip B. Crosby

   "Quality is the degree to which a specific product conforms to a design or specification."

   Harold L. Gilmore

3. **Product-based**
   "Differences in quality amount to differences in the quantity of some desired ingredient or attribute."

   Lawrence Abbott

   "Quality refers to the amount of the unpriced attribute contained in each unit of the priced attribute."

   Keith B. Leffler

4. **Value-based**
   "Quality is the degree of excellence at an acceptable price and the control of variability at an acceptable cost."

   Robert A. Broh

   "Quality means best for certain customer conditions. These conditions are (a) the actual use and (b) the selling price of the product."

   Armand V. Feigenbaum

5. **Transcendent**
   "Quality is neither mind nor matter, but a third entity independent of the other two . . . even though Quality cannot be defined, you know what it is . . . "

   Robert Pirsig

   ". . . a condition of excellence implying fine quality as distinct from poor quality . . . Quality is achieving or reaching the highest standard as against being satisfied with the sloppy or fraudulent."

   Barbara W. Tuchman

are gone. The new kind of quality American firms rediscovered in the 1980s is far more cultural than physical, far more the way things are done than the nature of the things themselves.

THE LANGUAGE OF QUALITY

Like any other field of study, "Quality First" brings with it a new set of ideas and a new vocabulary to express these ideas. But be careful. While the quality management literature is full of familiar sounding business terms, many take on a somewhat different meaning when used in a "Quality First" context. The language of quality vocabulary includes the following terms.

Process. The familiar definition of process is simply an agreed-upon set of steps. But, in the "Quality First" context the word *process* also means "the logical way things are done," in an organization. "Quality First" is based on a "continuous process improvement" approach, meaning it is a never-ending, cyclical search for ways to do things better.

Customer. In traditional management lore, attention is usually given only to the external customers. In "Quality First," however, a second, equally important customer is the internal customer. End users of a firm's product or service located inside the firm are the internal customers.

Patrick Townsend, in his book *Commit to Quality*, provides a simple model which splits quality into two halves. In Table 2–2, "Quality in Fact" represents the view of quality from the perspective of a supplier, while "Quality in Perception" examines how a customer looks at quality. A firm is located between its suppliers and its customers and, if the company is to serve as a world-class organization linking the two, it must also adopt a quality-focused—a "Quality First"—approach as its principal business objective.

But this seemingly simple supplier-customer model is complicated by the fact that the company is *both* a customer of its suppliers (internal and external) and a supplier to its customers (both internal and external). A "Quality First" approach is the means to bring the views of the suppliers and the views of the

TABLE 2–2.
Quality: Fact and Perception

Quality in fact

Doing the right thing
Doing it the right way
Doing it right the first time
Doing it on time

Quality in perception

Delivering the right product
Satisfying your customer's needs
Meeting your customer's expectations
Treating every customer with integrity, courtesy, and respect

---

customers into harmony with each other. In graphic form, this relationship of the company to its many suppliers and customers is shown in Figure 2–1.

Customer requirements. The needs of the customers—both internal and external users—constitute a company's customer requirements. The ultimate aim of the company is to satisfy these requirements, as shown in Figure 2–1, and thereby satisfy its customers.

Supplier specifications. Once customer requirements are known, you can then determine supplier specifications. "Quality First" companies reject the idea that their suppliers should be picked mainly on the basis of price. Far more emphasis is placed on whether a supplier can meet the company's customer-driven specifications on a continuous basis, thus avoiding the introduction of defects into the company's production process.

Conformance. This term is closely linked to customer requirements. In the "Quality First" context, conformance demands that products and services be measured against known and reliable customer requirements to ensure that they will, in fact, meet the customer's needs. Guesswork is not allowed. Dependence only on historical data is rejected. Conformance must be based on continuously updated data that reflect current, objective measures of customer needs.

Data. "Quality First" is a data-driven approach to qual-

FIGURE 2–1
"Quality First" Customer/Supplier Relationships

Note: C = internal customer; S = internal producer (supplier).

Source: *Continuous Improvement Process: Principles and Practices,* Logistics Management Institute, Bethesda, MD, August 1989.

ity improvement. Information or a set of facts are presented in descriptive form. There are two basic kinds of data: measured (variable data) and counted (known as attribute data).

Statistical process control. Statistical Process Control (SPC) is a disciplined way of identifying and solving problems in order to improve performance. It involves use of fishbone diagrams (see Chapter Ten) to identify causes and effects of problems. Data are then collected and organized in various ways (graphs, Pareto charts, and/or histograms) to further examine problems. The data may be tracked over time (control charts) to determine variation in the process. The process is then enhanced in some way and new data are collected and analyzed to determine whether the process has been improved.

Cross-functional teams. These teams are similar to quality teams but the members are from several work units that interface with one another. These teams are particularly useful when work units are dependent upon one another for systems integration, materials, information, and so forth.

Employee empowerment. In many companies, employees, by design, are doers, not thinkers. They are expected only to perform to minimum standards. In "Quality First" companies, on the other hand, all employees are expected to solve problems, participate in team-building efforts and, generally, expand the scope of their role in the organization. The goal of employee empowerment is to stop trying to motivate workers with extrinsic incentives, as is the case in traditional practices, and build a work environment in which all employees take pride in their work accomplishments and begin motivating themselves from within.

This enhanced role of the worker draws on the work of Douglas McGregor during the 1950s and his familiar Theory X and Theory Y assumptions about the nature of the worker. He argues that the Theory X view is fundamentally flawed. His Theory Y assumptions, on the other hand, many of which underlie the "Quality First" approach, invite a wider and more responsible role for the worker in an organization. A review of McGregor's two sets of assumptions, shown in Table 2–3, will facilitate a better understanding of the expanded role of the worker in "Quality First" firms in the 1990s.

Culture. Culture does not mean going to the opera. Rather, culture is the prevailing pattern of activities, interactions, norms, sentiments, beliefs, attitudes, values, and products in your company. Many executives want to ignore "culture." It is too nebulous, too difficult to "fix." Some believe "all is well," or "if it's not broke, don't fix it."

Recently a vice president for a large American company became a born-again quality advocate. He met late Friday with the CEO to outline his plan to improve the organization's quality by changing the corporate culture and adopt the "Quality First" concepts. All was well until the CEO jumped up, full of enthusiasm, and said he wanted the corporate culture changed by close of business Monday!

One of the most difficult tasks for top management is to understand the impact of culture modification on their near-term and long-term business strategy. Changing your corporate culture takes years, not days.

FUNDAMENTAL CONCEPTS OF QUALITY

The fundamental concepts and principles of "Quality First" include (1) need for a single interdependent system, (2) adoption of the "Quality First" paradigm, (3) enhanced leadership for management's new role, (4) constancy of purpose, (5) commitment to quality, (6) customer focus, (7) benchmarking, (8)

TABLE 2–3
McGregor's Theory X and Y

Theory X Assumptions of the Worker

1. The average human being has an inherent dislike of work and will avoid it if he can.

2. Because of this human characteristic of dislike of work, most people must be coerced, directed, threatened with punishment to get them to put forth adequate effort toward the achievement of organizational objectives.

3. The average human being prefers to be directed, wishes to avoid responsibility, has relatively little ambition, wants security above all.

Theory Y Assumptions of the Worker

1. The expenditure of physical and mental effort in work is as natural as play or rest.

2. External control and the threat of punishment are not the only means for bringing about effort toward organizational objectives. Man will exercise self-direction and self-control in the service of objectives to which he is committed.

3. Commitment to objectives is a function of the rewards associated with their achievement.

4. The average human being learns, under proper conditions, not only to accept but to seek responsibility.

5. The capacity to exercise a relatively high degree of imagination, ingenuity, and creativity in the solution of organizational problems is widely, not narrowly, distributed in the population.

6. Under the conditions of modern industrial life, the intellectual potentialities of the average human being are only partially utilized.

Source: Douglas McGregor, *The Human Side of Organizations* (New York: McGraw-Hill, 1960) pp. 33–34; pp. 47–48.

process orientation, (9) continuous process improvement, (10) system-centered management, (11) investment in knowledge, (12) teamwork, (13) total involvement, and (14) long-term commitment. These synergistic concepts and principles of "Quality First" are described below.

These "Quality First" concepts and principles work together in a logical and holistic manner to give substance and vitality to the continuously improving corporate culture. Figure 2–2 illustrates this holistic view.

FIGURE 2–2
Holistic View of "Quality First" Integration

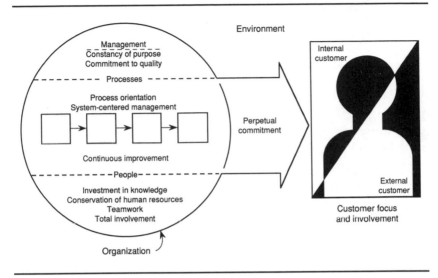

Environment

Management
Constancy of purpose
Commitment to quality

Processes

Process orientation
System-centered management

Perpetual
commitment

Continuous improvement

People

Investment in knowledge
Conservation of human resources
Teamwork
Total involvement

Organization

Internal
customer

External
customer

Customer focus
and involvement

Source: *An Introduction to the CIP Principles and Practices*, Logistics Management Institute, Bethesda, MD, 1989.

A Single Interdependent System

In traditional management, a company's product or service—its output—is the focal point of attention. Typically, the company's goal was to make sure its output was error-free before it left the plant. This was usually accomplished with an in-house inspection department designed to spot defective products. In other words, because each work unit was treated separately, the mistakes of one department could easily become the input for another department. Mistakes were not avoided, but detected and corrected.

In a "Quality First"–focused company, all work units, suppliers, and customers are viewed as part of a single, interdependent system. From a quality perspective, either the whole system is working well, or the whole system is not working well. "Quality First" rejects the notion that one unit's defects can be passed along to another unit and become its inputs. "Quality First" insists that each work unit does its job correctly,

the first time around, every time around. When the total process is designed to perform its tasks correctly, the system is said
to be healthy, the customer is satisfied, and the cost of maintaining the system is reduced to its minimum level.

A New Business Paradigm

A few of the characteristics associated with the traditional way
of managing a company have already been mentioned. Underlying these characteristics is a set of generally held but largely
invisible beliefs and values, including "the job of top management is to find answers to company problems, and workers
must be closely monitored if they are to be productive." The
sum of the common beliefs held by a majority of managers
today comprises what is called the traditional management
paradigm.

A different set of beliefs and assumptions about the nature of
life in the business organization underlies the "Quality First"
practices described throughout this book. "Quality First" is a
paradigm shift. A paradigm, according to futurist Joel Barker, is
a set of values and regulations that first establishes boundaries
and then establishes how to be successful in solving problems
within those boundaries. In the individual, a paradigm shift requires a profound change in one's thinking. In your company,
it requires cultural change. And, as you know, cultural change
does not come easily. For example, it is assumed in a quality
management company that workers are capable of managing
themselves (once given the tools to do so) and that solutions to
most problems faced in the work place can be found within the
work force itself, not in the CEO's office. Clearly, the belief systems of traditional management and "Quality First" are not
compatible. That is, a company operating under the traditional
paradigm cannot fully adopt "Quality First" practices without
first replacing the old belief system with a new one. A company
shifting its belief system is said to be undergoing a change in its
internal culture.

As the number of American business firms shifting from
the old to the new "Quality First" paradigm grows in the
1990s, as shown in Figure 2–3, there will come a point—some-

FIGURE 2–3
**American Business Adopts "Quality First" Principles by the
Year 2000**

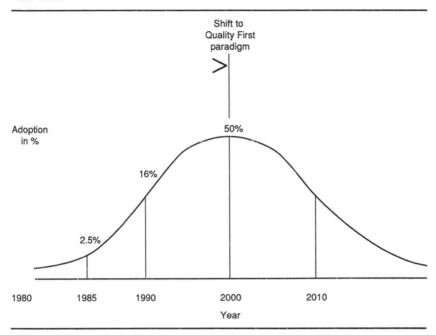

where around the 50 percent mark—when the entire competitive American business community will have made the paradigm shift. After that point any laggard firms wishing to remain competitive will, of necessity, have to shift to the new paradigm or retire their business. My estimate is that the turning point from the old to the new "Quality First" paradigm in the American business community will take place around the year 2000. After that point, the pros and cons of "Quality First" will no longer be debated, as they are today. After 2000, "Quality First" will become the operative belief system of the entire American business community, and the shift from only a bottom-line mentality to a customer-first way of corporate life will be complete.

Unfortunately, it is our view that the "Quality First" concept is all too frequently advocated without sufficient substance or understanding. It is much easier to jump on particular aspects

of the concept—such as statistical process control, employee involvement, structured problem solving, and other tools and
techniques—than it is to understand and embrace the concept
in its holistic sense. If the number of government and industry
organizations that claim to be doing quality improvement in its
fundamental sense were really doing it, world-class competitors of the United States would be begging for mercy. We cannot afford to settle for the easy way. We cannot take shortcuts.
And we cannot pretend that buzzwords, slogans, rhetoric, and
posturing are enough to meet the competitive challenges
American business faces.

Leadership and Management's New Role

"Quality First" is destined to alter both the definition of leadership in an organization as well as the role of top management. Read what *A Guide for Implementing Total Quality Management*, by the ITT Reliability Analysis Center (RAC), has to say
about the role of top management in implementing a "Quality
First" process:

> RAC recommends the top-down model because it has the
> highest probability for success, although it doesn't guaran-
> tee success. The top-down model fosters management
> commitment, the single most important requirement for
> . . . success. . . . Top-down implementation requires man-
> agement leadership as well as commitment. Management
> must lead the effort, providing . . . vision and philosophy
> for the organization. Management must lead the cultural
> change required.
>   The top-down approach assures the availability of the re-
> source support that is crucial for success. Time, money, and
> people are going to be required. . . . The bottom-up approach
> sends the message that quality management is something
> for the employees, but not necessarily for management.

Vision and Philosophy

Leadership is the key role for top managers. In more traditional
management cultures, the meaning given to the term *leadership*
is somewhat amorphous. In a "Quality First" culture, however,

leadership takes on a more precise definition. A quality leader must first establish a common vision of what the company is all about, its purpose. He or she must also put into place that vision through his or her unique "Quality First" philosophy—a set of guiding principles and practices—that will form a top-to-bottom, organization-wide belief system of the way in which the company will go about its business.

Management's New Role

Traditional management methods—the accepted norm today in America—are in conflict with "Quality First" practices. For example, traditional management practices require managers to hold employees accountable; yet in a firm practicing "Quality First" the customer, not top management, controls the actions of the workers. In traditionally managed firms, fighting daily fires consumes management's energies, and competition among work groups is encouraged. In "Quality First" organizations, however, these practices are replaced with a managerial focus on teamwork and continuous process improvement to permanently put out brush fires.

W. Edwards Deming describes the new role for top management in *Out of Crisis*:

> The job of management is not supervision, but leadership. Management must work on sources of improvement, the intent of quality of product and of service, and on the translation of the intent into design and actual product. The required transformation of Western style of management requires that managers be leaders. The focus on outcome (management by numbers, MBO, work standards, meeting specifications . . .) must be abolished, and leadership put in place.

Changing the Corporate Culture

Table 2–4 gives you a realistic idea of the magnitude of change often required when your company moves from a traditional to a "Quality First" culture. Don't underestimate the initial resistance to change that is likely to be generated in an organization once it is clear to its employees how deeply the proposed changes will alter the old way of doing things.

Constancy of Purpose

The constancy of purpose principle is a core "Quality First" concept. For the "Quality First" organization, constancy of purpose is generally articulated by management through a broad statement of corporate purpose.

Such a statement provides individuals with a steady and consistent vision of where they are going, what is expected of them, and what they expect of themselves. Likewise, a constancy of purpose demonstrated consistently by management's behavior enables each individual to construct a reliable mental road map on which to base decisions and actions.

Top management is responsible for providing constancy of purpose. It must be provided from the highest possible level so that it can be infused throughout all parts of an organization. It is conveyed by a clear statement of a vision for the company with a set of consistent goals and objectives, and it is supported by strategic and tactical plans. This constancy of purpose is reinforced by an ongoing stream of management

TABLE 2–4
**Culture Change from Traditional to "Quality First"
Implementation**

"Quality First" is . . .	"Quality First" is not . . .
• demonstrating executive leadership and commitment.	• assigning responsibility for quality to others.
• listening to customers to determine their requirements.	• assuming you know your customer's requirements.
• doing the right thing right the first time.	• doing it over to make it right.
• identifying cost of quality and focusing on prevention.	• overlooking the hidden costs of poor quality.
• continuous process improvement.	• one-time fix.
• taking ownership at all levels of the organization.	• assigning responsibility for quality to one department.

signals and actions that nurture and support the realization of the vision.

Commitment to Quality

Commitment to quality is a cornerstone of the "Quality First" concept. The concept of quality improvement must encompass both measurability and the customer's perceptions of usefulness. Improvement implies a comparison with past performance. Quality improvement implies increasing degrees of excellence with reference to specific and accepted points of reference. Those points of reference include specifications, cost, performance, schedule, responsiveness, and product or service improvement based on competitive benchmarks.

A commitment to quality must begin with top management. Consistent with its constancy of purpose, working within the corporate philosophy, top management must identify the external customers for the organization's products and services. Top management must understand the customer's needs and expectations and assure that those needs are translated into the attributes and characteristics of the products or services. Top management must direct the resources of the organization toward continuously improving the product or service with respect to the customer-relevant attributes.

Customer Focus and Involvement

Without customer focus and involvement, both constancy of purpose and commitment to quality become meaningless. Attracting, serving, and retaining customers is the ultimate purpose of any company, and those customers help the organization frame its quality consciousness and guide its improvement effort. A process, product, or service has no relevance without customers; everything done in an organization is done for the customer. The quality of a product or service is defined by customer behavior and response. Process improvement must be guided by a clear understanding of customer needs and expectations.

Increased customer satisfaction is the ultimate result of customer focus and involvement. The responsibility for assuring customer focus and involvement starts with a top-management focus on the organization's external customer and extends down through every level of activity to involve all customers in the improvement process. "Quality First" emphasizes satisfying all customers, internal and external.

Just as your company is dynamic, so are its customers. Customer requirements change for a variety of reasons, often uncontrollable and unpredictable. To serve its customers adequately, therefore, the organization must continually reassess its customers' needs and requirements and factor them into its improvement efforts. Failure to consider customers and to actively involve them in the improvement effort is a fatal flaw in a company's quality philosophy.

Benchmarking

A benchmark is a standard of excellence or achievement against which other similar things must be measured or judged. Simply speaking, benchmarking is the process of:

- Figuring out what to benchmark.
- Finding out what the benchmark is.
- Determining how it's achieved.
- Deciding to make changes or improvements in one's own business practices to meet or exceed the benchmark.

These four questions—while sounding fairly simple—require thinking and analysis. They require that you know your own business processes and practices down to the smallest detail. Benchmarking is a process of comparing—comparing results, outputs, methods, processes or practices in a systematic way. One of the purposes of this book is to help you through the process of self-assessment.

Process Orientation

The most effective means for an organization to address customer needs and improve itself is to focus improvement efforts on its processes. Process orientation requires a significant change in thinking for many American managers. American management practices, particularly quality functions, have traditionally focused on the postproduction identification and rejection of defective products.

While that approach may be reasonably successful in preventing most unsatisfactory products from reaching customers, it does little to change the processes that create defects.

"Quality First" forces management to think in terms of process rather than in terms of finished product. Everything that is done in an organization is accomplished through a process comprised of definable stages, steps, or activities. Each step of a process involves both producer and customer. The customer is always the step subsequent to the producer. Hence, the principle of customer focus and involvement provides a precise means for defining the purpose (and often the means) of the process.

Continuous Process Improvement
The central, unifying concept in the "Quality First" approach is the idea that everything a firm does is part of a continuous improvement process. Here is how Brian E. Mansir and Nicholas R. Schacht, both of the Logistics Management Institute, describe this key concept in their report entitled *An Introduction to the Continuous Improvement Process: Principles and Practices.*

Continuous process improvement is the fundamental principle around which quality is centered. It complements and animates the principles of process orientation and customer focus and involvement with the certain recognition that no process, product, or service ever attains perfection and that neither the customer's expectations nor the quality of the competition remains static. A deliberate positive change (improvement) is required to win and hold a customer base or to remain economically competitive. Devotion to continuous improvement is a demonstration of constant, purposeful commitment to quality.

Continuous improvement depends on both innovative and small incremental changes. Innovation is characterized by large dramatic changes (see Figure 2–4) resulting from new technologies or new ways of thinking and is often the product of research and development.

FIGURE 2–4
The Large-Step Innovation-Driven Improvement Process

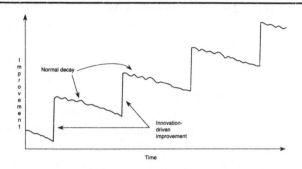

FIGURE 2–5
The Small-Step Improvements Process

FIGURE 2–6
Balance between Innovation and Incremental Improvement

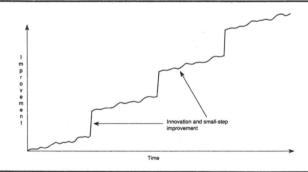

Source: *Continuous Improvement Process: Principles and Practices*, Logistics Management Institute, Bethesda, MD, 1989.

American management has traditionally focused on innovation as the primary engine of improvement. The "Quality First" organization also recognizes the importance of innovation for developing new processes, products, and services. It also recognizes small incremental improvements (see Figure 2–5) as essential for maintaining and building on the new performance standards achieved through innovation. "Quality First" organizations seek a better balance between innovation and small incremental improvement.

Eventually the opportunities from small incremental process improvements reach a point of diminishing returns. Before that occurs, the company should be prepared to introduce the next level of innovation and to begin again the incremental improvement cycle. The balance between innovation and incremental improvement is key and is illustrated by the growth curves in Figure 2–6.

System-Centered Management

System-centered management requires managers to actively improve the system within which they work. Management's new job is to study and reform the processes by which work is accomplished. This concept is anathema to many American managers. Many managers come to their positions with the idea that their job is to assure that work is accomplished in accordance with the established processes. They tend to see their role as keeping people busy and processing the paper that constitutes their deliverable products. True, a substantial part of their job is motivating the work force, providing better discipline, hiring better people, or performing administrative tasks. However, when managers assume that the fundamental structure and processes of the system are fixed and correct, they fail to address their most important job: system improvement.

The traditional attitude about management's role leads managers to deal with a continuous stream of momentary demands for attention. The demands of the "in-basket" never cease, squeaky wheels constantly need oiling, and most managers get bogged down in detail and are unable to step back and deal with the entire process or system. The manager becomes a mechanic, so busy tinkering with the sources of noise that he cannot see that the machine—the organizational system—is becoming obsolete and incapable of performing to modern standards.

Investment in Knowledge

Personal knowledge, teamwork, security, and personal involvement are among the key factors that govern how individuals function and interact within the company. Expanding knowledge is both a personal and a company responsibility. Both the individual and the company must commit to investing in knowledge.

Investment in knowledge is aimed at maximizing human potential and capital. All planned improvement comes from growth in understanding. Improvement is achieved through questioning why things are done and the ways they are done, by trying new ways of doing things, and by learning. Increased education and knowledge should be a lifelong opportunity and experience. In the workplace, every employee should be challenged to grow in value to the organization and in self-worth. An organization that practices "Quality First" makes this growth happen!

Teamwork

Although knowledgeable, skilled employees are crucial to the "Quality First" improvement process, the individual skills they provide may be substantially leveraged when employed in the context of teamwork. Teamwork is essential to the success of the "Quality First" culture in an organization. One universal goal is ultimately to involve every member of the organization in process-improvement team activity.

Teamwork does not necessarily imply that new organizational entities must be created. Rather, in most applications it means that existing groups will begin working as teams, using the techniques that take advantage of interpersonal dynamics.

Most process-improvement teams mirror the natural function or work group structures and thus overlay the existing organizational hierarchy. Additional teams are created to ensure cross-functional process improvement and attention to processes of special interest or broad application such as reward and recognition or quality-of-work-life issues.

For the most part, creation of the team network flows from the top down. Training team members within the team setting is an integral part of the deployment process to produce what H. James Harrington, author of *The Improvement Process*, calls a "waterfall effect" that systematically washes out the counterproductive ideas and signals as the culture is deployed down into the organization.

Each team, once created, engages in an ongoing process-improvement activity that is appropriate to its level and area of responsibility. These activities include customer recognition, process definition, performance requirements definition, performance measurement and assessment, and process-improvement cycle activity. Statistical information provides a common language for the examination of process performance and for the assessment of improvement efforts.

Conservation of Human Resources

Consistent with and embedded in its constancy of purpose, the organization must recognize that its people are its most important asset. This recognition is rooted in the principle of conservation of human resources. Often management behavior does not reflect an appreciation of this principle. Work force reduction is frequently the first avenue of cost reduction. Rank-and-file employees are too frequently perceived as pairs of hands or strong backs with too little regard for the available mind.

An enlightened and consistent approach to leadership is a cornerstone of every successful "Quality First" application. All of the leaders in the field, including Deming, Juran, Drucker, and Crosby, stress the importance of creating a stimulating, secure, and supportive environment in which teamwork, creativity, and pride of workmanship can thrive. Without this environment none of the other elements of "Quality First" can be totally successful.

A key message of the principle of human resource conservation is, "We expect the best from our people and we give them our best in return." The creation and maintenance of a work environment that is compatible with a "Quality First" culture is absolutely a top management responsibility.

Total Involvement

Ultimately, all the "Quality First" principles will guide the actions of every person in the organization. The principle of total involvement (participation and empowerment) addresses this universal involvement in "Quality First." It is concerned with ensuring continuity of appropriate signals throughout the organization and realizing process-improvement benefits in every area of activity. Total participation means that every individual gets involved and has a responsibility to seek continuous improvement at both the individual and team levels. Total empowerment means that individuals are given the necessary authority to make decisions and initiate improvement actions within their own work areas and expertise. Employees are encouraged through respect and trust to exercise self-direction and self-discipline. Empowerment is a source of pride, a wellspring of creativity, and an engine for improvement action.

This empowerment is essential if the principle of total involvement is to be followed. Participation and empowerment are stimulated, nurtured, and guided by management involvement, teamwork, clear objectives, and vigorous open communication.

Perpetual Commitment

Perpetual commitment makes it clear that "Quality First" is not a program that has starting and finishing points; rather, it is a process that, once begun, will be used by the company to conduct all future business. Commitment is a management action that implies a management responsibility to encourage and facilitate positive change even when such change is difficult or time-consuming, or lacks immediate return on the investment. Commitment is measured by behavior: It means holding a steady, long-term course in the face of short-term pressure; making improvement the top agenda item in communications and decisions; being willing to invest for the long-term benefit; supporting the creative improvement initiatives of the work force; structuring the recognition system to reward initiative and improvement; providing for extensive education and training, including everyone in the process; and becoming personally involved in improvement activity. In sum, it means making "Quality First" the company way of life.

Initial deployment of "Quality First" into an organization requires a considerable amount of time and effort. Many changes must occur—ways of thinking, individual and group behavior, methods of accomplishing tasks, attitudes, priorities, relationships, signals, and knowledge levels. These changes will not, and indeed cannot, happen overnight. Experience indicates that three to 10 years, depending on your current state of practice for quality, may be required for an organization to reach "Quality First" maturity. It may take that long before the "Quality First" process is fully in place and considered to be the standard way of doing business.

The length of time required to reach maturity should not be perceived as a reason for you not to begin the transition process to "Quality First." Experience shows that positive results and significant returns on investment start very early in the process. "Quality First," when managed correctly, should essentially pay for itself even in the first year. Companies that are only two or three years into the process report return on their investments of $4 or $5 for every $1 invested.

Top management in an organization is responsible for ensuring that "Quality First" is a perpetual commitment. Every member of the organization should know with certainty that "Quality First" is not just another fad that management will soon forget. Everyone should understand that getting on board is mandatory and that it is not possible to "wait until this 'Quality First' thing blows over." The responsibility for knowing what is going on and for providing the leadership to shape and guide the change process cannot be delegated. Each manager and each individual must recognize a personal role and responsibility and must be given a personal, intrinsic incentive in the "Quality First" effort.

THE COST OF QUALITY

One of the more compelling reasons prompting early quality leaders to trade in traditional practices for "Quality First" practices was the projected cost of poor quality if they did business as usual. Once CEOs realize how costly their old way of doing business is, mainly because it actually builds poor quality and unnecessary costs into the process, shifting to a new, defect-free process becomes very attractive cost wise. According to *A Guide for Implementing Total Quality Management*, of the ITT Reliability Analysis Center:

> The cost of poor quality has been quoted by various sources as being between 15 percent to 50 percent of the cost of doing business. . . . One of the most effective actions management can take to improve productivity in any organization is to improve the quality of its processes. Quality saves, it does not cost. . . . Reducing the cost of poor quality directly affects the bottom line. Improving quality is the most direct way for an organization to increase profit.

More specifically, in *Quality Is Free*, Crosby zeros in on the cost of quality, stating:

> Quality is free. It's not a gift, but it is free. What costs money are the unquality things—all the actions that involve not doing jobs right the first time.
>
> Quality is not only free, it is an honest-to-everything profit maker. Every penny you don't spend on doing things wrong, over, or instead becomes half a penny right on the bottom line. In these days of "who knows what is going to happen to our business tomorrow" there aren't many ways left to make a profit improvement. If you concentrate on making quality certain, you can probably increase your profit by an amount equal to 5 to 10 percent of your sales. That is a lot of money for free.

The key event then in a company's journey toward "Quality First" is an awareness among top management that their finan-

FIGURE 2–7
The Cost of Quality: Before and After "Quality First"

cial statements already reflect the costs of not doing things right the first time around, that they must change their definition of quality, and that to be successful, the "Quality First" program must be organization-wide and involve everyone at all levels.

Let's look at how Xerox Corporation learned to deal with the cost of quality. Simply stated, the cost of quality aims at spending capital wisely and avoiding wasting it. At Xerox Corporation, the Cost of Quality is defined as the measurement of what your division, department, teamwork group or family group is spending for its overall Quality. There are three kinds of measurements in Cost of Quality:

Conformance. Spending that is in conformance with customer requirements. Conformance means that work outputs are being measured against known customer requirements . . .

Cost of nonconformance. Spending that is not in conformance with customer requirements . . . and measured in time needed to go back and do a job over . . . *and* nonconformance can also cost money by exceeding your customer requirements . . .

Lost opportunities. A profit not earned because a customer is lost due to lack of quality.

Figure 2–7 will help you visualize the cost shifts that can be expected before and after a company adopts a "Quality First" approach to management.

Implicit in this Cost of Quality diagram is the notion that the firm will continuously set and achieve higher and higher quality standards.

THE CORPORATE QUALITY CHAMPION

Earlier in this chapter we discussed the anticipation of the coming paradigm shift from traditional management to "Quality First" practices. Once this shift takes place, "Quality First" practices will quickly displace existing practices—that is, they will become standard operating procedures—in most American firms. Until that paradigm shift takes place, however, the process of introducing and institutionalizing a set of new management ideas in an existing company is a very difficult task.

Each new procedure introduced into a firm is certain to upset an existing status quo. Workers who identify personally with the existing status quo will, in turn, feel vulnerable and insecure. Their response is likely to be resistance to the new ideas and the changes in behavior required to implement them. For this reason, if a new idea is to pass from simply a new concept to actual practice in an organization it needs a boost from a champion.

A full-time champion is needed to overcome the resistance the change process will generate and to settle the myriad of problems and barriers that will crop up from day to day. In the absence of a dedicated champion, the initiation of a new idea will soon falter before it is routinized. A "Quality First" champion—an individual that leads by his or her own participation—is needed to inspire others to participate fully in the change process. A successful "Quality First" champion will:

- Visibly support the company's "Quality First" strategy.

- Insist on the team approach.

- Measure his or her success by customer satisfaction.

- Build feedback loops within the firm and to suppliers and customers.

- Meet goals.

Figure 2–8 describes the four stages through which a new

idea such as "Quality First" must pass before it is institutionalized in your company.

Stage 1: The source of the new ideas such as the
"Quality First" concept are located *outside* of the target
organization. The "Quality First" concept captures the
interest of an organizational *insider*, such as the CEO or
quality manager.

FIGURE 2-8
The "Quality First" Idea—Adoption–Implementation Process

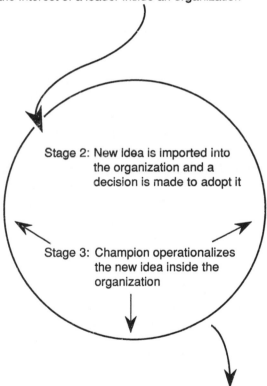

Stage 1: New idea originates outside of the organization, and captures
the interest of a leader inside an organization

Stage 2: New Idea is imported into
the organization and a
decision is made to adopt it

Stage 3: Champion operationalizes
the new idea inside the
organization

Stage 4: The new idea becomes routinized and becomes the "way
business is done" in the organization

Stage 2: An *insider* (or group of insiders) makes the decision to adopt the new idea.

Stage 3: Once the decision to adopt the idea is made, an internal change process must then be set in motion to make the new idea operate. Characteristically, a champion—a person with strong personal convictions concerning quality management, sufficient formal or informal authority, expertise, or some other mix of desired qualities—is given responsibility for the day-to-day implementation process.

Step 4: Only when the new idea is finally internalized and accepted as the "way things are done" in an organization is the champion's job complete.

In their book, *In Search of Excellence,* Thomas Peters and Robert Waterman, Jr., identified the "fired-up champion" as an indispensable part of all of the best-run companies. They define the champion's role like this: "The champion is not a blue-sky dreamer, nor an intellectual giant. The champion might even be an idea thief. But, above all, he's the pragmatic one who grabs onto someone else's theoretical construct if necessary and bullheadedly pushes it to fruition. . . . Champions are pioneers, and pioneers get shot at. The companies that get the most from champions, therefore, are those that have rich support networks so their pioneers will flourish. This point is so important it's hard to overstress. No support system, no champions. No champions, no innovation."

The question now is does your company have a "Quality First" champion? If not, why not you? The next chapters of this book will arm you with the concepts, principles, practices, tools, and techniques that will begin to help you become the "Quality First" champion in your company.

Chapter Three
Different Drummers

"There is nothing more difficult to plan, more doubtful of success, nor more dangerous to manage than the creation of a new order of things. . . . Whenever his enemies have occasion to attack the innovator they do so with the passion of partisans, while the others defend him sluggishly so that the innovator and his party alike are vulnerable."

Niccolo Machiavelli
The Prince, 1513

MORE THAN ONE WAY

The Innovators

A t the turn of the century, most Americans believed that leaders were born, not made. The idea that anyone could develop leadership traits was gradually accepted. Today, however, the study of leadership is a part of most business school curriculums. The diffusion of "Quality First" practices throughout American manufacturing and service industries has followed a similar path as managers cautiously redefine how they view, and perform, their work.

Like innovators before them, Philip Crosby, W. Edwards Deming, Joseph M. Juran, and Robert Costello are change agents,

47

FIGURE 3–1
Distribution of Adopters of Innovations

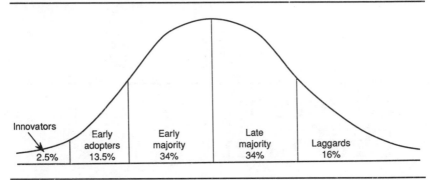

Source: Everett M. Rogers, *Diffusion of Innovations* (New York: Free Press, 1983).

spreading the notion that business and government leaders can, and must, learn to build quality performance into their enterprises; that quality is neither a matter of chance nor an act of magic. But since change involves risks for individuals and organizations alike, with each new idea also comes resistance to change. Familiar habits and beliefs are traded in slowly for new ones. Research has shown that the diffusion of new ideas and successful change processes—whether occurring society-wide or within individual companies—pass through predictable stages. Figure 3–1 is based on Professor Everett M. Rogers's grouping of innovation adopters into five categories, from "innovators" to "laggards."

Professor Rogers's classification scheme helps us better appreciate the process of quality-management change in several ways. First, it places the quality movement in America into a long-range historical context, and suggests that Crosby, Costello, Deming, and Juran—the "innovators" of new ideas—were the starting points of a society-wide change process. Second, we also learn from Rogers that the "early adopters," the risk-taking companies (such as the Malcolm Baldrige Award winners) that first embraced the new ideas, represent only a fraction of the potential adopters.

Finally, as quality management ideas spread into the business population at large, dependence on the guru-dominated diffusion

process used by the relatively few early adopting firms will probably be complemented by customized, mix-and-match approaches to better accommodate the needs of thousands upon
thousands of adopting companies in the years ahead.

Toward Customized Adoption

In Japan in the 1950s, quality management innovators achieved
a charismatic appeal. Only in the early 1980s, as these innovators spread their ideas among American clients who were
also feeling the impact of global competition, did quality management begin to gain a similar appeal in the United States. Under the influence of a single innovator, firms tended to adopt
a more or less pure approach—á la Deming, Juran, or some
other guru. Not until the middle and late 1980s were the ideas of
these innovators popularized and their various approaches
adopted.

Today, business and government organizations throughout
America are on the verge of mass adoption of "Quality First"
practices. In this emerging era, the one-on-one, guru-dominated approach will become less and less able to keep up with
the demand as the number of adopters skyrockets. Now that
both the experiences of the early adopters, and the wide variations in methodology promoted by the gurus, have percolated
through the business community, it seems only natural that
mix-and-match, customized approaches to "Quality First" will
replace the original, guru-dominated approach.

Is There One Best Approach?
The remainder of this chapter introduces the basic ideas and
concepts of a few leading quality management experts. These
experts, it should be stressed, are just a sampling of a still larger
community of quality management thinkers, including Armand V. Feigenbaum, Kaoru Ishikawa, and Rosabeth Moss-
Kanter. The four quality management experts highlighted here
do, nonetheless, offer the reader a wide range of approaches to
better understand quality in America today.

Deming's approach is selected because of his well-known role
in the reconstruction of Japan's industrial base following World

War II and his broad, philosophical approach to change with an emphasis on a statistically based implementation process. Juran's contribution, on the other hand, contains a distinct product-development flavor and a systematic, three-step methodology to help managers zero in on quality management.

Because Crosby stresses a well-structured, stage-by-stage development of an organization's culture, his model may have greater appeal for those executives interested in a more incremental road-map approach. Costello's work, leading to the adaptation by the federal government of a total quality management program predominantly based on Deming, is included here to round out our survey of the state of quality management in America in the early 1990s.

Caution: Don't assume that a single best method should, or does, exist. Maybe it does, maybe it doesn't. Only you can decide. If, after comparing the Crosby approach to those of Deming and Juran, for example, you conclude that Crosby's model fits exactly the needs of your firm, you might consider adopting it wholesale. On the other hand, after a careful comparison of the strengths and weaknesses of each approach, you may decide that a pick-and-choose approach is the way to go. For example, you might use a version of Crosby's maturity grid at the organization-wide level, and a version of Deming's control chart approach at the sub-unit level. The latter chapters in this book provide a description of the "Quality First" methodology that can be used as an aid in developing your own unique "Quality First" program.

The challenge facing America's business executives in the 1990s is not simply to decide whether to adopt any quality management program, but to adopt one that best fits their specific competitive business environment.

THE CROSBY SCHOOL

Like Chester Barnard, a 40-year veteran of AT&T and author of the 1938 classic study of management, *The Functions of the Executive*, Philip Crosby's quality management ideas also followed a long corporate career. Rising through managerial ranks, Crosby was a vice president of ITT for 14 years. Crosby's insider corporate perspective is reflected in a down-to-earth approach to quality management. He believes an organization can "learn" and that top management should adopt a quality-management style, not because it is the right thing to do, but because it is "free" and good for the bottom line.

The problem organization. Crosby believes "the problem organization" will benefit most from his quality-management program. In his book, *Quality Without Tears*, Crosby identifies a problem organization by the presence of five symptoms:

- The outgoing product or service normally contains deviations from the published, announced, or agreed-upon requirements.

- The company has an extensive field service or dealer network skilled in rework and resourceful corrective action to keep the customers satisfied.

- Management does not provide a clear performance standard or definition of quality, so the employees each develop their own.

- Management does not know the price of nonconformance. Product companies spend 20 percent or more of their sales dollars doing things wrong and doing them over. Service companies spend 35 percent or more of their operating costs doing things wrong and doing them over.

- Management denies that it is the cause of the problem.

In other words, virtually every business firm is, by Crosby's definition, a "problem organization." Why? Because, managers traditionally attack problems as they crop up in the organization and seek random improvements. Top management, according to Crosby, is too quick to " . . . send everyone else to school, set up programs for the lowest levels of the organization, and make speeches with impressive-sounding words. It is not until all the problems are pulled together, particularly the financial ones, that the seriousness of the situation is exposed."

Crosby's View of Quality

The real meaning of quality, Crosby asserts in *Quality Is Free*, suffers from several erroneous assumptions. Quality is not:

- Goodness, or luxury, or shininess.
- Intangible, therefore not measurable.
- Unaffordable.
- Originated by the workers.
- Something that originates in the quality department.

Quality is:

- Conformance to requirements; nonquality is nonconformance.

To put this definition into practice, Crosby assumes that quality either is or is not present in the whole organization; that quality is the responsibility of everyone in the organization; and that quality is measurable. In addition, he cautions the quality-bound executive, "The process of instilling quality improvement is a journey that never ends. Changing a culture so that it never slips back is not something that is accomplished quickly."

Crosby's Quality Management Maturity Grid

The first step for an organization moving toward a quality management profile is to determine its current level of "management maturity." Table 3–1, Crosby's Quality Management Maturity Grid, is used for this purpose. Along the left-hand margin are six measures of the sophistication of an organization's management style, including how the organization handles problems, the attitude of top management, and the cost of quality to the firm. Across the top are five levels, or stages, of quality management

TABLE 3–1
Crosby's Quality Management Maturity Grid

Measurement Categories	Stage I: Uncertainty	State II: Awakening	Stage III: Enlightenment	Stage IV: Wisdom	Stage V: Certainty
Management understanding and attitude	Fails to see quality as a management tool.	Supports quality management in theory but is unwilling to provide the necessary money or time.	Learns about quality management and becomes supportive.	Participates personally in quality activities.	Regards quality management as essential to the company's success.
Quality organization status	Quality activities are limited to the manufacturing or engineering department and are largely appraisal and sorting.	A strong quality leader has been appointed, but quality activities remain focused on appraisal and sorting and are still limited to manufacturing and engineering.	Quality department reports to top management, and its leader is active in company management.	Quality manager is an officer of the company. Prevention activities have become important.	Quality manager is on the board of directors. Prevention is the main quality activity.
Problem handling	Problems are fought as they occur and are seldom fully resolved; "fire-fighting" dominates.	Teams are established to attack major problems, but the approach remains short term.	Problems are resolved in an orderly fashion, and corrective action is a regular event.	Problems are identified early in their development.	Except in the most unusual cases, problems are prevented.
Cost of quality as percentage of sales	Reported: unknown Actual: 20%	Reported: 5% Actual: 18%	Reported: 8% Actual: 12%	Reported: 6.5% Actual: 8%	Reported: 2.5% Actual: 2.5%
Quality improvement actions	No organized activities.	Activities are motivational and short term.	Implements the 14-step program with full understanding.	Continues the 14-step program and starts Make Certain.	Quality improvement is a regular and continuing activity.
Summation of company quality posture	"We don't know why we have quality problems."	"Must we always have quality problems?"	"Because of management commitment and quality improvement programs, we are identifying and resolving our quality problems."	"We routinely prevent defects from occurring."	"We know why we don't have quality problems."

Source: Adapted from Philip B. Crosby *Quality is Free*, (New York: McGraw-Hill, 1979).

maturity. These range from Stage I, "Uncertainty," in which an organization is characterized by the statement, "We don't know why we have quality problems," to Stage V, "Certainty," reserved for organizations in which top management can proclaim, "We know why we don't have quality problems."

Once a firm has located its current maturity stage on the grid, it then implements a quality improvement program based on Crosby's Fourteen (14) Steps of Quality Improvement (delineated in Table 3–2). Each step is designed as a building block to move the organization's management style toward the right-hand side of the management grid, passing through progressively higher level maturity stages—titled "Awakening," "Enlightenment," and "Wisdom"—and ultimately, to Stage V. Only at this final stage is conformance to the firm's stated quality requirements assured. A zero-defects culture—a set of beliefs held throughout the organization that says, in effect, "Do it right the first time"—is established and the cost of quality is reduced to its lowest possible level.

The Crosby Quality College

A mood of intellectual progress established by the labels Crosby has given to each stage on his management maturity grid—"awakening," "enlightenment," and "wisdom"—reinforces the role of organizational learning in his "do it right the first time" approach to quality management. Wishful thinking won't work. Only constant, top-level effort will move an organization toward the right-hand side of the grid. To make sure this happens, the Crosby Quality College offers a no-nonsense environment that reinforces again and again one basic theme: zero-defect management is possible.

In *Quality Without Tears*, Crosby says,

> The main problem of quality as a management concern, is that it is not taught in management schools. It is not considered to be a management function, but rather a technical one. . . . However, with the pressure on quality erupting worldwide and the difficulty in getting senior management to do something about it, it becomes apparent that a new measurement is needed for quality. The best measurement for this subject is the same as for any other—money.

TABLE 3–2
Crosby's Fourteen-Step Program

Step 1.   **Management Commitment**
           Top management must become convinced of the need for
           quality improvement and must make its commitment clear
           to the entire company. This should be accompanied by a
           written quality policy, stating that each person is expected to
           "perform exactly like the requirement, or cause the
           requirement to be officially changed to what we and the
           customers really need."

Step 2.   **Quality Improvement Team**
           Management must form a team of department heads (or
           those who can speak for their departments) to oversee quality
           improvement. The team's role is to see that needed actions
           take place in its departments and in the company as a whole.

Step 3.   **Quality Measurement**
           Quality measures that are appropriate to every activity must
           be established to identify areas needing improvement. In
           accounting, for example, one measure might be the percentage
           of late reports; in engineering, the accuracy of drawings; in
           purchasing, rejections due to incomplete descriptions; and in
           plant engineering, time lost because of equipment failures.

Step 4.   **Cost of Quality Evaluation**
           The controller's office should make an estimate of the costs of
           quality to identify areas where quality improvements would be
           profitable.

Step 5.   **Quality Awareness**
           Quality awareness must be raised among employees. They
           must understand the importance of product conformance and
           the costs of nonconformance. These messages should be
           carried by supervisors (after they have been trained) and
           through such media as films, booklets, and posters.

Step 6.   **Corrective Action**
           Opportunities for correction are generated by Steps 3 and 4, as
           well as by discussions among employees. These ideas should be
           brought to the supervisory level and resolved there, if possible.
           They should be pushed up further if that is necessary to get action.

Step 7.   **Zero-Defects Planning**
           An ad hoc defects committee should be formed from members
           of the quality improvement team. This committee should start
           planning a zero defects program appropriate to the company
           and its culture.

Step 8.   **Supervisory Training**
           Early in the process, all levels of management must be trained
           to implement their part of the quality improvement program.

TABLE 3–2 *(continued)*

Step 9.   **Zero-Defects Day**
           A Zero-Defects Day should be scheduled to signal to
           employees that the company has a new performance standard.

Step 10.   **Goal Setting**
           To turn commitments into action, individuals must establish
           improvement goals for themselves and their groups.
           Supervisors should meet with their people and ask them to set
           goals that are specific and measurable. Goal lines should be
           posted in each area and meetings held to discuss progress.

Step 11.   **Error Cause Removal**
           Employees should be encouraged to inform management of any
           problems that prevent them from performing error-free work.
           Employees need not do anything about these problems them-
           selves; they should simply report them. Reported problems must
           then be acknowledged by management within 24 hours.

Step 12.   **Recognition**
           Public, nonfinancial appreciation must be given to those who
           meet their quality goals or perform outstandingly.

Step 13.   **Quality Councils**
           Quality professionals and team chairpersons should meet
           regularly to share experiences, problems, and ideas.

Step 14.   **Do It All Over Again**
           To emphasize the never-ending process of quality improvement,
           the program (Steps 1–13) must be repeated. This renews the com-
           mitment of old employees and brings new ones into the process.

The Crosby Quality College does not educate individuals per
se. According to Crosby, "The college deals with whole companies, not with individuals." While at this college, every action taken by the student, from the manner in which he or she
registers at the hotel upon arrival to ownership of problems in
class, is designed to reinforce *the* central message: Conformance to requirements—the definition of quality—is both beyond compromise and financially wise.

THE DEMING PHILOSOPHY

Born in 1900, and recipient of a Ph.D. in mathematics and
physics from Yale University, W. Edwards Deming was first in-

troduced to the basic tenets of traditional management principles in the late 1920s, as a summer employee at Western
Electric's famous Hawthorne plant in Chicago. Here the revo-
lutionary human relations studies of Harvard University
Professor Elton Mayo began to raise a fundamental question:
How can firms best motivate workers? Deming found the traditional motivation system in use at that time to be degrading
and economically unproductive. Under that system, worker incentives were linked to piecework to maximize worker output,
followed by an inspection process in which defective items
were subtracted from the worker's piecework credits. The vir-
tues of an equalitarian work place is an enduring theme found
throughout Deming's philosophy.

During the 1930s, Deming's collaboration with Walter A.
Shewhart, a statistician working at Bell Telephone Laborato-
ries, led to his conviction that traditional management methods
should be replaced with statistical control techniques. Deming
recognized that a statistically controlled management process
gave the manager a newfound capacity to systematically determine when to intervene and, equally important, when to leave
an industrial process alone. During World War II, Deming got
his first opportunity to demonstrate to government managers
how Shewhart's statistical-quality-control methods could be
taught to engineers and workers and put into practice in busy
war production plants.

Following the war, Deming left government service and set
up a private consulting practice. The State Department, one of
his early clients, sent him to Japan in 1947 to help prepare a national census in that devastated country. While American managers soon forgot their wartime quality-control lessons—and
continued their prewar love affair with traditional management
practices, which prized production over quality—Deming's
evolving quality-control methods received a warm reception in
Japan.

In fact, the Japanese now credit much of their postwar industrial renaissance to Deming's statistical process control (SPC),
based philosophy of quality. Each year in his name, the Union
of Japanese Scientists and Engineers awards the Deming Prize
to companies that have demonstrated outstanding contribu-

tions to product quality and dependability. In addition, in 1960 the Japanese emperor awarded Deming with Japan's Second Order Medal of the Sacred Treasure, a tribute rarely paid to a foreigner.

The Quality Crisis

In his book *Out of the Crisis*, Deming holds American managers responsible for causing a society-wide quality crisis.

> Western style of management must change to halt the de-
> cline of Western industry, and to turn it upward. . . .
> There must be an awakening to the crisis, followed by ac-
> tion, management's job. . . . The transformation can only
> be accomplished by man, not by hardware (computers,
> gadgets, automation, or new machinery). A company can-
> not buy its way into quality.

Deming's philosophy is prone to put quality in human terms. When a firm's work force is committed to doing a good job, and has a solid managerial process in which to act, quality will flow naturally. A more practical, composite definition of quality might read: Quality is a predictable degree of unifor-mity and dependability at low cost, and suited to the market.

Since Japan adopted statistical-based control techniques in the early 1950s, it has had a 30-year head start on the United States. Deming estimates it will take American managers another 30 years to achieve the advanced level of statistical con-trol now in wide practice in Japan. While Western managers have focused on outcome and practiced "retroactive manage-ment," such as management by objective, the Japanese have perfected quality. In 1985, as quoted in *The Deming Management Method*, by Mary Walton, Deming summed up his indict-ment this way: "Failure to understand people is the devasta-tion of Western management." The American quality crisis is being prolonged by what Deming calls the Seven Deadly Dis-eases (see Table 3–3) associated with traditional management practices.

TABLE 3–3
The Seven Deadly Diseases

---

1. Lack of constancy of purpose. A company that is without constancy of purpose has no long-range plans for staying in business. Management is insecure, and so are employees.
2. Emphasis on short-term profits. Looking to increase the quarterly dividend undermines quality and productivity.
3. Evaluation by performance, merit rating, or annual review of performance. The effects of these are devastating—teamwork is destroyed, rivalry is nurtured. Performance ratings build fear and leave people bitter, despondent, beaten. They also encourage defections in the ranks of management.
4. Mobility of management. Job-hopping managers never understand the companies they work for and are never there long enough to follow through on long-term changes that are necessary for quality and productivity.
5. Running a company on visible figures alone. The most important figures are unknown and unknowable—the "multiplier" effect of a happy customer, for example.
6. Excessive medical costs for employee health care, which increase the final costs of goods and services.
7. Excessive costs of warranty, fueled by lawyers who work on the basis of contingency fees.

Deming's Fourteen Points

To eliminate these underlying managerial diseases, Deming prescribes his fourteen-point cure, found in Table 3–4 on pages 61 and 62. Both the philosophical foundation for Deming's managerial transformation, and the role assigned to statistical quality control in the execution of that philosophy, are present in his fourteen-point program of quality management. These points are so central to his approach that Deming will not accept a new company client until its president has promised to faithfully implement *all* fourteen points. Halfway measures will not do. If a company is unwilling to change its management philosophy 100 percent to the Deming way, Deming passes that client by. Why? Because Deming is convinced that about 85 percent of all quality problems are caused by harmful management practices. Consequently, a CEO intent on changing the way production workers perform—without changing the obsolete management system—will, at best, only address 15 percent of the problems.

FIGURE 3–2
A Typical Deming Control Chart

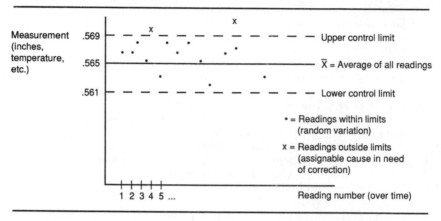

Statistical Process Control

Identifying the Problem
The methodological core of Deming's quality management approach is the use of simple statistical techniques to continuously improve a firm's management process. Only through statistical verification, according to Deming, can the manager (1) know that he or she has a problem, and (2) find the cause of the problem. Deming uses quality-control charts, like the one shown in Figure 3–2, to identify the absence or presence of a quality problem. Since all human activity will contain unavoidable variations—that is, every product or service is slightly different from all the others—an acceptable range of "random variations" must be established for every product or service.

Once measurable upper and lower control limits have been set for a product or service, and a control chart prepared to reflect these limits, the workers performing the activity periodically plot actual measurements on the chart. When these measurements fall outside of the acceptable, "random variation" range, the worker immediately knows a "non-random" quality problem exists.

TABLE 3–4
Deming's Fourteen Points

1. Create constancy of purpose for improvement of product and service. Deming suggests a radical new definition of a company's role: Rather than to make money, it is to stay in business and provide jobs through innovation, research, constant improvement, and maintenance.

2. Adopt the new philosophy. Americans are too tolerant of poor workmanship and sullen service. We need a new religion in which mistakes and negativism are unacceptable.

3. Cease dependence on mass inspection. American firms typically inspect a product as it comes off the assembly line or at major stages along the way; defective products are either thrown out or reworked. Both practices are unnecessarily expensive. In effect, a company is paying workers to make defects and then to correct them. Quality comes not from inspection but from improvement of the process. With instruction, workers can be enlisted in this improvement.

4. End the practice of awarding business on the price tag alone. Purchasing departments customarily operate on orders to seek the lowest price vendor. Frequently, this leads to supplies of low quality. Instead, buyers should seek the best quality in a long-term relationship with a single supplier for any one item.

5. Improve constantly and forever the system of production and service. Improvement is not a one-time effort. Management is obligated to continually look for ways to reduce waste and improve quality.

6. Institute training. Too often, workers have learned their job from another worker who was never trained properly. They are forced to follow unintelligible instructions. They can't do their jobs well because no one tells them how to do so.

7. Institute leadership. The job of a supervisor is not to tell people what to do, nor to punish them, but to lead. Leading consists of helping people do a better job and of learning by objective methods who is in need of individual help.

8. Drive out fear. Many employees are afraid to ask questions or to take a position, even when they do not understand what their job is or what is right or wrong. They will continue to do things the wrong way, or not do them at all. The economic losses from fear are appalling. To ensure better quality and productivity, it is necessary that people feel secure.

9. Break down barriers between staff areas. Often a company's departments or units are competing with each other, or have goals that conflict. They do not work as a team so they cannot solve or foresee problems. Worse, one department's goals may cause trouble for another.

TABLE 3–4
Deming's Fourteen Points *(continued)*

---

10. Eliminate slogans, exhortations, and targets for the work force. These never helped anybody do a good job. Let workers formulate their own slogans.

11. Eliminate numerical quotas. Quotas take into account only numbers, not quality or methods. They are usually a guarantee of inefficiency and high cost. A person, to hold a job, meets a quota at any cost, without regard to damage to the company.

12. Remove barriers to pride of workmanship. People are eager to do a good job and distressed when they cannot. Too often, misguided supervisors, faulty equipment, and defective materials stand in the way of good performance. These barriers must be removed.

13. Institute a vigorous program of education and retraining. Both management and the work force will have to be educated in the new methods, including teamwork and statistical techniques.

14. Take action to accomplish the transformation. It will require a special top management team with a plan of action to carry out the quality mission. Workers cannot do it on their own, nor can managers. A critical mass of people in the company must understand the Fourteen Points, [and] the Seven Deadly Diseases.

Classifying the Problem's Cause

The next step is to identify the cause behind the problem. Two possibilities exist. The cause could be a "common cause"—one rooted in the basic management system in use and, therefore, a problem that is potentially company-wide in scope. Fundamental design errors or the use of imprecise machinery are examples of common causes. Alternatively, the problem could be the result of a "special cause," or one stemming from a more isolated source—a few poorly trained workers in one department, for example.

Deming recommends using several additional charting methods to learn more about the factors causing the quality problems exposed in a control chart. Mary Walton, in *Deming Management at Work*, sums up the crucial role of statistics this way: "American managers pride themselves on hunches and intuition. When they succeed, they take credit. When they fail, they find someone to blame. But a quality transformation rests on a different set of assumptions: decisions must be based on facts . . . [and] . . . it is helpful to display information graphically." Figure 3–3 summa-

FIGURE 3–3
Doing It with Data—Seven Helpful Charts

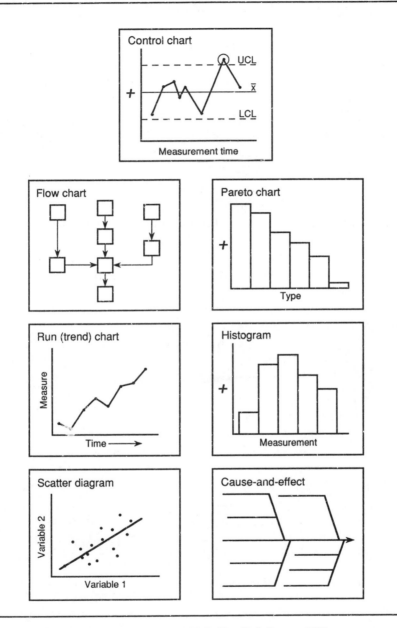

Source: Mary Walton, *Deming Management at Work*, (New York: Putnam, 1990).

rizes the full array of Deming's charting techniques. More is said concerning the specific uses of these charting methods in Chapter 10, Quality First Tools and Techniques.

Correcting the Problem

The final step in the quality-management cycle is for the manager and the workers to eliminate the cause of the quality problem by taking the necessary actions contained in the fourteen points. These actions may range from redesign of a faulty manufacturing assembly line, to a one-day training course for workers to learn how to operate a new machine or how to better serve a new type of customer.

Boosting Performance

While finding and curing quality problems keep a firm's activities within *established* quality limits, there is another way Deming uses control charts to actually boost a firm's performance. By narrowing the established range between the upper and lower random variation limits for an activity, a firm will, in effect, artificially and deliberately create and then solve self-inflicted quality problems. The result is an increase in the firm's attainable level of quality. In this way, managers can plan for and implement a long-range quality-improvement program to stay ahead of the competition.

The Plan-Do-Check-Act (PDCA) Cycle

Deming envisions a never-ending, circular management process. The Plan-Do-Check-Act (PDCA) Cycle, an adaptation of the work of Shewhart, links the seven diseases, the fourteen points, and the statistical techniques into a continuous process, without a starting or ending point. Only through the ongoing application of the four-stage cycle shown in Figure 3–4 can an organization attain and retain a superior quality-management process. There are no shortcuts.

THE JURAN TRILOGY

Joseph M. Juran was educated during the first quarter of this century in engineering and law. His outlook, in general,

FIGURE 3–4
The Shrewhart/Deming PDCA Cycle

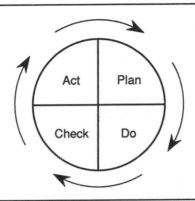

reflects a rational, matter-of-fact approach to business organization and one heavily dependent on sophisticated "shop
floor" planning and quality-control processes. The focal point
of Juran's quality management philosophy is the firm's individual product or service, not the organization per se. By making
sure the building blocks—each individual product or service—
meet the customers' requirements, a company-wide quality
program will emerge.

Like Deming, Juran also played a significant role in rebuild-
ing Japan after World War II, and he also received the Second
Class of the Order of the Sacred Treasure for "the development
of Quality Control in Japan and the facilitation of U.S. and Japanese friendship." His search for underlying principles of the
management process led to his focus on quality as the ultimate
goal. Before becoming a quality management consultant and
lecturer, Juran worked in both government and business organizations.

A National Quality Crisis

The basic society-wide problem, according to Juran, is that
American industry is caught up in a quality crisis. And while
many U.S. managers agree with him on the existence of the crisis, too few understand how to end it. Juran identifies two

widely held but wrong assumptions that are preventing American managers from finding solutions to their problems.

The first error in thinking is that many managers have not yet accepted the fact that they, not the workers, must shoulder most of the responsibility for the performance of their companies. Juran's conclusion is that, until top management redirects its energies toward planning quality into their products—rather than actually planning a lack of quality into them, as is presently the case—the quality crisis will continue. Complementing the first erroneous assumption is the fact that managers also fail to realize the great financial gains to be made once quality becomes their top priority.

The result of this obsolete mindset is summarized in Juran's book, *Juran on Planning for Quality*:

> Many companies are facing serious losses and wastes that have their main origin in deficiencies in the quality planning process:
>
> • Loss of sales due to competition in quality.
>
> • Costs of poor quality, including customer complaints, product liability lawsuits, redoing defective work, products scrapped, and so on.
>
> • The threats to society . . . [since the ability of] the products of an industrial society . . . to lengthen the human life span; relieve people of drudgery; provide opportunities for educational, cultural, and entertainment . . . depend absolutely on the continuing and proper performance of those products, that is, on their quality.

Juran's Quality Trilogy

The challenge facing American managers, according to Juran, is to abandon the traditional approach to product planning, which carelessly introduces quality flaws into the product's original design. The traditional approach depends on an inspection-and-rejection process to find and correct quality problems in individual products, without ever redesigning the planning process itself.

Adoption of Juran's quality trilogy requires that a firm, once and for all, redesign its product and service planning and control systems and then, through an ongoing improvement program, ensure that the basic causes of quality flaws are permanently eliminated. This means a firm's planning system should contain a single, *universal* thought process that supersedes the *particular* processes used in the production of an individual product. It also requires the adoption of Juran's definitions of quality presented in *Juran on Planning for Quality*:

> Quality is (1) product performance that results in customer satisfaction, (2) freedom from product deficiencies, which avoids customer dissatisfaction. A shorthand expression that conveys both meanings is "fitness for use."

Trilogy Parts

Conceptually, Juran divides quality management into three parts:

- Quality planning
- Quality control
- Quality improvements

While planning, controlling, and improving managerial processes have long been considered fundamental executive functions, Juran asserts they are seldom combined in a structured way—as they are in the quality trilogy—for managing product quality. Figure 3–5 describes the way in which Juran's three-part approach is designed to reduce the cost of quality over time.

Quality Planning

In Juran's approach to quality management, the central task is "the activity of developing the products and processes required to meet customers' needs." To accomplish this task, he recommends the road map shown in Figure 3–6. During the quality planning stage, a firm *prepares* to meet established quality goals. The result of the planning stage is *a dependable process* that can be trusted to perform as planned under operating conditions.

FIGURE 3–5
The Juran Trilogy Reduces the Cost of Quality

Source: J. M. Juran, *Juran on Planning for Quality* (New York: The Free Press, 1988).

Quality Control

Control processes are designed to ensure that the quality goals set in the planning stage are, in fact, being met during the actual production or rendering of the firm's products and services. Figure 3–7 illustrates Juran's quality-control process.

Quality Improvement

Unlike quality planning and quality-control processes that logically fit together to form a step-by-step, product idea-to-quality-product continuum, quality improvement is the means by which a firm selectively identifies and implements change on a subsystem level. Quality planning and quality control establish a stabilized product quality "culture," or foundation, throughout an organization. The third part of the trilogy, however, known both as quality improvement and Juran's "breakthrough sequence," provides managers the means to find and

FIGURE 3–6
The Quality Planning Road Map

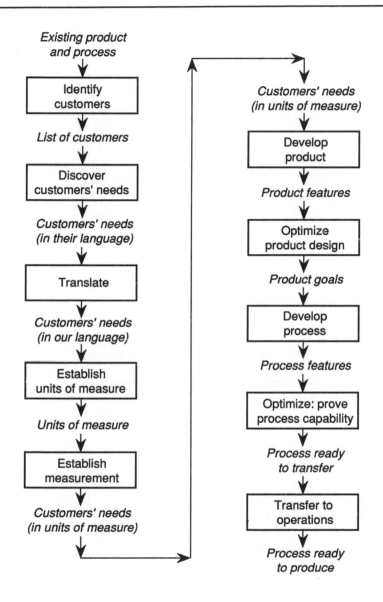

Source: J. M. Juran, *Planning for Quality* (New York: The Free Press, 1988).

FIGURE 3–7
Juran's Quality Improvement Process

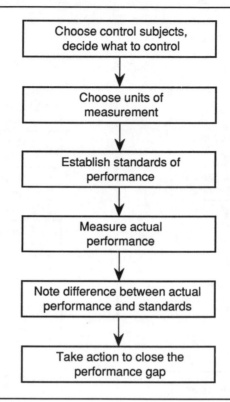

remedy the basic quality-limiting causes imbedded in the organization. Juran expressly does not consider the improvement phase of his trilogy to be a quick-fix exercise. Instead, whenever a basic cause leading to a quality failure is identified, Juran insists that the planning-control processes be altered to permanently prevent that cause from occurring again in the future.

The "breakthrough" process described in Table 3–5 is used in conjunction with Juran's planning and control processes while the trilogy is first being installed in an organization, and as a trouble-shooting tool to keep the planning-control sequence running smoothly after it is established in the organization. Juran uses the term *breakthrough* to emphasize that this part of the

TABLE 3–5
Juran's Breakthrough Sequence

1. Breakthrough in attitudes. Managers must first prove that a breakthrough is needed and then create a climate conducive to change. To demonstrate need, data must be collected to show the extent of the problem; the data most convincing to top management are usually cost-of-quality figures. To get the resources required for improvement, expected benefits must be presented in terms of cost and return on investment.

2. Identify the vital few projects. Pareto chart analysis is used to distinguish the vital few projects from the trivial many and to set priorities based on problem frequency.

3. Organize for breakthrough in knowledge. Two organizational entities should be established: a steering group and a diagnostic group. The steering group, composed of people from several departments, defines the program, suggests possible problem causes, gives the authority to experiment, helps overcome resistance to change, and implements the solution. The diagnostic group, composed of quality professionals and sometimes line managers, is responsible for analyzing the problem.

4. Conduct the analysis. The diagnostic group studies symptoms, develops hypotheses, and experiments to find the problem's true causes. It also tries to determine whether defects are primarily operator-controllable or management-controllable. (A defect is operator-controllable only if it meets three criteria: operators know what they are supposed to do, have the data to understand what they are actually doing, and are able to regulate their own performance.) Theories can be tested by using past data and current production data and by conducting experiments. With this information, the diagnostic group then proposes solutions to the problem.

5. Determine how to overcome resistance to change. The need for change must be established in terms that are important to the key people involved. Logical arguments alone are insufficient. Participation is therefore required in both the technical and social aspects of change.

6. Institute the change. Departments that must take corrective action must be convinced to cooperate. Presentations to these departments should include the size of the problem, alternative solutions, the cost of recommended changes, expected benefits, and efforts taken to anticipate the change's impact on employees. Time for reflection may be needed, and adequate training is essential.

7. Institute controls. Controls must be set up to monitor the solution, see that it works, and keep abreast of unforeseen developments. Formal follow-up is provided by the control sequence used to monitor and correct sporadic problems.

trilogy is the means to achieve unprecedented levels of quality performance in an organization. Juran estimates that approximately 80 percent of the problems identified with breakthrough analysis, including defect rates, are correctable only by improving the management control system. The remaining 20 percent are attributable to the actions of the operating work force.

Cost of Quality Accounting System

To keep top management interested in, and supportive of, the department-level quality-planning process, Juran uses a cost of quality (COQ) accounting system to demonstrate how cost-effective it really is to shift to a quality management process. Here is how it works.

By comparing the rising costs of implementing Juran's appraisal and prevention process to the decreasing costs of detecting internal and external product failures, an executive can determine his optimal level of effort. Figure 3–8, for example, indicates that, in the early stages of implementing a quality management process, every dollar invested in appraisal and prevention activities cuts the firm's external and internal failure costs by far more than one dollar. As the defect rate and failure costs drop in response to the widespread adoption of quality management processes, the firm's level of investment will be optimal whenever a dollar spent on appraisal and prevention equals one dollar reduction in detecting and fixing failures. Since the costs of finding and preventing the last few defects in a production system are extremely high—higher than the costs saved if these defects were eliminated—the optimal quality level is somewhat less than a 100 percent, defect-free system.

ROBERT COSTELLO AND TOTAL QUALITY MANAGEMENT

Long before his appointment as the Under Secretary of Defense for Acquisitions on January 15, 1988, Robert Costello, an engineer by training, was quite familiar with corporate buyer-seller relations. Before going to Washington, Costello was the executive director, purchasing activities, for General Motors Corp.

FIGURE 3–8
Minimal Cost of Quality Curve

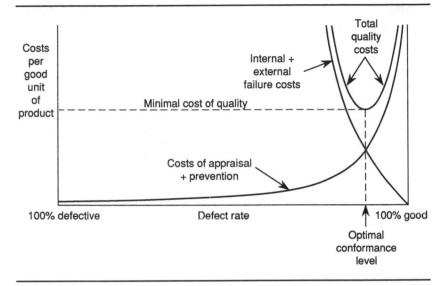

Source: J. M. Juran, *Planning for Quality* (New York: The Free Press, 1988).

(GM) and in charge of acquiring parts and materials from worldwide suppliers in excess of $50 billion per year. This experience would, of course, be useful at the Department of Defense (DoD), where about one-third of the agency's budget goes for the acquisition of weapons, supplies, and military research services. While at GM, Costello also became familiar with, and applied, statistical methods in his quality management process.

By coincidence, Costello arrived at DoD just as the federal government in general, and the DoD's acquisition bureaus in particular, were about to adopt their first large-scale quality management program. In 1986, President Reagan set the stage by issuing Executive Order 12552, which calls for all of the federal government to improve its productivity by 20 percent by 1992. While Costello is not the intellectual source of the ideas that were ultimately put into practice in DoD's Total Quality Management (TQM) program, his hand was very much on the tiller during the crucial formative period and, for this reason, his name is linked with TQM at DoD.

Total Quality Management: A Synthesis Approach

Costello set the tone for the development of DoD's Total Quality Management Master Plan by declaring:

> It is critical at this time that DoD, its contractors, and their vendors focus on quality as the vehicle for achieving higher levels of performance. The DoD budget leaves no room for solving problems that flow from poor quality. Quality is synonymous with excellence. It cannot be achieved by slogans and exhortation alone, but by planning for the right things and setting in place a continuous quality improvement process.
>
> Total Quality Management is a concept that demands top management leadership and continuous involvement in the process activities. The successful TQM operation is characterized by an organization of quality trained and motivated employees, working in an environment where managers encourage creativity, initiative, and trust, and where each individual's contributions are actively sought to upgrade quality. . . . The ultimate goal is the satisfied, quality-equipped, quality-supported soldier, sailor, airman, and Marine.

DoD's Total Quality Management Master Plan, issued in August 1988, defined TQM as:

> . . . a strategy for continuously improving performance at every level, and in all areas of responsibility. It combines fundamental management techniques, existing improvement efforts, and specialized technical tools under a disciplined structure [or model, as shown in Figure 3–9] focused on continuously improving all processes. Improved performance is directed at satisfying such broad goals as cost, quality, schedule, and mission need and suitability. Increasing user satisfaction is the overriding objective. The TQM effort builds on the pioneering work of Dr. W. Edwards Deming, Dr. Joseph H. Juran, and others, and benefits from both private and public sector experience with continuous process improvement.

FIGURE 3–9
A TQM Model

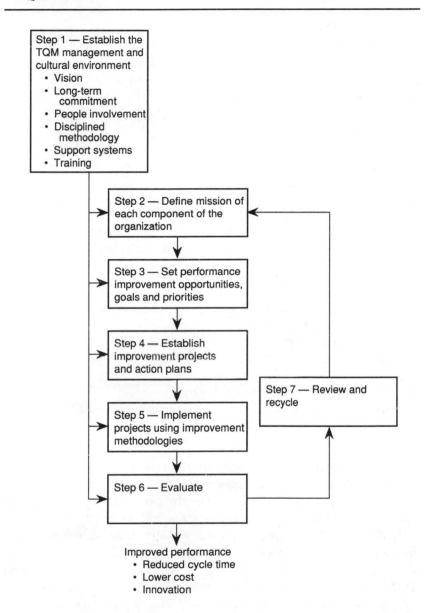

Source: Department of Defense, *Quality and Productivity Self-Assessment Guide for Defense Organizations*. (Washington, D.C.: Department of Defense, 1990).

TABLE 3–6
Two Views of Quality

Traditional View

- Productivity and quality are conflicting goals.
- Quality is defined as conformance to specifications or standards.
- Quality is measured by degree of nonconformance.
- Quality is achieved through inspection.
- Some defects are allowed if the product meets minimum quality standards.
- Quality is a separate function and focused on evaluating production.
- Workers are blamed for poor quality.
- Supplier relationships are short-term and cost-oriented.

Total Quality Management View

- Productivity gains are achieved through quality improvements.
- Quality is conformance to correctly defined requirements satisfying user needs.
- Quality is measured by continuous process/product improvement and user satisfaction.
- Quality is determined by product design and is achieved by effective process controls.
- Defects are prevented through process-control techniques.
- Quality is part of every function in all phases of the product life cycle.
- Management is responsible for quality.
- Supplier relationships are long-term and quality-oriented.

Among his first steps to build an awareness of TQM among the top DoD executives, and implement the new plan, Costello invited Deming to stand by his side in the presentation of Deming's approach to DoD's top military officers and senior managers.

DoD's synthesis approach to quality management is reflected in Table 3–6, a vision of what the DoD leadership wants the organization to look like by the mid-1990s. The eight-part TQM View contained in this table functions as the guiding "principles" for the DoD's quality management program. Note that these "principles" reflect a mixture of the quality improvement ideas of Crosby, Deming, and Juran.

TABLE 3-7
DoD's Total Quality Management Master Plan

Mid-Range (Three-Year) Goals:

- Harmonize DoD regulations with TQM goals.
- Eliminate attitudinal and policy barriers to TQM.
- Cultivate TQM champions in Congress.
- Promote TQM programs in top defense contracting firms.

Long-Range (Seven-Year) Goals:

- Establish TQM as a way of life.
- Have all DoD personnel directly participating in continuous process improvement.
- Gain Congressional understanding and support for TQM.

The Key: Cultural Change

Costello was well aware that the fate of TQM within a federal agency the size of DoD depended largely on the ability of its managers to gain outside support from congress, and to control cultural changes within its 3-million-person work force. Culture is a set of beliefs, values, and attitudes that guides how members of an organization perceive and interpret events. Consequently, DoD's TQM Master Plan stresses a three-stage strategy of cultural change both within DoD and within the organization's environment.

Since Costello launched the DoD quality management effort, a number of government-wide TQM support and recognition systems have been put into place. These include a 1987 Presidential Executive Order setting out agency productivity and implementation guidelines, formation of the Federal Quality Institute in 1988 to serve as a clearinghouse for TQM techniques and methods, and the President's Award for Quality and Productivity Improvement. Because public-sector quality management programs face institutional barriers not normally found in private firms—unsteady commitment for TQM among elected leaders, for example—federal TQM support systems will take on an extra measure of importance.

COMPARATIVE ASSESSMENT

Before comparing the specific quality management approaches of Crosby, Deming, and Juran, let's first place the ideas of these innovators into their larger, societal framework. As a group, they are all advocates of the need for a greater commitment to quality in the work place. But each holds a somewhat different view of what causes the quality vacuum. Table 3–8 attempts to identify the genesis, or the root causes, of the quality challenge facing America. Of the three, Crosby tends to locate the roots of the problem within the firm itself. Juran and Deming, on the other hand, seem to trace company-based quality problems back to the values found in the general, post-World War II American society.

The Early Adopters

A measure of the adoption of "Quality First" principles and practices in America in the last 10 years is shown in Table 3–9. The table provides a partial listing of some of the growing number of well-known companies that have adopted the ideas of Crosby, Deming, Juran, and other gurus.

Common Ground

The various "Quality First" approaches explored here build on a solid base of commonly held expectations and assumptions. In many respects they are far more alike than they are different from one another. Each approach:

- Requires a very strong top-management commitment.
- Shows that quality management practices will save, not cost, money.
- Places the responsibility for achieving quality primarily on the managers and the systems they control, not on the workers.
- Stresses that "Quality First" is a never-ending, continuous improvement process.

TABLE 3-8
The Genesis of the Quality Management Movement

	Nature of the Crisis	Cause of the Crisis	The Solution	Their Definition of Quality
Crosby	Communication of failure within the firm	Lack of commitment to quality	Company culture committed to quality	Conformance to company's own quality requirements
Deming	Loss of international competitiveness	Society and company acceptance of low quality	Society and company committed to quality	Dependable, customer-satisfying product or service at a low cost
Juran	Loss of international competitiveness	Company acceptance of low quality	Company committed to quality	Product or service that is fit for use
Costello	Unresponsive management process	Rule-based standards	Total Quality Management—a synthesis approach	Meeting customer's expectations

TABLE 3–9
Some of the Early "Quality First" Adopters*

	Crosby	Deming	Juran	TQM
AT&T		X		
Bechtel	X			
Burroughs	X			
Campbell Soup		X		
DoD Contractors				
Hewlett-Packard				X
McDonnell Douglas				X
Westinghouse				X
Boeing				X
Chrysler	X			
Dow Chemical		X		
Du Pont			X	
Federal Agencies				
Defense				X
IRS				X
Social Security				X
Veterans Administration				X
Postal Service				X
Ford		X		
GM	X	X		
Hughes Aircraft		X		
IBM	X			
Johnson & Johnson	X			
Mobil			X	
Monsanto			X	
Texas Instruments			X	
Xerox			X	

*Note: Reflects primary initial quality philosophy

- Is customer-oriented.

- Assumes a shift from an old to a new organizational culture.

- Is founded on building a strong management/worker problem-solving team.

But, the differences do matter. The differences among the approaches, then, will most influence a manager's decision to adopt portions of one over the other. Let's compare and contrast Crosby, Deming, and Juran on a number of key issues in terms of balancing the strengths and weaknesses of each approach.

What Is the Nature of the Organization?

Crosby
More so than the others, Crosby's approach has an unmistakable, organization-wide, team-building flavor. The organization is treated almost as if it were a whole, living organism that evolves through time toward higher and higher levels of self-awareness.

Deming
Resident in Deming's view of the business organization is a deep current of social responsibility. The purpose of the organization is to stay in business. But why? Not to make a lot of money, but to lend stability to the community it serves and to treat workers throughout the organization with the respect naturally due every human being. There is a moral tone to the Deming approach that is absent in the others.

Juran
Of the three, Juran's outlook focuses more on the parts rather than the whole organization. The whole does matter, but the path to a healthy organization is to make sure each part is finely tuned. Juran seems to invite the use of his trilogy on an isolated, troubled department.

Is a Step-by-Step Implementation Process Readily Apparent?

Crosby and Juran
In both of these approaches, we have a feeling that a starting point and an end point is visible. Crosby's maturity grid and Juran's trilogy might be called "user-friendly."

Deming

With Deming, there is a feeling that a road map does not exist, that without a tutor's guiding hand one would not readily know where to start on the journey.

Can the Approach Be Implemented Piecemeal?

Crosby and Deming

Both of these approaches are holistic and do not invite a piecemeal implementation strategy. That said, however, the Crosby model does lend itself more to prudent modifications to suit the host organization. Deming, on the other hand, calls for an almost instantaneous belief and total adoption of a new way of organizational life—one filled with radical value shifts.

Juran

A danger, perhaps, in the Juran model is the apparent ease with which his methodology could be targeted at parts of the organization only. A manager attempting a piecemeal implementation of Juran's methods might forget that, in the end, the entire organization must subscribe to the same deep commitment to quality. While Juran selectively picks his sub-units for application of the quality improvement process, he still requires an organization-wide commitment.

How Well Does Each Approach Handle Resistance?

Crosby and Juran

Resistance to change is inevitable, but it need not be a barrier. Crosby's learning-based model is perhaps best suited to accommodating resistance by allowing the individual to acknowledge his or her doubts and, then, to satisfy them through education and training. Juran also accommodates resistance by insisting that changes be justified through analysis and team-building processes.

Deming

On the surface, one can easily conclude that Deming's approach is dogmatic and uncompromising, and in many respects Deming himself cultivates this image. Yet his statistical methods are, in effect, learning tools that not only objectively structure problems in ways that make them easily understood, but also objectively disarm critics of change by depending on facts, not gospel.

WHERE TO FROM HERE?

Adopting a "Quality First" program is a big decision and one that should be made with care and after consultation with others in your organization. Consider the advice given to Alice by the Cheshire Cat when, during her adventures in Wonderland, she could not decide which of two paths to take:

> "Cheshire Puss," Alice began, rather timidly . . . "Would you tell me please, which way ought I go from here?"
> "That depends a good deal on where you want to get to," said the Cat.
> "I don't much care where—" said Alice.
> "Then it doesn't matter which way you go," said the Cat.
> "—so long as I get somewhere," Alice added as an explanation.
> "Oh, you're sure to do that," said the Cat, "if you only walk long enough."*

If, like Alice, you really don't care where you and your company are going, then it really doesn't matter what you do regarding quality management. But if you do care, then which way you go will make all the difference in the world.

JUST PICK ONE

As Tom Peters notes in his book, *Thriving on Chaos*:

> You should have a system. There's a lot of controversy here: Should you follow W. Edwards Deming, father of the Japanese quality revolution via statistical process control?

---

*From *Alice's Adventures in Wonderland* by Lewis Carroll, 1865.

Or Phil Crosby, author of *Quality is Free*, and so prominent that GM bought a 10 percent stake in his firm? . . . Or Joseph Juran? Or invent a system of your own? Eventually you will develop your own scheme if you are successful.

During the mid-1980s, when quality management was first gaining some acceptance in America, it really didn't matter which approach—Crosby, Deming, or Juran—was adopted. Simply by being among the leaders, the early adopting firms were easily well ahead of competitors still operating under traditional management practices. Those days are over. In the 1990s, as more and more firms turn to "Quality First" strategies out of necessity—just to maintain their competitive positions nationally and internationally—there will be a growing need to carefully compare approaches and to adopt the quality initiatives that best fit a company's situation.

The Situational Approach

Perhaps the single most crucial step for a CEO preparing to adopt and implement a "Quality First" program is an honest and frank appraisal of the current status of the organization. For starters, the following questions should be carefully answered:

- How will the organization react to change?
- Who are the potential champions of the change?
- What are realistic expectations for the organization?
- How much time is available to make changes?
- Will it be an organization-wide effort, or will you target a single sub-unit?
- How will you measure results?

During your situational assessment, keep good notes. It will be to your advantage to construct your own version of an "As-Is/To-Be" table that summarizes and compares your organization's current quality situation to your vision of it in the future. Table 3–10 can be used as a prototype.

TABLE 3–10
Where to from Here?

"As-Is" State	"To-Be" State
From an environment that . . .	**To one that . . .**
has many different and often conflicting goals among its divisions and departments.	has a common vision shared by everyone.
punishes mistakes, and hides or rationalizes problems.	openly discusses problems and sees defects as opportunities for improvement.
rewards following established policies.	rewards risk-taking and creative thinking.
lets short-term problems drive and dominate work activity.	focuses on long-term continuous process improvement.
relies on inspection to catch mistakes before the customer receives the product.	improves work processes to prevent mistakes from occurring.
gives management full authority for top-down decisions for change.	trusts and empowers employees to contribute to decision making.
tolerates turf battles as inevitable.	facilitates and rewards cross-functional cooperation.
makes decisions arbitrarily.	bases all decisions on objective data.
has a negative or indifferent self-image.	feels like a winner, with achievements creating good morale.

Source: David Carr and Ian Littman, *Excellence in Government* (Coopers and Lybrand, 1990).

Picking a Strategy

In Chapters 8 and 9, you will find a step-by-step methodology for putting together your own "Quality First" program. In anticipation of that more detailed involvement, this chapter has been designed to first introduce you to, and then compare, the ideas of a few of the leading quality gurus. Once you have a feel for your organization's current needs and the depth of your initial step toward "Quality First" management, you can begin to consider how the strategies of Crosby, Deming, and Juran apply specifically to your situation.

As discussed earlier, each approach has a number of common elements. The decision to adopt elements of one approach over another, therefore, will probably hinge on the appeal you find in a unique aspect present in one approach but absent in the others. For example, a highly technical firm employing many engineers may find Juran far more appealing than the idealistic approach favored by Deming. A firm with a history of organizational development may find Crosby's organizational stage model culturally more comfortable.

Table 3–11 is a comparison of Crosby's fourteen steps, Deming's fourteen points, and Juran's seven-point breakthrough sequence. Each of the steps and/or points was allotted to one of eight generic "Quality First" implementation tasks. Four of the task categories deal with people-oriented tasks, and four are more technical in nature. The resulting table will help you compare the relative weight given by the quality gurus to each of the eight "Quality First" categories. With an idea of the strengths and weaknesses of your current organization in mind, try to decide which of the eight categories will be your greatest challenge to begin your "Quality First" program.

If, for example, you anticipate that building an awareness of quality in your organization will be a particularly difficult challenge, you may want to take a closer look at Crosby and Deming since their approaches have a strong awareness-building focus.

QUALITY DEMYSTIFIED

This chapter has been both a historical and an intellectual introduction to the central ideas behind the American "Quality First" movement. As with all innovations that challenge a long-held set of beliefs and practices, "Quality First" has not been quickly accepted in the American business community. While the ideas of Deming are as American as apple pie, they were first exported in the 1950s to Japan, where they ripened, and only recently have they been imported back into the United States.

Having surveyed a range of definitions of quality, and a variety of well-known approaches to implanting "Quality First" in an organization, you are ready to seriously consider the development of a specific "Quality First" methodology for your

TABLE 3–11
Comparative Assessment Matrix: Quality Management Tasks

	Crosby's 14 steps (Table 3–2)*	Deming's 14 points (Table 3–4)*	Juran's 7 points (Table 3–5)†
People oriented tasks			
Build top management commitment	1	1	1
Teamwork	2,10,13	9,4	3,5,6
Improve quality awareness	5,7,9,12	2,3,8,10,11,12	5
Expand training	8	6,7,13	5
Technically oriented tasks			
Measure quality	3	3,4	4
Quality of cost recognition	4	4,3	2†
Take corrective action	6,11	14	6,7
Continuous improvement process	14	5	7

*Refer to table noted for detailed description of each step/point delineated in quality leaders philosophy.
†Also see Juran's Cost of Quality Curve.

firm. The background you have gained here will help you better appreciate the step-by-step guidelines contained in Chapters six through ten. While there are risks whenever an organizational status-quo is upset, I hope you have gained a solid appreciation for the enormous benefits that the introduction of "Quality First" offers American industry.

It is hoped that this chapter has also helped "demystify" the aura that often surrounds the quality management gurus. Crosby, Deming, and Juran do, indeed, offer new insights into a leader's role in the management process. But there is no magic hidden behind their ideas. With determination, every American executive can learn to achieve a higher level of quality. What the gurus cannot do, however, is supply that precious ingredient—the will to act. That comes from within, and is developed bit by bit. By the time you have finished this book, you should have acquired both the tools and the desire to put "Quality First" into practice.

The final message contained in this chapter is this: There is no one best way. A situational approach, where business leaders must carefully match their unique organizational environment to a customized "Quality First" program, is the recommended route to achieving world-class quality products and services in the 1990s.

Chapter Four
The American Quality Awards

"The process of applying for the Malcolm Baldrige National Quality Award gives us an opportunity to look at our company as our customers see us, which in the end is the only thing that counts. If we get out of this process what we really have to, we will identify our frailties, our shortcomings. The benefits go way beyond winning the award; winning will be only 10 percent of the real impact."

David T. Kearns, Chairman and CEO
Xerox Corporation, February 10, 1989

THE MALCOLM BALDRIGE NATIONAL QUALITY AWARD

The quality of U.S. goods and services is central to the nation's trade balance, competitiveness improvement, and standard of living. Some American firms are rising to the challenge of the quality imperative. They are working hard to meet the ever-increasing requirements of customers who now have broader market choices. More businesses must join in quality improvement efforts to help themselves—and the nation—in the quest for excellence.

On August 20, 1987, President Reagan signed the Malcolm Baldrige National Quality Improvement Act, establishing an annual National Quality Award, shown in Figure 4–1. The purposes of the award are to promote quality awareness, recognize quality achievements of U.S. companies, and publicize successful quality strategies.

The award program is managed by the National Institute of Standards and Technology, United States Department of Commerce. It is administered by the Malcolm Baldrige National Quality Award Consortium, a joint effort of the American Society for Quality Control and the American Productivity and Quality Center. All funding for the program is from private contributions.

The Malcolm Baldrige National Quality Award recognizes American companies that excel in quality achievement and quality management. The award promotes:

- Awareness of quality as an increasingly important element in competitiveness.

- Understanding of the requirements for quality excellence.

- Sharing of information on successful quality strategies and on the benefits derived from implementation of these strategies.

There are three eligibility categories of the award:

- Manufacturing companies.
- Service companies.
- Small businesses.

Up to two awards may be given in each category each year. In addition to publicizing the receipt of the award, recipients are expected to share information with other U.S. organizations about their successful quality strategies.

Companies participating in the award process submit applications that include completion of the award examination. The award examination is based upon quality-excellence criteria created through the public/private partnership. In responding

FIGURE 4–1
The Malcolm Baldrige National Quality Award

to these criteria, applicants are expected to provide information and data on their quality processes and quality improvement. Information and data submitted must be adequate to demonstrate that the applicant's approaches could be replicated or adapted by other companies.

The award examination is designed not only to serve as a reliable basis for making awards but also to permit a diagnosis of the applicant's overall quality management. All award applicants receive feedback reports prepared by teams of U.S. quality experts.

SHOULD YOU APPLY?

The question is often asked of Malcolm Baldrige National Quality Award winning companies if one should apply for the award. Newt Hardie, vice president of quality for Milliken & Company, said he is often asked if companies "should go for the Baldrige" award. He responded "What is your objective? If your objective is to win an award—don't do it. But if you want to improve your company, you cannot afford not to apply." From the, perspective of a small business, Mike Spiess, executive vice president of the Wallace Company, one of the 1990 Malcolm Baldrige Award winners, said that he believed that applying for the award is the "best investment you will ever make." The major benefits described by Spiess are:

1. The award changed Wallace Co. forever. The winning of the award made a significant difference in the company's level of visability and in its "credibility for a small business to compete in world markets." Wallace Co. gained new business in America, Canada, and Australia as a result of its enhanced reputation.

2. He believes that the small business investment in the award filing fee of $1,000 is the best bargain in quality in America, because small businesses normally could not buy the level of consulting analytical support that is provided in the feedback reports provided by the award examiners. Many small companies just couldn't

afford to spend the thousands of dollars for the advice provided by the award examiners for the $1,000 filing fee.

3. By going through the preparation of the requirements of the examination application, your company will learn more about itself than you thought possible. The self-examination of your company causes you to improve and take a new look at how you are operating your business.

In summary, after dozens of interviews I could not find a company that was not enhanced by participation in the Malcolm Baldrige Award process. Make the investment now. See how good you really are!

THE XEROX QUALITY AWARD STRATEGY

In order to present a case study of the typical process used to apply for the Malcolm Baldrige National Quality Award, Xerox Corporation's strategy in winning the award is briefly described here.

The award process enabled Xerox to look at itself through the eyes of the customer, and every aspect of the business came under this scrutiny. The company was able to assess its strengths and identify areas that needed improvement against the strict and demanding total-quality-control criteria of the award.

The decision for Xerox to apply in 1989 was made by David Kearns and Paul Allaire in the fourth quarter of 1988. On December 8, 1988, Wayland R. Hicks, executive vice president of the Business Products and Systems Group (later renamed Development and Manufacturing), and A. Barry Rand, president, United States Marketing Group, announced that Xerox was making a major commitment to achieve the Malcolm Baldrige National Quality Award. Although it was felt that the award would be a symbol of their dedication to customer satisfaction, there was a stronger feeling that through the process of competing for the award, substantial opportunities for improvement in the company's business effectiveness would be identified.

A National Quality Award Office was established to lead the two organizations in the achievement of this award. James E. Sierk was appointed to head the effort, with team members drawn from both organizations to provide support.

The number of core Xerox National Quality Award (NQA) team members varied as the team entered various stages of the process. The core team comprised approximately 20 full-time employees and 8 part-time employees.

Xerox had multiple objectives, according to Norman E. Rickard, corporate vice president of quality, for the application process: to intensify the focus on leadership through quality; to build teamwork; and to involve all employees, including corporate officers and senior managers, in the process. This was accomplished through meetings consisting of senior managers, the NQA-team steering committees, category-sponsoring executives, and specific site teams, as well as through a concentrated company-wide communications effort. Throughout the various stages of the process, a large percentage of the 50,200 employees of the Business Products and Systems Organization in the United States became actively involved and supported the effort.

The National Quality Award team had its first meeting January 3, 1989, to determine the approach and strategy for developing the Xerox application by the May 5, 1989, deadline. The team identified three deliverables:

1. An application for the National Quality Award.

2. Development, implementation, and coordination of site-visit logistics.

3. An assessment report to senior management on Xerox's quality efforts to date, based on insights gained by the team during the application process.

Figure 4–2 represents the team's assessment of the allocation of their time for the three outputs identified.

The team researched and subsequently wrote the first draft of the Xerox application, which was completed February 22. The initial draft was 175 pages, more than double the number permitted.

FIGURE 4–2
Xerox National Quality Award Team Time Allocation

Team Outputs	January 3–May 1	May 1–August	August
1. Application	90%		
2. Site Examination	5%	70%	
3. Assessment	5%	30%	100%

The application was subsequently refined and edited through three additional drafts before submission on May 1.

Senior management was actively involved, providing valuable input and direction, throughout the application and site-visit process.

Xerox was one of 40 companies submitting an application in 1989. On May 25, Xerox received notification that its application had been judged and was one of 23 in the manufacturing category to undergo a preliminary screening. The preliminary screening evaluation, conducted by a team of examiners, was based on an evaluation of 16 of the 44 questions responded to in the application.

Xerox was notified on July 10 that its application had been selected to move forward to the second stage of the review process, which entailed a complete evaluation of the entire application.

On August 17, 1989, Xerox was notified that it had been selected to receive a site visit a month later.

A team of five members of the board of examiners conducted the site visit on Monday, Tuesday, and Wednesday of that week. In addition, two observers representing the National Institute of Standards and Technology accompanied the examiners. The examiners spent three days at Xerox Corporation facilities, including Xerox Square in Rochester, New York; Joseph C. Wilson Center for Technology in Webster, New York; the Denver, Colorado, District Office; and Development and Manufacturing facilities in El Segundo, California.

The team of examiners talked with more than 400 employees during their three-day visit in order to clarify issues and verify the contents of the application submitted by Xerox. Examiners were also checking the extent to which the company's quality efforts were deployed across the breadth of the Business Products and Systems organization. To accomplish this, examiners talked to three different groups of employees:

- Category teams: Groups of five to eight employees were formed and met with examiners to answer specific questions on each of the seven categories contained in the application.

- Teams: Examiners, during the course of their visit, requested to meet with many employee-involvement and quality improvement teams to discuss their project, process, and results.

- Individual employees: During walk-arounds and in cafeterias, examiners met at random with employees to discuss quality within Xerox.

Following their visit to Xerox, the examiners submitted their site-visit report to the nine-member panel of judges. During the first week in October, the judges met to review all the site-visit reports and select the award recipients.

The 1989 awards were presented at the Department of Commerce on November 2, 1989, to the following companies:

- Milliken & Co.

- Xerox Corporation.

BENCHMARK YOUR QUALITY PERFORMANCE

The purpose of the balance this chapter is twofold. First, it is designed as a guide for award applicants. It includes a description of award processes and requirements, and the award examination. Second, it provides an evaluation framework for use by all American organizations that are pursuing quality excellence.

Reliable evaluation of the examination criteria requires experience with quality improvement systems. Nevertheless, the examination may also be used as a self-assessment tool. Thousands of organizations—businesses, government, healthcare, and education—they are currently eligible for or plan to apply for the award, are using the examination for a variety of purposes. These purposes include training, self-assessment, quality-system development, quality improvement, and strategic planning.

DESCRIPTION OF THE EXAMINATION[1]

The award examination is based on criteria designed to be a quality-excellence standard for organizations seeking the highest levels of overall performance and competitiveness. The examination addresses all key requirements to achieve quality excellence as well as the important interrelationships among these key requirements. By focusing not only on results but also on the conditions and processes that lead to results, the examination offers a framework that can be used by organizations to tailor their systems and processes toward ever-improving quality performance. Moreover, the mechanisms for tailoring are themselves included in the examination.

Key Concepts in the Award Examination Criteria

The award examination is built on a number of key concepts. Together, these concepts are the basis for all requirements in the examination, including the following:

- Quality is defined by the customer.
- The senior leadership of businesses needs to create clear quality values and build the values into the way the company operates.
- Quality excellence derives from well-designed and well-executed systems and processes.
- Continuous improvement must be part of the management of all systems and processes.

---

[1]This section is based on the 1991 Application Guidelines for the Malcolm Baldrige National Quality Award.

- Companies need to develop goals as well as strategic and operational plans to achieve quality leadership.

- Shortening the response time of all operations and processes of the company needs to be part of the quality improvement effort.

- Operations and decisions of the company need to be based on facts and data.

- All employees must be suitably trained and developed and involved in quality activities.

- Enhanced design quality and defect prevention should be major elements of the quality system.

- Companies need to communicate quality requirements to suppliers and work to improve supplier quality performance.

Several of these concepts are described in greater detail below.

Customer-Driven Quality

Quality is judged by the customer. All product and service attributes that contribute to value to the customer, lead to customer satisfaction, and affect customer purchase preferences must be addressed appropriately in quality systems. Value, satisfaction, and preference may be influenced by many factors throughout the overall purchase, ownership, and service experiences of customers. This includes the relationship between the company and customers—the trust and confidence in products and services—that leads to loyalty and preference. This concept of quality includes not only the product and service attributes that meet basic requirements. It also includes those that enhance them and differentiate them from competing offerings. Such enhancement and differentiation may include unique product-product, service-service, or product-service combinations. "Quality First" customer-driven quality is thus a strategic concept. It demands constant sensitivity to customer and market information and rapid response to requirements. These requirements extend well beyond defect and error reduction, merely meeting specifications, or reducing complaints. Nevertheless, defect and error reduction and elimination of causes of dissatisfaction contribute significantly to the customers' view of quality and therefore are important parts of customer-driven quality.

Leadership

A company's senior leaders must create clear quality values, specific goals, and well-defined systems and methods for achieving the goals. The systems and methods need to guide all activities of the company and encourage participation by all employees. Through their regular personal involvement in visible activities such as goal setting, planning, review of company quality performance, and recognizing employees for quality achievement, the senior leaders reinforce the values and encourage leadership in all levels of management.

Continuous Improvement

Achieving the highest levels of quality and competitiveness requires a well-defined and well-executed approach to continuous improvement of all operations and of all work unit activities of a company. Improvements may be of several types: (1) enhancing value to the customer through improved product and service attributes, (2) reducing errors and defects, (3) improving responsiveness and cycle-time performance, and (4) improving efficiency and effectiveness in use of all resources. Therefore, improvement is driven not only by the objective to provide superior quality but also by the need to be responsive and efficient. Both provide additional marketplace advantages. To meet all of these requirements, the process of continuous improvement must contain regular cycles of planning, execution, and evaluation. It must be accompanied by a basis— preferably a quantitative basis—for assessing progress, and for deriving information for the next cycle of improvement.

Fast Response

Meeting customer requirements and expectations and achieving success in competitive markets increasingly demand evershorter product and service introduction cycles and more rapid response to customers. Indeed, fast response itself is often a major quality attribute. Reduction in cycle times and lead times and rapid response to customers can occur only when quality systems and processes are designed to meet both quality and response goals, and when response time is included as a major focus of quality improvement processes. This requires that all designs, objectives, and work-unit activities include measurement and monitoring of cycle time and responsiveness to seek opportunities for improvement. Major gains in response may occur when work processes and paths are simplified and shortened. Such improvements are often accompanied by simultaneous improvements in quality. Therefore, it is highly beneficial to consider response time and quality together.

Actions Based on Facts, Data, and Analysis

Meeting quality improvement goals of the company requires that actions in setting, controlling, and changing systems and processes be based on reliable information, data, and analysis. Facts and data needed for quality assessment and quality improvement are of many types—including customer, product and service performance, operations, market, competitive comparisons, supplier, and employee-related concerns. Analysis refers to the process of extracting larger meaning from data to support evaluation and decision making at various levels within the company. Such analysis may entail using data individually or in combination to reveal information—such as trends, projections, and cause and effect—that might not be evident without analysis. Facts, data, and analysis support a variety of company purposes, such as planning, reviewing company performance, improving operations, and comparing quality performance with that of competitors.

The creation and use of performance indicators are a major consideration of data analysis in connection with quality system development, competitive performance, and continuous improvement. Performance indicators are measurable characteristics of products, services, processes, and operations that the company uses to evaluate performance and to track progress. The indicators should be selected to best represent the attributes that link customer requirements to customer satisfaction and competitive performance, as well as to operational effectiveness and efficiency. A system of indicators represents a clear and objective basis for aligning all activities of the company toward well-defined goals and for tracking progress toward those goals. Through the analysis of data obtained in the tracking process, the indicators themselves may be evaluated and changed. For example, indicators selected to measure product and service quality may be judged by how well they correlate with customer satisfaction.

Participation by All Employees

Meeting the company's quality objectives requires a fully committed, well-trained work force that is encouraged to participate in the company's continuous-improvement activities. Reward and recognition systems need to reinforce participation and emphasize achievement of quality objectives. Factors bearing on the safety, health, well-being, and morale of employees need to be part of the continuous-improvement objectives and activities of the company. Employees need to receive training in basic quality skills in performing their work and understanding and solving quality-related problems.

Key Characteristics of the Award Examination

1. The examination is nonprescriptive.

The examination is based on the set of values embodied in the key concepts outlined above. However, the examination does not prescribe approaches to implementation. This means that there are no specific tools, techniques, technologies, or types of organizations required to demonstrate excellence. These may vary greatly among businesses, depending on business size and type.

2. The examination is part of a diagnostic system.

The examination and the scoring system make up a two-part diagnostic system. The examination items represent *what* is to be evaluated. The scoring system represents *how* evaluations are made.

3. The examination stresses quality-system integration.

The examination criteria represent a system of requirements. Integration is achieved through numerous direct and indirect relationships among examination items. Many items link directly to others. Also, information is requested on company-level and unit-level quality performance. This information allows an assessment of how well the overall system is coordinated.

FRAMEWORK OF THE MALCOLM BALDRIGE NATIONAL QUALITY AWARD EXAMINATION

The Malcolm Baldrige National Quality Award examination consists of a framework designed for reliable evaluation and diagnosis. Applicants are required to provide information on their quality management systems, methods, and results using this framework.

THE EXAMINATION

The examination comprises seven categories that represent the major components of a quality management system. The categories are:

1.0 Leadership—senior management's success in creating and sustaining a quality culture.

2.0 Information and analysis—the effectiveness of the company's collection and analysis of information for quality improvement and planning.

3.0 Strategic quality planning—the effectiveness of the integration of quality requirements into the company's business plans.

4.0 Human resource utilization—the success of the company's efforts to utilize the full potential of the work force for quality.

5.0 Quality assurance of products and services—the effectiveness of the company's systems for assuring quality control in all operations.

6.0 Quality results—the company's results in quality achievement and quality improvement.

7.0 Customer satisfaction—the effectiveness of the company's systems to determine customer requirements and its demonstrated success in meeting them.

Each examination item, such as 1.0 Leadership, includes a set of areas to address as shown in Table 4–1. The areas serve to illustrate and clarify the intent of the items to place limits on the types and amounts of information the applicant should provide. Areas are not assigned individual point values, because their relative importance depends on factors such as the applicant's type and size of business and quality system

The following text describes the basic examination based on the 1991 requirements. This text is keyed to the paragraph numbers used in the examination.

1.0 Leadership (100 pts.)

The leadership category examines how senior executives create and sustain clear and visible quality values along with a management system to guide all activities of the company toward quality excellence. Also examined are the senior executives' and the company's quality leadership in the external community and how the company integrates its public responsibilities with its quality values and practices.

1.1 Senior executive leadership (40 pts.)

Describe the senior executives' leadership, personal involvement, and visibility in developing and maintaining an environment for quality excellence.

1.2 Quality values (15 pts.)

Describe the company's quality values, how they are projected in a consistent manner, and how adoption of the values throughout the company is determined and reinforced.

TABLE 4–1
Examination Categories and Items

Examination Categories/Items		Maximum Points
1.0 Leadership		100
1.1 Senior executive leadership	40	
1.2 Quality values	15	
1.3 Management for quality	25	
1.4 Public responsibility	20	
2.0 Information and Analysis		70
2.1 Scope and management of quality data and information	20	
2.2 Competitive comparisons and benchmarks	30	
2.3 Analysis of quality data and information	20	
3.0 Strategic Quality Planning		60
3.1 Strategic quality planning process	35	
3.2 Quality goals and plans	25	
4.0 Human Resource Utilization		150
4.1 Human resource management	20	
4.2 Employee involvement	40	
4.3 Quality education and training	40	
4.4 Employee recognition and performance management	25	
4.5 Employee well-being and morale	25	
5.0 Quality Assurance of Products and Services		140
5.1 Design and introduction of quality products and services	35	
5.2 Process quality control	20	
5.3 Continuous improvement of processes	20	
5.4 Quality assessment	15	
5.5 Documentation	10	
5.6 Business process and support service quality	20	
5.7 Supplier quality	20	
6.0 Quality Results		180
6.1 Product and service quality results	90	
6.2 Business process, operational, and support service quality results	50	
6.3 Supplier quality results	40	
7.0 Customer Satisfaction		300
7.1 Determining customer requirements and expectations	30	
7.2 Customer relationship management	50	
7.3 Customer service standards	20	
7.4 Commitment to customers	15	
7.5 Complaint resolution for quality improvement	25	
7.6 Determining customer satisfaction	20	
7.7 Customer satisfaction results	70	
7.8 Customer satisfaction comparison	70	
Total Points		**1,000**

1.3 Management for quality (25 pts.)

Describe how quality values are integrated into day-to-day leadership, management, and supervision of all company units.

1.4 Public responsibility (20 pts.)

Describe how the company extends its quality leadership to the external community and includes its responsibilities to the public for health, safety, environmental protection, and ethical business practices in its quality policies and improvement activities.

2.0 Information and Analysis (70 pts.)

The information and analysis category examines the scope, validity, use, and management of data and information that underlie the company's overall quality-management system. Also examined is the adequacy of the data, information, and analysis to support a responsive, prevention-based approach to quality and customer satisfaction built on "management by fact."

2.1 Scope and management of quality data and information (20 pts.)

Describe the company's base of data and information used for planning, day-to-day management, and evaluation of quality, and how data and information reliability, timeliness, and access are ensured.

2.2 Competitive comparisons and benchmarks (30 pts.)

Describe the company's approach to selecting quality-related competitive comparisons and world-class benchmarks to support quality planning, evaluation, and improvement.

2.3 Analysis of quality data and information (20 pts.)

Describe how data and information are analyzed to support the company's overall quality objectives.

3.0 Strategic Quality Planning (60 pts.)

The strategic quality planning category examines the company's planning process for achieving or retaining quality leadership and how the company integrates quality improvement planning into overall business planning. Also examined are the company's short-term and longer-term plans to achieve and/or sustain a quality leadership position.

3.1 Strategic quality planning process (35 pts.)

Describe the company's strategic quality planning process for short-term (one to two years) and longer term (three years or more) quality leadership and customer satisfaction.

3.2 Quality goals and plans (25 pts.)

Summarize the company's goals and strategies. Outline principal quality plans for the short term (one to two years) and longer term (three years or more).

4.0 Human Resource Utilization (150 pts.)

The human resource utilization category examines the effectiveness of the company's efforts to develop and realize the full potential of the work force, including management, and to maintain an environment conducive to full participation, quality leadership, and personal and organizational growth.

4.1 Human resource management (20 pts.)

Describe how the company's overall human resource management effort supports its quality objectives.

4.2 Employee involvement (40 pts.)

Describe the means available for all employees to contribute effectively to meeting the company's quality objectives; summarize trends and current levels of involvement.

4.3 Quality education and training (40 pts.)

Describe how the company decides what quality education and training is needed by employees and how it uses the knowledge and skills acquired; summarize the types of quality education and training received by employees in all employee categories.

4.4 Employee recognition and performance measurement (25 pts.)

Describe how the company's recognition and performance-measurement processes support quality objectives; summarize trends in recognition.

4.5 Employee well-being and morale (25 pts.)

Describe how the company maintains a work environment conducive to the well-being and growth of all employees; summarize trends and levels in key indicators of well-being and morale.

5.0 Quality Assurance of Products and Services (140 pts.)

The quality assurance of products and services category examines the systematic approaches used by the company for assuring quality of goods and services based primarily on process design and control, including control of procured materials, parts, and services. Also examined is the integration of process control with continuous quality improvement.

5.1 Design and introduction of quality products and services (35 pts.)

Describe how new and/or improved products and services are designed and introduced and how processes are designed to meet key product and service quality requirements.

5.2 Process quality control (20 pts.)

Describe how the processes used to produce the company's products and services are controlled.

5.3 Continuous improvement of processes (20 pts.)

Describe how processes used to produce products and services are continuously improved.

5.4 Quality assessment (15 pts.)

Describe how the company assesses the quality of its systems, processes, practices, products, and services.

5.5 Documentation (10 pts.)

Describe documentation and other modes of knowledge preservation and knowledge transfer to support quality assurance, quality assessment, and quality improvement.

5.6 Business process and support service quality (20 pts.)

Summarize process quality, quality assessment, and quality improvement activities for business processes and support services.

5.7 Supplier quality (20 pts.)

Describe how the quality of materials, components, and services furnished by other businesses is assured, assessed, and improved.

6.0 Quality Results (180 pts.)

The quality results category examines quality levels and quality improvement based on objective measures derived from analysis of customer requirements and expectations and from analysis of business operations. Also examined are current quality levels in relation to those of competing firms.

6.1 Product and service quality results (90 pts.)

Summarize trends in quality improvement and current quality levels for key product and service features; compare the company's current quality levels with those of competitors and world leaders.

6.2 Business process, operational, and support service quality results (50 pts.)

Summarize trends in quality improvement and current quality levels for business processes, operations, and support services.

6.3 Supplier quality results (40 pts.)

Summarize trends and levels in quality of suppliers and services furnished by other companies; compare the company's supplier quality with that of competitors and with key benchmarks.

7.0 Customer Satisfaction (300 pts.)

The customer satisfaction category examines the company's knowledge of the customer, overall customer-service systems, responsiveness, and its ability to meet requirements and expectations. Also examined are current levels and trends in customer satisfaction.

7.1 Determining customer requirements and expectations (30 pts.)

Describe how the company determines current and future customer requirements and expectations.

7.2 Customer relationship management (50 pts.)

Describe how the company provides effective management of its relationships with its customers and uses information gained from customers to improve products and services as well as its customer relationship management practices.

7.3 Customer service standards (20 pts.)

Describe the company's standards governing the direct contact between its employees and customers and how these standards are set and modified.

7.4 Commitment to customers (15 pts.)

Describe the company's commitment to customers

on its explicit and implicit promises underlying its products and services.

7.5 Complaint resolution for quality improvement (25 pts.)

Describe how the company handles complaints, resolves them, and uses complaint information for quality improvement and for prevention of recurrence of problems.

7.6 Determining customer satisfaction (20 pts.)

Describe the company's methods for determining customer satisfaction, how satisfaction information is used in quality improvement, and how methods for determining customer satisfaction are improved.

7.7 Customer satisfaction results (70 pts.)

Summarize trends in the company's customer satisfaction and in indicators of adverse customer response.

7.8 Customer satisfaction comparison (70 pts.)

Compare the company's customer satisfaction results and recognition with those of competitors that provide similar products and services.

HOW IT'S SCORED

The system for scoring examination items is based on three evaluation dimensions: approach, deployment, and results. All examination items require applicants to furnish information relating to one or more of these dimensions. Specific criteria associated with the evaluation dimensions are described in the following text. Scoring guidelines are outlined in Table 4–2.

Approach

"Approach" refers to the methods the company uses to achieve the purposes addressed in the examination items. The scoring criteria used to evaluate approaches include one or more of the following:

TABLE 4–2
Scoring Guidelines

Score	Approach	Deployment	Results
0%	• Anecdotal, no system evident	• Anecdotal	• Anecdotal
10-40%	• Beginnings of systematic prevention basis	• Some to many major areas of business	• Some positive trends in the areas deployed
50%	• Sound, systematic prevention basis that includes evaluation/ improvement cycles	• Most major areas of business	• Positive trends in most major areas
	• Some evidence of integration	• Some support areas	• Some evidence that results are caused by approach
60-90%	• Sound systematic prevention basis with evidence of refinement through evaluation/ improvement cycles	• Major areas of business	• Good to excellent in major areas
	• Good integration	• From some to many support areas	• Positive trends— from some to many support areas • Evidence that results are caused by approach
100%	• Sound, systematic prevention basis refined through evaluation/ improvement cycles	• Major areas and support areas	• Excellent (world-class) results in major areas
	• Excellent integration	• All operations	• Good to excellent in support areas • Sustained results • Results clearly caused by approach

- The degree to which the approach is prevention-based.

- The appropriateness of the tools, techniques, and methods to the requirements.

- The effectiveness of the use of tools, techniques, and methods.

- The degree to which the approach is systematic, integrated, and consistently applied.

- The degree to which the approach embodies effective evaluation and improvement cycles.

- The degree to which the approach is based on quantitative information that is objective and reliable.

- The indicators of unique and innovative approaches, including significant and effective new adaptations of tools and techniques used in other applications or types of businesses.

Deployment

"Deployment" refers to the extent to which the approaches are applied to all relevant areas and activities addressed and implied in the examination items. The scoring criteria used to evaluate deployment include one or more of the following:

- The appropriate and effective application to all product and service characteristics.

- The appropriate and effective application to all transactions and interactions with customers, suppliers of goods and services, and the public.

- The appropriate and effective application to all internal processes, activities, facilities, and employees.

Results

"Results" refer to outcomes and effects in achieving the purposes addressed and implied in the examination items. The scoring criteria used to evaluate results include one or more of the following:

- The quality levels demonstrated.
- The contributions of the outcomes and effects to quality improvement.
- The rate of improvement.
- The breadth of quality improvement.
- The demonstration of sustained improvement.
- The significance of improvements to the company's business.
- The comparison with industry and world leaders.
- The company's ability to show that improvements derive from their quality practices and actions.

Business Factors Considered in the Evaluation of Applications

The award examination is designed to permit evaluation of the widest range of quality systems for manufacturing and service companies of any size, type of business, or scope of market. The 32 items and 99 areas to address have been selected because of their importance to virtually all businesses. Nevertheless, the importance of the items and areas to address may not be equally applicable to all businesses, even to businesses of comparable size in the same industry. Specific business factors that may bear on the evaluation are considered at every stage of preparation for evaluations as well as in the evaluations themselves. Below is an outline of the key business factors and how they are considered in the award examination.

Key Business Factors

The key business factors include:

- Size and resources of the applicant.

- Number and type of employees.

- Nature of the applicant's business: products, services, and technologies.

- Special requirements of customers or markets.

- Scope of the applicant's market: local, regional, national, or international.

- Regulatory environment within which the applicant operates.

- Importance of suppliers, dealers, and other external businesses to the applicant, and the degree of influence the applicant has over its suppliers.

DOES YOUR COMPANY RANK AMONG THE BEST?

You can obtain a copy of the latest application guidelines for the Malcolm Baldrige National Quality Award by contacting:

Malcolm Baldrige National Quality Award
National Institute of Standards and Technology
Route 270 and Quince Orchard Road
Administration Building, Room A537
Gaithersburg, MD 20899
Telephone: (301) 975-2036
Telefax: (301) 948-3716

Since 1988, more than nine American companies have won the Malcolm Baldrige National Quality Award. Their approach to "Quality First" principles and practices is described for each of these world-class, quality-driven organizations in Chapter 5, which follows. You can tell how you rank by reviewing the award requirements described in this chapter and evaluating your organization's quality status. You may wish to apply for the award, but if you decide not to, consider reviewing these award requirements, ask your staff to review them, and determine by self-examination the areas in which you can improve your business.

Chapter Five
American Quality Leaders

"The winners of the Malcolm Baldrige National Quality Award have made quality improvement a way of life. Quality is their bottom line, and that kind of can-do attitude makes for world-class products and services."

Robert A. Mosbacher, Secretary of Commerce,
1990 Award Announcement

The Malcolm Baldrige National Quality Award, as described in Chapter 4, has been awarded to Cadillac Motor Car Division of General Motors Corporation (1990 winner), Federal Express Corporation (1990), Globe Metallurgical, Inc. (1988), IBM Rochester (1990), Milliken & Co. (1989), Motorola, Inc. (1988), Wallace Co. Inc. (1990), Westinghouse Commercial Nuclear Fuel Division (1988), and Xerox Business Products and Systems (1989). Several of these American quality leaders are described briefly in this chapter. The corporate mission, objectives, and unique approach to quality are described to provide a reference point in determining how your organization's quality efforts can be enhanced.

FEDERAL EXPRESS CORPORATION

The Federal Express Corporation was the Malcolm Baldrige National Quality Award's first winner in the service category. Federal Express Corporation launched the air-express delivery industry 18 years ago. By constantly adhering to a management philosophy emphasizing people, service, and profit, in that order, the company achieved high levels of customer satisfaction and experienced rapid sales growth. Annual revenues topped $1 billion within 10 years of the company's founding, an exceptional achievement.

But past accomplishments do not ensure future success. That's why the management of Federal Express is setting ever-higher goals for quality performance and customer satisfaction, enhancing and expanding service, investing heavily in advanced technology, and building on its reputation as an excellent employer. Company leaders are increasingly stressing management by fact, analysis, and improvement.

Through a quality improvement process focusing on 12 Service Quality Indicators (SQIs), all tied to customer expectations and articulated at all levels of its international service business, the Memphis-based firm continues to set higher standards for service and customer satisfaction. Measuring themselves against a 100 percent service standard, managers and employees strive to continuously improve all aspects of the way Federal Express does business.

Federal Express at a Glance

Conceived by Chairman and Chief Executive Officer Frederick W. Smith, Federal Express began operations in 1973. At that time, a fleet of eight small aircraft was sufficient to handle demand. Five years later, the company employed 10,000 people, who handled a daily volume of 35,000 shipments. Today, approximately 90,000 Federal Express employees at more than 1,650 sites process 1.5 million shipments daily, all of which must be tracked through a central information system, sorted in a short time at facilities in Memphis, Indianapolis, Newark, Oakland, Los Angeles, Anchorage, and Brussels, and delivered by a highly decentralized distribution network. Federal Express's air cargo fleet is now the world's largest.

Federal Express revenues totaled $7 billion in fiscal year

1990. Domestic overnight and second-day deliveries accounted for nearly three-forths of the total, with the remainder being international deliveries. The company's share of the domestic market in 1989 was 43 percent, compared with 26 percent for its nearest competitor.

People-Service-Profit

Federal Express Corporation's "people-service-profit" philosophy guides management policies and actions. The company has a well-developed and thoroughly deployed management evaluation system called Survey/Feedback/Action (SFA), which involves a survey of employees, analysis of each work group's results by the work group's manager, and a discussion between the manager and the work group to develop written action plans for the manager to improve and become more effective. Data from the SFA process are aggregated at all levels of the organization for use in policy making.

Training of frontline personnel is a responsibility of managers, and "recurrency training" is a widely used instrument for improvement. Teams regularly assess training needs, and a worldwide staff of training professionals devises programs to address those needs. To aid these efforts, Federal Express has developed an interactive video system for employee instruction. An internal television network, accessible throughout the company, also serves as an important avenue for employee education.

Consistently included in listings of the best U.S. companies to work for, Federal Express has a "no layoff" philosophy, and its "guaranteed fair treatment procedure" for handling employee grievances is used as a model by firms in many industries. Employees can participate in a program to qualify frontline workers for management positions. In addition, Federal Express has a well-developed recognition program for team and individual contributions to company performance. Over the last five years, at least 91 percent of employees responded that they were "proud to work for Federal Express."

Service Quality Indicators (SQI)

To spur progress toward its ultimate target of 100 percent customer satisfaction, Federal Express replaced its old measure of
quality performance—percent of on-time deliveries—with an
index that comprehensively describes how its performance is
viewed by customers. Federal Express established the service
quality indicators (SQI) to determine what the main areas of the
customers' perception of service are and how they are meeting
them. *The purpose of the SQI is to identify and eliminate causes, not
place blame.*

The SQI has 12 components weighted to reflect the customers' view of the company's performance by placing greater
weight on SQI categories that have the greatest impact on the
customers' perception of service received. The number of average daily failure points for each component is calculated by
multiplying the number of daily occurrences for that component by its assigned importance weight. Factors such as abandoned calls are included in order to measure internal performance that can significantly affect external customer service.
SQI categories are expanded and adjusted as necessary.

The SQI is the sum of the average daily failure points for all
12 components and is tracked and reported on a weekly basis,
with monthly summaries.

The service goal will always be 100 percent failure-free performance, with the emphasis on finding the root causes of failure and implementing solutions that *prevent* the failures rather
than simply fix the consequences of failures. For example, if
courier-mislabeled packages are a major cause of wrong day/
late failures, the SQI team would focus on creating effective
new solutions to prevent courier-miscoding at the source,
rather than perfecting the expensive expediting system. Effective quality improvement programs and teamwork such as this
are essential to achieving the SQI goal. Knowing what makes a
customer unhappy is important, but it is even more important
to understand it and solve it through a concerted effort by several areas. Goal congruence, improved methods, contingency
plans, and teamwork are vital parts of the total commitment to
service.

To reach its aggressive quality goals, Federal Express has set up one cross-functional team for each service component in the SQI. A senior executive heads each team and assures the involvement of frontline employees, support personnel, and managers from all parts of the corporation when needed. Two of these corporate-wide teams have a network of more than 1,000 employees working on improvements.

The SQI measurements are directly linked to the corporate-planning process, which begins with the CEO and COO and an executive planning committee. SQIs form the basis on which corporative executives are evaluated. Individual performance objectives are established and monitored. Executive bonuses rest on the performance of the whole corporation in meeting performance improvement goals. And, in the annual employee survey, if employees do not rate management leadership at least as high as they rated them the year before, no executive receives a year-end bonus.

Quality Improvement at Federal Express

Although Federal Express is an acknowledged leader in the air freight industry, a formal Quality Improvement Process (QIP) has been implemented throughout the entire corporation to continue meeting the needs of its customers. The objectives of the QIP are to:

- Achieve a 100 percent service level.

- Increase profits.

- Make Federal Express a better place to work by focusing everyone's attention on the corporate policy of "Doing Right Things Right" and catching and fixing problems when they happen.

The corporate mission supports the philosophy that quality must be a part of the way it does business. Themes such as "Do it right the first time," "Make the first time you do it the only time anyone has to," "Fedexcellence" and "Q=P" (Quality = Productivity) have always been a part of the Federal Express culture. Even the people/service/profit philosophy is an expression of their commitment to quality. Now, in light of intense competition and expansion into global markets, quality becomes more than a slogan at Federal Express—it is the normal way of life.

Experts say that in an organization committed to quality as a way of life, three things happen:

- The level of customer satisfaction increases and satisfied customers bring more business, which ensures the financial health of the corporation and continued job security.

- Profits increase because employees don't waste time and money correcting mistakes.

- The quality of work-life is improved because they have fewer customer complaints, less hassle, and less rework to deal with.

Quality improvement means the company meets the needs of its internal and external customers. While it is easy to recognize the ultimate customer, the company also must recognize that it has many customer-supplier relationships with other Federal Express employees. Quality improvement activities are critical to the continued success of Federal Express. Constantly striving to improve the system and finding better ways of doing things will make it possible for the company to keep its leadership position in the industry as it expands into the global marketplace. The competition will continue to get tougher and customers will continue to demand the best quality of service available for the price they pay. Federal Express must meet all of these challenges, and do so better than anyone else can.

Continuous Improvement

Quality improvement requires you to continuously develop ways to do better work. Continuous improvement means "Fix it now!" and "Prevent problems before they happen" and "Look for new ways to meet customer needs." The theory of

"If it ain't broke, don't fix it," has no place in a quality organization. Instead, the approach needs to be, "If it ain't broke, improve it."

Satisfying Internal and External Customers

Quality begins and ends with the customer. The customer tells what the right thing to do is, and then the company has to find the right way to do it. As the supplier of a service, Federal Express is famous for doing whatever it takes to satisfy the customer. Federal Express's team recognizes who the ultimate customer is and knows how important it is to meet their customer needs. However, team members also need to recognize and meet the needs of their internal customers—other Federal Express employees with whom they exchange information, products, and services every day. All of you have people who depend on you for products or services to do their jobs and each of you depends on services or products from others in order to do your job.

To make the work process flow smoothly and deliver a quality product to external customers, Federal Express builds positive working relationships with its internal customers. This can be accomplished by asking three questions:

- What do you need from me?
- What do you do with what I give you?
- Are there any gaps between what I give you and what you need?

The answers to these questions are the key to "Doing Right Things Right."

Quality Action Teams

In a quality organization, everyone, not just management, must be committed to improving both quality and productivity. Everyone must share responsibility for achieving corporate goals. Quality Action Teams (QATs) get employees involved in designing the work process for maximum quality at minimum cost. Teams are generally more effective than individuals in solving problems or improving the way things get done. When you start your quality improvement actions, employees often ask "What's in it for me?" Federal Express's experience has shown that:

- Doing right things the first time makes your job easier.

- Quality of work-life is improved because you have fewer customer complaints, less hassle, and less rework to deal with.

- Profits increase because time and money aren't wasted correcting mistakes.

- Quality work keeps Federal Express financially healthy and ensures job security.

- You have the opportunity to actively participate in problem solving.

- You are eligible to receive awards and recognition through various corporate programs.

Quality improvement activities are critical to the continued success of Federal Express. The competition will continue to get tougher and customers will continue to demand the best quality of service available for the prices they pay. Federal Express must meet all of these challenges and do so better than anyone else can. Constantly striving to improve the system and finding better ways of doing things will make it possible for Federal Express to keep its leadership position in the industry as it moves aggressively into the global marketplace.

GLOBE METALLURGICAL, INC.

Globe Metallurgical, Inc., a small business, is a major producer of silicon-metal and ferrosilicon products, with plants located in Beverly, Ohio, and Selma, Alabama. The company was founded in 1873 as the Globe Iron Company in Jackson, Ohio, and subsequently built the Beverly plant in 1955 and acquired the Selma plant in the mid-1960s. At the Beverly plant, Globe operates five submerged-arc electric furnaces, and has the capability to produce silicon metal and a full range of ferrosilicon products. The furnaces range in size from 10 to 20 megawatts. Once a specialist in the production of ferrochromium products, Globe abandoned the environmentally hazardous ferrochromium lines in 1985 to concentrate its ferrosilicon effort in the production of magnesium ferrosilicon products to serve the foundry industry. Magnesium ferrosilicon is used to convert gray iron to ductile iron in foundries, and ductile iron represents a growing segment of the iron castings market. The Selma plant contains two submerged-arc electric furnaces, and the plant specializes in the production of high-grade, low-impurity silicon metal. The furnaces at Selma are both in the 15 to 16 megawatt range. The silicon metal produced at Selma is devoted primarily to the chemical silicones industry and to applications requiring extremely low iron levels in silicon metal, such as the electronics and solar cell industries.

Development of the Globe Quality System

In 1985, the Ford Motor Co. approached its suppliers with its quality certification program, called Q-1. Since Globe supplied Ford with a number of alloys for its foundries, Globe management recognized that the criteria specified in the Q-1 program would have to be satisfied to sustain a long-term relationship with Ford. The first step to obtaining Q-1 certification was to undergo an extensive audit of the quality system by Ford personnel, called the Q-101 audit. If the supplier passes, with a score of 140 or more out of 200, the supplier becomes eligible for an internal review of its performance history at all Ford locations using its products. If all the locations approve the supplier, the Q-1 Award is forthcoming. Since the criteria are demanding, the Q-1 Award is recognized as a significant quality achievement in the U.S. auto industry.

The Ford Q-1 program has had the greatest initial impact on the development of the quality system at Globe. A self-assessment of the Q-101 criteria indicated to Globe management that the quality system in place was inadequate to satisfy the criteria, so a new quality system was built around the criteria. The primary inadequacies of the system were that it was detection-based as opposed to prevention-based, and lacked implementation of statistical process control techniques, quality planning, and employee participation in the improvement process.

Since Globe was deficient in so many areas, the building of the quality system was begun simultaneously in three areas: (1) training the entire work force in Statistical Process Control (SPC), (2) establishing a quality manual and the mechanics of the quality system, and (3) educating and training Globe's suppliers in the necessity for implementing statistical process control and a quality system.

Quality-Efficiency-Cost Committee

To establish the mechanics of a workable quality system, a Quality-Efficiency-Cost (QEC) committee was established at each plant, with a QEC steering committee overseeing the activities of the plant committees. The committees provide ideas for improvement in all three areas: quality, efficiency, and cost. The QEC steering committee comprises the top management of the company and is chaired by the president and chief executive officer. It meets monthly and discusses the broader issues of development and maintenance of the quality system, such as allocation of significant resources and planning. The plant QEC committees meet daily and are chaired by the plant manager. All department heads attend the meetings, and the discussion is much narrower in scope than the steering committee meetings, concentrating on specific projects and implementation techniques. Since the plant manager serves on the steering committee with upper management, he acts as the conduit for bringing plant issues up to the steering-committee level, and for bringing steering committee issues down to the plant level for implementation. Initially, the Beverly plant QEC committee was given the task of identifying the critical process variables within each of the plant's processes which must be controlled through SPC or other techniques. This was done to assure that the final product will always be consistent with the customers' requirements without the need for 100 percent inspection of the final product. Thus, the emphasis was to build a quality system based on prevention techniques as opposed to the historical protection methodologies.

Globe Project Teams

Project teams are called on an ad hoc basis to address a particular problem or project. Unlike the other teams, salaried employees with particular expertise are invited onto project teams. This expertise includes Taguchi design of experiments, storyboarding, brainstorming techniques, and other statistical tools and techniques. Since all the salaried employees utilize personal computers, the computers are frequently used to facilitate the team's activities. Historically, the activities now undertaken by project teams were done solely by salaried employees, and the implementation of their ideas was dictated by management within a given department. In many instances, the hourly employees, whose ideas were not solicited in the development of the project, resented the implementation technique, or felt that they knew of more effective techniques. Now that input is actively solicited from hourly employees, the hourly employees take pride of ownership in the decision process, and are much more likely to assist in implementation. Typically, there are seven departmental teams, three interdepartmental teams, two project teams, and two interplant teams in operation at any given time. More than 60 percent of the work force of both plants is involved in quality circle teams. An average of 70 ideas per week are generated to improve the quality, efficiency, and/or cost of the operation.

Quality Planning

Prior to 1986, quality was not given consideration in the planning process. Today, the Continuous Improvement Plan is a vital document that is updated annually and distributed widely both internally and outside of the company. The current plan is 20 pages, with 96 items for improvement identified. Each item in the plan fully supports items found in the company's Strategic Plan. Both plans cover a period of five years.

The structure of the Continuous Improvement Plan includes the goal of the improvement, the objective of the improvement item, individual projects that support the objectives, and assigned responsibilities and target dates. The QEC steering committee is responsible for developing the goals that are found in the plan, but the plant QEC committees are responsible for the much more specific activities of project determination and assignment of responsibilities. To ensure that the hourly employees have input and the ability to comment on the plan, copies are distributed, and hourly employees are invited to attend planning meetings. Many quality circle ideas that require large capital expenditures are incorporated into the plan each year. To track the progress of individual projects, an audit system has been established that requires the persons responsible to file update reports quarterly. The update reports are distributed by the quality manager, to whom they are returned. To assist the responsible parties in remembering their assignments, the projects have all been translated into a calendar format, which each employee receives, to hang on the wall. As project deadlines approach, employees can readily be aware of their responsibilities by looking at the calendar. On due dates, the employee's name, project number, and a brief description of the specific project are printed on the calendar.

Quality Pays!

Since QEC emphasizes quality, efficiency, and cost, many productivity improvements have been realized through the implementation of both quality-enhancing and productivity-enhancing techniques. In 1986, management became interested in the works of Shigeo Shingo, and began to apply many Shingo methods, such as Just In Time (JIT), to the manufacturing process. It has been found that the Shingo techniques work in harmony with the techniques of Deming, Taguchi, and others. Using the formula

(Net Sales-Total Cost) + (Total Cost EQ)

the index for productivity has improved 36 percent company-wide in the period 1986 through 1988. Documented savings of $10.3 million per year have been realized through the implementation of quality-related techniques.

MOTOROLA, INC.

Motorola, Inc., is one of the world's leading manufacturers of electronic equipment, systems, and components produced for both United States and international markets. Motorola products include two-way radios, pagers, and cellular radiotelephones, other forms of electronic communications systems, integrated circuits and discrete semiconductors, defense and aerospace electronics, data communications, and information processing and handling equipment.

Ranked among the United States' 100 largest industrial companies, Motorola has about 102,000 employees worldwide.

As a leader in its high-technology markets, Motorola is one of the few end-equipment manufacturers that can draw on expertise in both semiconductor technology and government electronics.

The company was founded in Chicago by Paul V. Galvin in 1928 as the Galvin Manufacturing Corporation. Its first product was a "battery eliminator," allowing customers to operate radios directly from household current instead of from the batteries supplied with early models. In the 1930s, the company successfully commercialized car radios under the brand name "Motorola," a new word suggesting sound in motion. During this period, Motorola also established home radio and police radio departments; instituted pioneering personnel programs; and began national advertising. The name of the company was changed to Motorola, Inc., in 1947—during a decade that also saw the company enter government work and open a research laboratory in Phoenix, Arizona, to explore solid-state electronics.

Motorola's attention to quality also has shown up on the bottom line, according to Richard Buetow, vice president and director of quality, who says that defects have been cut by 80 percent during the past few years, and the company has saved about $962 million in inspection and rework costs.

It wasn't always that way. Ten years ago, admits Motorola President Gary L. Tooker, the company faced the grim fact that many of its products and operations simply weren't making the grade. Top executives had a choice: Motorola could either continue losing its customers to Japan (as it had in consumer electronics during the late 1970s) or it could go back to basics.

Robert W. Galvin (then Motorola's chairman and head of the company's executive committee) chose the latter by personally visiting key customers around the world, then calling for a tenfold improvement in quality within five years. But even that wasn't tough enough, says Tooker; Galvin's goal eventually became one of "total customer satisfaction." Motorola now aims for a condition of six sigma—3.4 defects per million opportunities—not just in manufacturing, but within every one of the company's operations by 1992. Buetow puts it another way: "We're striving for absolute perfection."

At Motorola, the quality culture is pervasive. Motorola top management formally restated their company objectives, beliefs, goals, and key initiatives in 1987, and quality remained as a central theme. Total customer satisfaction is Motorola's fundamental objective. It is the overriding responsibility of everyone in the company, and the focus of all of their efforts.

Motorola top management also reaffirmed two key beliefs that have been part of the Motorola culture since the company began in 1928: uncompromising integrity, and constant respect for people. The CEO has identified the following key goals for Motorola:

1. Increased global market share.
2. Best in class in terms of people, technology, marketing product, manufacturing, and service.
3. Superior financial results.

Quality and Productivity at Motorola

In an era of intense international competition, Motorola has maintained a position of leadership in the electronics industry through a combination of aggressive product innovation, strategic long-range planning, and a unique philosophy that allows each employee to contribute insights to the achievement of quality standards. This philosophy is translated into action through the teams to openly and effectively communicate ideas to help improve processes and products. The Participative Management Program (PMP) assumes that under the right conditions, employees will suggest better ways to do their jobs. For many years, Motorola has sought the ideas of its employees. For about 10 years, a process of participatory management has been in place. Each U.S. employee of the company who is not part of the Motorola Executive Incentive Program (MEIP) is a member of a PMP team. Teams are usually organized by function within an organization. Their purpose is to continually assess the process of performing their work, and to change it in ways that will reduce defects and reduce cycle time. The problem-solving efforts of these teams are directly analogous to quality circles. The quality and cycle-time improvement rates for these teams are the same as the corporate goal, thereby providing incentives that directly support the quality improvement process.

The Motorola Quality Improvement Process

Management of the quality improvement process is based on Motorola's practice of Management by Measurement. This style of management says that by establishing measurements that are correlated to the desired end result, and regularly reviewing the actual measurements, the organization will focus on those actions necessary to achieve the required improvement.

In 1986, the communications sector adopted a uniform metric, called "total defects per unit." In addition, because all operations were using the same measurement, the goal for defect reduction was uniformly applied to all operations. The required percent reduction was the same, regardless of the absolute level. The improvement rate achieved by the communications sector was much greater than had been achieved in the five-year Ten Times program, and so the measurement was adopted by the entire corporation.

In January 1987, Motorola restated its corporate quality goals to be:

1. Improve 10 times by 1989.

2. Improve 100 times by 1991.

3. Achieve six-sigma capability by 1992.

This goal is applied to all areas of the business, not just product quality.

Motorola's Quality Initiatives

The first of these initiatives is the achievement of six-sigma quality. Motorola intends that all products and services are to be at the six-sigma quality level (3.4 defects/million products) by 1992. This means designing products that will accept reasonable variation in component parts, and developing manufacturing processes that will produce minimum variation in the final output product. It also means analyzing all the services provided, breaking them down into their component parts, and designing systems that will achieve six-sigma performance. Motorola, Inc., is taking statistical technologies and making them a part of each and every employee's job, regardless of assignment. Measuring this begins by recording the defects found in every function of their business, then relating these defects to a product or process by the number of opportunities to fabricate the product or carry out the process. Motorola has converted their yield language to parts per million (ppm), and the six-sigma goal is 3.4 ppm defect levels across the company. Despite the wide variety of products and services, the corporate goal is the same six-sigma quality level by 1992.

The company's second key initiative, total cycle-time reduction, is closely related to six-sigma quality. Motorola defines cycle time as the elapsed time from the moment a customer places an order for an existing product to the time the company delivers it. In the case of a new product, it is from the time the company conceives of the product to the time it ships. Motorola examines the total system, including design, manufacturing, marketing, and administration.

The third initiative, product and manufacturing leadership, also emphasizes the need for product development and manufacturing disciplines to work together in an integrated world, applying principles of teamwork and simultaneous engineering.

Motorola's fourth initiative, profit improvement, is a long-term, customer-driven approach that shows the company where to commit its resources to give customers what they need, thus improving long-term profits. It recognizes that investing in quality today will produce growth in the future.

The final initiative is participatory management within, and cooperation among organizations. This team-work approach is designed to achieve more synergy and greater efficiency, and to improve quality.

WALLACE COMPANY, INC.

Wallace Company, Inc., a Houston-based industrial distribution company, bucked the conventional business wisdom during the mid-1980s. With the Texas Gulf Coast economy in the doldrums and new construction activity—its primary source of revenues—at a standstill, Wallace avoided short-term remedies, and pursued a long-term strategy of continuous quality improvement.

In only a few years, Wallace has distinguished itself from its competitors by setting new standards for service. It has emerged as a stronger firm with a rapidly growing sales volume, steadily increasing market share, and better profit performance.

Now entering the final stage of the three-phase quality program it initiated in 1985, Wallace has effectively merged business and quality goals, built new partnerships with customers and suppliers, and instilled associates with a commitment to one overriding aim: total customer satisfaction.

Wallace at a Glance

Founded in 1942, Wallace is a family-owned distribution company primarily serving the chemical and petroleum industries.

Its 10 offices, located in Texas, Louisiana, and Alabama, distribute pipe, valves, and fittings, as well as value-added specialty products such as actuated valves and plastic-lined pipe. Wallace distributes directly in the Texas Gulf Coast area but serves international markets as well.

In tandem with its move to continuous quality improvement, Wallace shifted its marketing focus from engineering and construction activities to maintenance and repair operations, now the source of 70 percent of its sales. In 1989, sales totaled $79 million. The company employs 280 associates, all of whom have been trained in quality improvement concepts and methods.

Continuous Quality Improvement

The seeds of the Wallace quality process were sown and cultivated by the company's five top leaders, directed by John W. Wallace, chief executive officer, and C.S. Wallace, Jr., president. Comprising the quality-management steering committee, each of the five top leaders has undergone more than 200 hours of intensive training on the methods and philosophy of continuous quality improvement. Their hands-on involvement is typified by the participation of at least one senior leader in all quality activities, including on-the-job training for associates.

Leadership drafted the company's quality mission statement, which was circulated throughout the company. Embodying input from all associates, the final document serves as Wallace's public commitment to continuous quality improvement. It is distributed to all associates, customers, and suppliers. Furthermore, Wallace developed 16 quality strategic objectives— nine of which focus on improving customer satisfaction—to guide business decision making. In fact, business and quality aims are one and the same, formulated in Wallace's quality business plan.

Associates are responsible for devising and carrying out plans to accomplish objectives under the company's cooperative, yet centralized, approach to quality improvement. Since 1985, participation on teams, whose membership is voluntary and cuts across department and district-office boundaries, has increased sixfold. Team planning and decision making are greatly aided by an extensive set of customer-focused databases, accessible to all associates through the company's computer system. Teams are assisted by 12 statistical process control (SPC) coordinators, who chart trends, conduct failure-mode effects analysis to isolate real and potential problems, and evaluate progress in accomplishing quality objectives. Each district office has at least one SPC coordinator on staff, and at all sites, one day a week is devoted to evaluating and planning quality improvements.

Wallace has fixed its sights on providing the products and services that best meet the needs of its regional market, but the scope of its quality improvement efforts is truly worldwide. Measurable quality benchmarks are identified in global searches for the top-performing companies in each category of service or business operation, from on-time delivery to safety performance.

Not only does Wallace comprehensively monitor its activity—it has identified and now measures 72 discrete processes that contribute to on-time delivery and accurate invoicing—but it also invites the scrutiny of customers. Customers receive computer-generated reports that document how well the company has been servicing its accounts. Customer feedback is ensured through four types of surveys, "partner building" meetings, frequent contacts by sales representatives, and a total customer-response network that must respond to all inquiries and complaints within 60 minutes.

Moreover, customers have access to some of Wallace's databases. Wallace also has led the way in converting customers to electronic data interchange. Both Wallace and its customers reap the advantages of better inventory management, time savings, error reduction, and more accurate data. About 40 percent of Wallace's sales orders are now handled electronically, compared with less than five percent in 1988.

Wallace holds suppliers to its same high standards, requiring firms to provide statistical evidence of the quality of their shipments and to guarantee their products for a minimum of 12 months. Based on its quality surveillance measures, the distributor has trimmed the number of its suppliers to 325, down from more than 2,000 in 1987. To ensure that suppliers consistently provide products meeting the expectations of customers, Wallace provides training in continuous quality improvement to its suppliers, a first in the industry. Last year, 15 suppliers initiated processes based on the Wallace model. In another pioneering initiative spawned by a committee of Wallace customer and supplier representatives, the company has implemented a vendor-certification process, in which Wallace and its major customers will jointly assess the quality processes of suppliers.

Because associates drive quality improvement, Wallace has invested about $2 million in formal training between 1987 and the end of 1990. Teams of associates closest to a specific area targeted for improvement are charged with identifying the steps necessary to accomplish a quality objective, with standardizing the methods to ensure consistent performance, and with conducting the necessary training at all departments and offices.

"Quality wins" are reported in the company's monthly newsletter, acknowledged in congratulatory letters from the CEO, and rewarded with dinners for the responsible associates and their families, or with team picnics.

Simultaneous with management's efforts to increase associate involvement in continuous quality improvement, rates of absenteeism, turnover, and work-related injuries have dropped sharply. New associate-led projects are intended to foster greater dedication and higher levels of job satisfaction. For example, teams are studying ways to enhance career development opportunities. In a newly begun program, each associate will visit at least one customer site to discuss service performance.

These and other initiatives have paid numerous dividends. Since 1987, Wallace's market share has increased from 10.4 percent to 18 percent. Its record of on-time deliveries has jumped from 75 percent in 1987 to 92 percent in 1990. By July 1991, the distributor has committed to guarantee all customers an on-time delivery rate of 98 percent. Its customer base has grown, while existing clients have increased their business. As a result, sales volume has grown 69 percent and, because of greater efficiency, operating profits through 1989 have increased 7.4 times.

WESTINGHOUSE COMMERCIAL NUCLEAR FUEL DIVISION

Westinghouse Electric Corporation is involved in many aspects of nuclear power plant design, manufacturing, and operation. The Commercial Nuclear Fuel Division (CNFD) is responsible for the engineering, manufacturing, and supply of Pressurized Water Reactor (PWR) fuel assemblies for commercial nuclear power reactors. The fuel contained in these assemblies generates heat (through nuclear fission), which is converted to electricity.

CNFD is a division within the Energy Systems Business Unit of Westinghouse. It is a fully integrated fabricator of commercial PWR fuel comprised of the Western Zirconium Plant, near Ogden, Utah (which became part of CNFD in 1988), where zircalloy extrusions and other components are produced from zircon sands; the Specialty Metals Plant (SMP) in Blairsville, Pennsylvania, where nuclear-grade tubing is produced from the extrusions; the Fuel Manufacturing Plant in Columbia, South Carolina, where enriched uranium is converted into ceramic pellets and loaded into the fuel-rod assemblies; and nuclear engineering, marketing, and administrative activities in Monroeville, Pennsylvania.

CNFD currently supplies 40 percent of the U.S. light-water reactor fuel market and 20 percent of the free-world market. This market leadership can be directly attributed to the quality of the division's products and services. Fuel produced at the Columbia plant is responsible for more than 7 percent of the electricity produced in the United States.

Value Creation at Westinghouse

In the early 1980s, dramatic changes in the global marketplace caused Westinghouse corporate leadership to create a new management vision for the corporation. The corporation was becoming concerned about maturing market conditions and international competition. The new vision of Westinghouse was based on a management strategy independent of changes in technology or market conditions. It was based on the principle of "value creation."

As Westinghouse CEO John Marous has stated, the primary mission of both corporate- and division-level managers is to create value for the people who have a stake in the corporation—primarily its customers, stockholders, employees, and the community. Westinghouse believes that managing all of its businesses around the concept of "Quality First" is the fundamental strategy for value creation.

The Westinghouse model for "Quality First" is built on four imperatives: management leadership, product and process leadership, human resource excellence, and customer orientation. These imperatives, in turn, are broken down into conditions of excellence. Under the imperative of management leadership, there are four conditions required of management in a "Quality First" environment. The first task of management is to create the right culture. The next task is planning, followed by communications, and, last, accountability.

Strategic Quality Planning

Westinghouse has discovered that the "Quality First" concept must be viewed as an all pervasive operating strategy for managing a business every day.

"Quality First" begins with a strategic decision—a decision that can only be made by top management—and that decision, simply put, is the decision to compete as a world-class company. "Quality First" concentrates on quality performance—in every facet of a business—as the primary strategy to achieve and maintain competitive advantage. It requires taking a systematic view of an organization—looking at how each part interrelates to the whole process. In addition, it demands continuous improvement as a "way of life."

The Westinghouse "Quality First" model is built on four imperatives. These imperatives simply state that an organization must have quality management systems, quality products and technology, and quality people—and that the combined energies of its management, products, and people must be focused on customer satisfaction.

Today, CNFD has programs in place to improve quality on a continuous basis in every segment of the organization. Management has discovered that "Quality First" is not merely the sum of a lot of individual quality improvement programs. The power of "Quality First" is much greater than that. "Quality First" results from the synergy of all components of an organization working together.

Results Count

"Quality First" has been the single most important factor in the division's overall business strategy. It has helped to reinforce CNFD's position as a world leader in the marketplace. But more importantly, it has given division personnel a totally new perspective and a new way of thinking. CNFD people constantly come up with new ideas for making things better.

The division is also living up to its commitment to deliver software—proposals, reports, documentation, and the like—to its customers on time and devoid of errors. Accurate and timely data is crucial to customers, and the division rating is 98 percent on both scores.

In 1988, CNFD completed a record of 42 consecutive months of 100 percent on-time delivery of finished assemblies and related hardware.

"Quality First" costs, which include internal and external failure costs as well as prevention and appraisal costs, have been reduced by 30 percent in four years, due mainly to reduced rework and scrap costs. CNFD has been able to increase its customer satisfaction rating, a relatively new measure, by about 6 percent in less than one year. That means customers are attaching greater value to the division's products and services than they did a year ago.

Lessons Learned

From its experience in quality improvement, Westinghouse CNFD has learned a number of lessons, which it believes can be applied with reasonable success to any business.

First, an organization must have a common vision, and all people in that organization must embrace a common mission.

Next, a framework for "Quality First" is absolutely critical.

This is the model or blueprint that keeps everyone focused on continuous improvement in all aspects of the business.

The third lesson can be summarized as: measure, measure, and measure. In addition, CNFD discovered that no quality improvement program can be successful unless both employees and customers are intimately involved in the process.

And finally, "Quality First" requires a long-term commitment to continuous quality improvement. A "Quality First" culture cannot be built overnight. "Quality First" is not a short-term proposition. But neither are the rewards. The benefits of Quality First are long-term for a company willing to make the commitment.

Long-term customer satisfaction and long-term industry leadership are what "Quality First" is all about.

XEROX BUSINESS PRODUCTS AND SYSTEMS

For its first 15 years, Xerox was without equal, best in an industry whose products were synonymous with its name. But challenges came in the mid-1970s from foreign and U.S. competitors that surpassed Xerox reprographic products in both cost and quality.

Not even second best in some product categories, Xerox launched an ambitious quality improvement program in 1984 to arrest its decline in the world market it created. Today, the company can once again claim the title as the industry's best in nearly all copier product markets. As a result, Xerox has not only halted loss of world market share, but also reversed it.

Xerox Business Products and Systems (BP&S), headquartered in Stamford, Connecticut, attributes the turnaround to its strategy of Leadership Through Quality. The company defines quality through the eyes of the customer. Xerox BP&S knows what customers want in products and services.

Analyses of a wide variety of data, gathered with exhaustive collection efforts that include monthly surveys of 55,000 Xerox equipment owners, enable the company to identify customer requirements. The company uses this information to develop concrete business plans with measurable targets for achieving the quality improvements necessary to meet customers' needs.

Xerox at a Glance

One of two Xerox Corporation businesses, Business Products and Systems employs 50,200 people at 83 U.S. locations. BP&S makes more than 250 types of document-processing equipment, generating $6 billion in 1988 U.S. sales, or 54 percent of the company's domestic revenues. Copiers and other duplicating equipment account for nearly 70 percent of BP&S revenues. The remainder is divided among sales of electronic printers and typing equipment, networks, work stations, and software products.

Leadership through Quality

Customer satisfaction is the number one priority at Xerox. The corporation's strategy for achieving that priority is Leadership Through Quality, the Xerox total quality initiative that pervades the entire organization. Personally driven by CEO David T. Kearns and his senior management team, Leadership Through Quality, initiated in 1983, is guided by the simple but powerful Xerox Quality Policy:

> Xerox is a quality company. Quality is the basic business principle for Xerox. Quality means providing our external and internal customers with innovative products and services that fully satisfy their requirements. Quality improvement is the job of every Xerox employee.

At Xerox, quality is defined as "fully meeting customer requirements." To do this, Leadership Through Quality encompasses a wide range of initiatives. Key initiatives are the *benchmarking* of Xerox's performance against its competitors and industry leaders; *employee involvement* to fully realize all of their people's talents and capabilities to satisfy customers; and the use of *quality tools and processes* developed specifically for Xerox to achieve continuous quality improvement. Among these processes are a six-step problem-solving process and a nine-step quality-improvement process. The thrust of Leadership Through Quality is prevention; both processes are used at all

levels of the organization to identify and correct potential diffi-
culties, as well as to act on quality opportunities.

Leadership Through Quality has transformed the way Xerox
does business. Establishing objectives with individual units,
planning for future products, delivering current products,
reviewing progress—all of these activities start with a focus on
customer requirements, proceed through work processes built
around quality, and are reviewed and evaluated against the
original set of customer requirements. Decisions at every point
are guided by Leadership Through Quality processes and
based on factual data. Data for decision making in all these activities comes from over 375 major information systems—of
which 175 relate specifically to the management, evaluation,
and planning of quality.

To support this massive quality effort, Xerox created an extensive training program. All Xerox employees have received at
least the basic 28-hour Leadership Through Quality training;
many have been trained in advanced quality techniques. Over
the last four years, Xerox has invested four million man-hours
and $125 million in Leadership Through Quality training.

Training and empowerment have furthered the basic Xerox
strategy of employee involvement. Xerox estimates that at any
given time, 75 percent of its employees are actively working on
one or more of 7,000 quality improvement teams. The empowerment of field managers has been greatly enhanced by the creation of district partnerships, in which employees involved
with sales, service, and administration functions work closely
to make customer-oriented decisions once made at higher organization levels. And on the front lines, the service organization's work-group strategy empowers customer service engineers to manage their work loads in ways that deliver better
service to customers.

An important factor in Xerox's quality initiative is the Amal-
gamated Clothing and Textile Workers Union. Xerox and the
union jointly encourage participation by union members in
quality improvement processes, with such success that the
partnership, unique in American industry, is considered a role
model by other corporations. The recently ratified contract
states that "every employee shall support the concept of con-

tinuous quality improvement while reducing quality costs through teamwork and the tools and processes of Leadership Through Quality." Union/management study teams have found ways to retain work inside the corporation—with resulting savings of $7 million annually and 250 jobs.

Xerox is proud of the results realized by Leadership Through Quality. Among those results achieved over the last 5 years are:

- A 78 percent improvement in the quality of Xerox machines.

- Year after year, Xerox copiers and printers continuously set new benchmarks for copy quality.

- More than 40 percent improvement in product reliability.

- The introduction of the industry's first three-year warranty, now offered on five Xerox copiers.

- A 73 percent reduction in production-line defective parts.

Xerox suppliers are made full partners with Xerox through continuous supplier involvement. Xerox supplier parts are process-qualified, which means a step-by-step procedure is in place to analyze and qualify suppliers' production and control processes. Xerox provides training and follow-up in such areas as statistical process control, just-in-time, and total quality techniques.

But Xerox's proudest achievement is the response of their customers to Xerox's efforts to improve quality. They are actively soliciting their customers' requirements and reactions, surveying 55,000 of them monthly about performance in equipment, sales, service, and administrative support. Results have shown a 38 percent improvement in their customers' perceptions of Xerox's performance. Customers also show their satisfaction with Xerox in other ways: Their purchases of Xerox products enabled Xerox to reverse the erosion of their market share by Japanese firms—one of the very few American companies to have accomplished this. Customers also respond to Xerox quality through formal ratings.

In Xerox's continuous drive for quality improvement, the corporation has set very demanding future targets. For example, their targets for 1993 include:

- Benchmark performance in the corporation's product development cycle schedule.
- A 50 percent reduction in unit manufacturing cost.
- A fourfold improvement in reliability.

Xerox is committed to continuous quality improvement because it is committed to customer satisfaction. Using Leadership Through Quality, the corporation is determined to constantly upgrade those processes and decisions that deliver world-class products to the most important members of Team Xerox: its customers.

Xerox Benchmarking System

In its quest to elevate its products and services to world-class status, Xerox BP&S devised a benchmarking system that has, in itself, become a model. The company measures its performance in about 240 key areas of product, service, and business performance. Derived from international studies, the ultimate target for each attribute is the level of performance achieved by the world leader, regardless of industry.

Returns from the company's strategy for continuous quality improvement have materialized quickly as noted below:

Customer Processes

- Highly satisfied customers have increased 38 percent and 39 percent for copier/duplicator and printing systems, respectively.
- Customer satisfaction within Xerox sales processes have improved 40 percent; service processes, 18 percent; and administrative processes, 21 percent.
- Billing quality has improved 35 percent.

- Service response time has improved 27 percent.

- Supply order returns have improved 38 percent.

Productivity

- Service visits per day have been increasing 4 percent a year.

- Product performance during the first 30 days of installation has increased 40 percent.

- Manufacturing lead times have been reduced 50 percent.

- Manufacturing labor and material overhead rates have been improved by 31 percent and 46 percent, respectively.

- Customer retention rate is 20 percent better than U.S. industry average and Xerox is gaining customers at a rate of more than four new customers for every three customers lost.

People

- 75 percent of all Xerox employees are actively involved with quality-improvement or problem-solving projects.

- 94 percent of Xerox employees acknowledge that customer satisfaction is their top priority.

- Employee turnover is 17 percent better than the average reported by the Bureau of National Affairs.

Safety

- Product safety has improved 70 percent with an associated 90 percent decrease in claims. Xerox has not had a product liability judgment in the last five years.

- Xerox employees are three times safer on the job than around the home. There has never been an industrial fatality or a major OSHA citation in Xerox.

These improvements have enabled Xerox BP&S to take additional steps to distinguish itself from the competition; for instance, it was the first in the industry to offer a three-year product warranty.

The thrust of Leadership Through Quality is ongoing with Xerox BP&S. The process of continuous quality improvement, directed toward greater customer satisfaction and enhanced business performance, is currently targeting a 50 percent reduction in unit manufacturing cost and fourfold improvement in reliability by 1993. Such goals illustrate the commitment concentrated in the Xerox quality policy, which states that "quality is the basic business principle at Xerox."

FOLLOW BY EXAMPLE!

This chapter has presented the approaches taken by some of America's quality leaders who are world-class providers of products and/or services—from very large to small companies involved in diverse business, from Federal Express overnight package delivery to Xerox's turnaround of its copier business. Each of these companies has developed its own customized approach at improving quality. Each has recognized that "Quality First" is not a buzzword but a bedrock upon which these American quality leaders are now prospering.

After examination of these American quality leaders' efforts to improve their business by adopting "Quality First" principles, you may wish to assess your own organization's quality climate, implementation processes, management tools, and accomplishments by completing the "Quality First" self-assessment provided in the next chapter.

Chapter Six
Quality First
Self-Assessment

*"Look for the ways you trip yourself up—how you get in your own way
without meaning to. It will help you anticipate where problems and setbacks
will likely occur."*

Tom Peters and Nancy Austin
A Passion for Excellence

SELF-ASSESSMENT APPROACH

This chapter provides a method to assess the current practices, policies, procedures, and attitudes throughout your
own organization as they relate to quality enhancement, and
provides the opportunity to assess the effects of any changes as
they relate to quality enhancement. It also provides an opportunity to check your progress by occasionally re-evaluating
your performance.

This self-assessment asks questions concerning:

- Climate—People's perceptions about their organization
  and/or work units.

- Processes—The organization's or work unit's policies,
  practices, and procedures.

- Management tools—The specific techniques used to promote quality improvements throughout the organization or work units.

- Outcomes—Mission accomplishment.

The self-assessment questions are divided into four groups: climate, processes, tools, and outcomes. Some of the questions ask you to consider the entire organization in your response, and others ask you to think only about your immediate work unit. The definitions of these two terms need to be clear in your mind prior to the use of this self-assessment so that you are referring to the organization and work unit in the same way as the self-assessment.

Decide which organization and work unit you wish to examine and enter the names below. For example, you may be in charge of a corporation. The corporation may contain three divisions. The divisions, in turn, may be composed of several departments. Depending on your interest, the corporation may be designated as the organization, and one of the three divisions as the work unit.

Name of organization = _____

Work unit = _____

Another term you will encounter is "customer," defined as anyone who receives the work that your work unit(s), or your organization, performs. Note that customers can be another organization, another work unit, or any organization member. The traditional notion of customer as someone outside your immediate organization or work unit that uses or buys your product or service can also apply. In all cases, consider that your customer relies on and judges the quality of the work that you do.

The source of this evaluation structure is the "Quality and Productivity Self-Assessment Guide," a public-domain federal report. You may reproduce this chapter to aid in your use of this self-assessment tool.

To conduct the "Quality First" self-assessment, complete the following worksheets for each self-assessment element (climate, processes, tools, outcomes). There are 215 self-assessment questions, which can be answered in approximately 15 minutes. The scoring rationale follows the questions.

ASSESSMENT OF ORGANIZATION CLIMATE

The following list of statements is presented for your evaluation and ranking. There are no wrong answers. Circle the number 1, 2, 3, 4, 5, or 6 that you feel best indicates the extent of your agreement with the statement. The legend for the questionnaire is: (1) strongly disagree, (2) disagree, (3) somewhat disagree, (4) somewhat agree, (5) agree, and (6) strongly agree.

	Strongly Disagree					Strongly Agree
1. People in this organization are aware of its overall mission.	1	2	3	4	5	6
2. In general, this organization's customers believe that we care about what they think.	1	2	3	4	5	6
3. People in this organization are aware of how their jobs contribute to the organization's mission.	1	2	3	4	5	6
4. It's in everyone's best interests that this organization be successful.	1	2	3	4	5	6
5. People in this organization are aware of how the organization's mission contributes to higher-level missions and objectives.	1	2	3	4	5	6
6. In general, this organization's customers would not go elsewhere even if it were possible.	1	2	3	4	5	6

Legend: (1) strongly disagree, (2) disagree, (3) somewhat disagree, (4) somewhat agree, (5) agree, and (6) strongly agree.

	Strongly Disagree				Strongly Agree

People in this organization:

7. try to plan ahead for changes (such as in policy) that might impact our mission performance.   1 2 3 4 5 6

8. try to plan ahead for technological changes (such as new development in computer software) that might impact our mission performance.   1 2 3 4 5 6

9. regularly work together to plan for the future.   1 2 3 4 5 6

10. see continuing improvement as essential.   1 2 3 4 5 6

11. care about what will happen to the organization after they are reassigned.   1 2 3 4 5 6

---

12. Creativity is actively encouraged in this organization.   1 2 3 4 5 6

13. Innovators are the people who get ahead in this organization.   1 2 3 4 5 6

---

14. The quality of our work is second only to mission accomplishment as the overriding focus of this organization.   1 2 3 4 5 6

15. Every member of this organization is concerned with the need for quality.   1 2 3 4 5 6

Legend: (1) strongly disagree, (2) disagree, (3) somewhat disagree, (4) somewhat agree, (5) agree, and (6) strongly agree.

	Strongly Disagree			Strongly Agree		

16. Continuous quality improvements within this organization can lead to more productive use of our resources.   1   2   3   4   5   6

17. People in this organization know how to define the quality of what they do.   1   2   3   4   5   6

18. Every member of this organization needs to contribute to quality improvement.   1   2   3   4   5   6

People in this organization:

19. live up to high ethical standards.   1   2   3   4   5   6

20. like to do a good job.   1   2   3   4   5   6

21. emphasize doing things right the first time.   1   2   3   4   5   6

The leader(s) in this organization (people at the highest level):

22. are committed to providing top-quality services/products/work.   1   2   3   4   5   6

23. regularly review the quality of work produced.   1   2   3   4   5   6

24. ask people about ways to improve the work produced.   1   2   3   4   5   6

25. follow up suggestions for improvement.   1   2   3   4   5   6

The leader(s) in this organization (people at the highest level):

26. set examples of quality performance in their day to day activities.   1   2   3   4   5   6

Legend: (1) strongly disagree, (2) disagree, (3) somewhat disagree, (4) somewhat agree, (5) agree, and (6) strongly agree.

	Strongly Disagree				Strongly Agree	

27. regularly review the organization's progress toward meeting its goals and objectives.
    1 2 3 4 5 6

28. attempt to find out why the organization may not be meeting a particular goal/objective.
    1 2 3 4 5 6

People in my work unit:

29. turn to their supervisors for advice about how to improve their work.
    1 2 3 4 5 6

30. know how their supervisors will help them find answers to problems they may be having.
    1 2 3 4 5 6

31. are challenged by their supervisors to find ways to improve the system.
    1 2 3 4 5 6

The supervisors in my work unit:

32. make the continuous improvement of our work top priority.
    1 2 3 4 5 6

33. regularly ask our customers about the quality of work they receive.
    1 2 3 4 5 6

34. The structure of our organization makes it easy to focus on quality.
    1 2 3 4 5 6

35. The way we do things in this organization is consistent with quality.
    1 2 3 4 5 6

Legend: (1) strongly disagree, (2) disagree, (3) somewhat disagree, (4) somewhat agree, (5) agree, and (6) strongly agree.

	Strongly Disagree				Strongly Agree	

36. People in my work unit understand how a quality emphasis leads to more productive use of resources.

1 2 3 4 5 6

37. People in my work unit can describe the organization's quality and productivity policy.

1 2 3 4 5 6

---

38. People in my work unit believe that quality and productivity improvement is their responsibility.

1 2 3 4 5 6

39. People in my work unit take pride in their work.

1 2 3 4 5 6

40. People in my work unit share responsibility for the success or failure of our services/products.

1 2 3 4 5 6

41. People in my work unit believe that their work is important to the success of the overall organization.

1 2 3 4 5 6

---

42. We have good relationships between departments in this organization.

1 2 3 4 5 6

43. Co-workers in this organization cooperate with each other to get the job done.

1 2 3 4 5 6

44. A spirit of cooperation and teamwork exists in this organization.

1 2 3 4 5 6

45. We have good relationships with other organizations that we work with.

1 2 3 4 5 6

Legend: (1) strongly disagree, (2) disagree, (3) somewhat disagree, (4) somewhat agree, (5) agree, and (6) strongly agree.

	Strongly Disagree					*Strongly Agree*
46. Supervisors in my work unit request employee opinions and data.	1	2	3	4	5	6
47. People in my work unit are involved in improving our services/products/work.	1	2	3	4	5	6
48. We have the appropriate personnel in my work unit to get the job done properly.	1	2	3	4	5	6
49. The work goals or standards in my work unit are generally fair.	1	2	3	4	5	6
50. The supervisors in my work unit do a good job of setting work expectations.	1	2	3	4	5	6
51. People in my work unit are friendly with one another.	1	2	3	4	5	6
52. People in my work unit enjoy their co-workers.	1	2	3	4	5	6
53. We have the right tools, equipment, and materials in my work unit to get the job done.	1	2	3	4	5	6
54. The materials and supplies we need in my work unit are delivered on time as ordered.	1	2	3	4	5	6
55. The distribution of work among the people in my work unit is well-balanced.	1	2	3	4	5	6

Legend: (1) strongly disagree, (2) disagree, (3) somewhat disagree, (4) somewhat agree, (5) agree, and (6) strongly agree.

	Strongly Disagree					Strongly Agree
56. In my work unit, we have enough time to perform our jobs in a professional manner.	1	2	3	4	5	6
57. My work unit is structured properly to get the job done.	1	2	3	4	5	6
58. People in my work unit are rewarded for good work.	1	2	3	4	5	6
59. People in my work unit are paid fairly for the work that they do.	1	2	3	4	5	6
60. Attempts are made to promote the people in my work unit who do good work.	1	2	3	4	5	6
61. People in my work unit receive promotions because they have earned them.	1	2	3	4	5	6
62. Supervisors in my work unit give credit to people when they do a good job.	1	2	3	4	5	6
63. There are penalties for people in my work unit.	1	2	3	4	5	6
64. There is quick recognition for people in my work unit for outstanding performance by an individual or team.	1	2	3	4	5	6
65. People in my work unit know who their customers are.	1	2	3	4	5	6
66. People in my work unit care about our customers.	1	2	3	4	5	6

Legend: (1) strongly disagree, (2) disagree, (3) somewhat disagree, (4) somewhat agree, (5) agree, and (6) strongly agree.

	Strongly Disagree				Strongly Agree	
67. There are effective communication channels between departments in this organization.	1	2	3	4	5	6
68. People in my work unit do not have to rely on "the grapevine" or rumors for information.	1	2	3	4	5	6
69. People in my work unit have ample opportunity to exchange information with their supervisors.	1	2	3	4	5	6
70. People in my work unit get the facts and the information they need to do a good job.	1	2	3	4	5	6

ASSESSMENT OF PROCESSES

The statements in the following sections are varied in format. In each case, circle the response number to the right of each statement that most closely represents the extent of your perception about your organization.

	Yes	No	Not Sure
This organization has:			
71. used surveys of some/all of its members in order to determine whether improvements in quality are needed.	2	1	1
72. used formal interviews with some/all of its members in order to determine whether improvements in quality are needed.	2	1	1

	Yes	No	Not Sure
73. informally asked some/all of its members for their opinions about whether improvements in quality are needed.	2	1	1
74. asked senior management people for their opinions about whether improvements in quality are needed.	2	1	1
75. analyzed data concerning goal/ objective accomplishments in order to determine whether improvements in quality are needed.	2	1	1
76. relied on "higher order" directives in order to determine whether improvements in quality are needed.	2	1	1
77. asked established team members to report periodically.	2	1	1

This organization is (or might become) committed to quality improvement because:

	Yes	No	Not Sure
78. we are mandated to do so by a higher authority.	2	1	1
79. the people at the top level of this organization are/were dissatisfied with the quality being achieved.	2	1	1
80. we want to improve an already acceptable quality record.	2	1	1
81. we want to maintain a specified level of service in the face of budget reductions.	2	1	1

	Yes	*No*	*Not Sure*
82. the people we serve deserve our best efforts.	2	1	1

	Yes	*No*	*Don't Have Policy*
This organization has a quality improvement policy that:			
83. is written.	2	1	1
84. has specific goals and objectives.	2	1	1
85. everyone in the organization has seen.	2	1	1
86. is taken seriously by people.	2	1	1
87. holds people accountable for success/failure.	2	1	1

	Yes	*No*	*Does Not Apply*
Responsibility for quality performance improvement:			
88. is accepted by senior management.	2	1	1
89. is accepted by middle management.	2	1	1
90. is accepted by almost all organizational members.	2	1	1

| 91. This organization has a separately identified office that oversees its quality improvement efforts. | 2 | 1 | 1 |

	Yes	No	Does Not Apply
92. Quality improvement concerns are discussed/monitored at least on a quarterly basis.	2	1	1
93. Managers at all levels have clearly defined roles in our quality improvement process.	2	1	1
94. This organization uses teams to monitor quality improvement projects.	2	1	1
95. Managers at all levels are responsible for the success or failure of our quality improvement efforts.	2	1	1
96. This organization has a database or tracking system for relevant quality information.	2	1	1

	Yes	No	Not Sure

In order to determine what our customers think about our products/services work, we:

	Yes	No	Not Sure
97. conduct surveys on a regular basis.	2	1	1
98. ask them informally.	2	1	1
99. monitor complaints.	2	1	1
100. ask our employees who have contact with our customers.	2	1	1

The leaders at the top level in this organization:

	Yes	No	Not Sure
101. have agreed upon a definition of quality improvement.	2	1	1

	Yes	No	*Not Sure*
102. have set long-term goals concerning quality improvement.	2	1	1
103. have set short-term objectives concerning quality improvement.	2	1	1
104. have defined performance measures to monitor progress toward reaching objectives and goals.	2	1	1

	Almost None			*Almost All*		

How many work units within this organization:

105. know how the organization defines quality improvement?   1 2 3 4 5 6

106. have set long-term goals concerning quality improvement?   1 2 3 4 5 6

107. have set short-term objectives concerning quality improvement?   1 2 3 4 5 6

108. have defined performance measures to monitor progress toward reaching their objectives and goals?   1 2 3 4 5 6

How many organizational members:

109. can specify, if asked, what goals or objectives they are working toward?   1 2 3 4 5 6

110. were invited to participate in setting goals or objectives related to their work?   1 2 3 4 5 6

Legend: (1) almost none, (2) very few, (3) some, (4) quite a few, (5) most, and (6) almost all.

	Almost None				Almost All

111. know how the goals/objectives they are working toward relate to their work unit's mission?	1	2	3	4	5	6
112. know how performance measures relate to monitoring their accomplishment of goals and objectives?	1	2	3	4	5	6

Legend: (1) almost none, (2) very few, (3) some, (4) quite a few, (5) most, and (6) almost all.

	Yes	No	Not Sure
Long-range planning in this organization includes:			
113. integration of quality improvement planning into general business planning.	2	1	1
114. prioritizing quality improvement issues.	2	1	1
115. customer input.	2	1	1
116. employee input.	2	1	1
117. quality improvement implementation strategies for all work units.	2	1	1
118. a means for monitoring quality improvement effectiveness over time.	2	1	1

	Yes	No	Not Sure
In terms of setting organizational improvement priorities, we have considered or evaluated:			
119. changing our business strategy.	2	1	1
120. improving our work methods or procedures.	2	1	1
121. bettering our employee utilization.	2	1	1

	Yes	No	*Not Sure*
122. revising or instituting training programs.	2	1	1
123. acquiring recent technological improvements (equipment, materials).	2	1	1

	Strongly Disagree					*Strongly Agree*
124. The structure of this organization supports its efforts to carry out its mission.	1	2	3	4	5	6
125. Organizational members have the information they need to do their work.	1	2	3	4	5	6
126. This organization has a realistic schedule for replacing outdated equipment.	1	2	3	4	5	6
127. Organizational members have been adequately trained to use the equipment they have.	1	2	3	4	5	6
128. Before equipment is bought by or issued to this organization, plans have been made concerning how it will be used and who will use it.	1	2	3	4	5	6
129. Efforts are made to update work methods in this organization (e.g., the way work is organized and the tools or materials used to accomplish it).	1	2	3	4	5	6

Legend: (1) strongly disagree, (2) disagree, (3) somewhat disagree, (4) somewhat agree, (5) agree, and (6) strongly agree.

	Strongly Disagree					*Strongly Agree*
130. People in charge of similar work units frequently share information about their work methods and practices.	1	2	3	4	5	6
131. Updating work methods can be the key to quality improvement.	1	2	3	4	5	6

Organization members with good ideas are likely to:

	Strongly Disagree					*Strongly Agree*
132. formally submit them through a suggestion system.	1	2	3	4	5	6
133. tell their supervisors.	1	2	3	4	5	6
134. be asked periodically what they think.	1	2	3	4	5	6

	Yes	*No*	*Not Sure*
135. This organization has a suggestion program.	2	1	1
136. This organization has conducted "brainstorming" sessions that included lower-level organizational members.	2	1	1
137. This organization has used teams to gather information or solve problems.	2	1	1

	Strongly Disagree					*Strongly Agree*
138. Creative thinking is rewarded in this organization.	1	2	3	4	5	6

Legend: (1) strongly disagree, (2) disagree, (3) somewhat disagree, (4) somewhat agree, (5) agree, and (6) strongly agree.

	Strongly *Disagree*					*Strongly* *Agree*

139. Taking risks is rewarded in this organization.   1 2 3 4 5 6

140. Managers at all levels have the authority to try a promising new approach.   1 2 3 4 5 6

141. A promising new approach is likely to be approved quickly for a trial.   1 2 3 4 5 6

142. The future strength of this organization is dependent on the continuing growth of its members through appropriate training.   1 2 3 4 5 6

Legend: (1) strongly disagree, (2) disagree, (3) somewhat disagree, (4) somewhat agree, (5) agree, and (6) strongly agree.

143. Circle the response number next to the *one* statement that best represents your organization.

    Most nonsupervisory members have direct input in setting goals or expectations for their work.   6

    Most nonsupervisory members have indirect input through representatives in setting goals or expectations for their work.   4

    Most nonsupervisory members can negotiate with management after they are assigned goals or expectations for their work.   3

    Most nonsupervisory members have no input about goals or expectations for their work.   1

144. Circle the response number next to the *one* statement that best represents your organization.

    Most organizational members attend mandatory in-house training programs to learn about quality improvement techniques.   6

    Most organizational members attend in-house training programs on a voluntary basis to learn about quality improvement techniques.   5

Most organizational members attend outside seminars to learn about quality improvement techniques.   4

Most organizational members review resources
(books, tapes) that are available in-house to learn
about quality improvement techniques.   3

None of the above.   1

	Yes	No	Not Sure

In order to tell how well we are doing as an organization, we
monitor data about:

		Yes	No	Not Sure
145.	our efficiency.	2	1	1
146.	our effectiveness.	2	1	1
147.	our productivity.	2	1	1
148.	the quality of our services/ products/work.	2	1	1
149.	the timeliness of our work.	2	1	1
150.	our innovativeness.	2	1	1
151.	the quality of working life for our members.	2	1	1
152.	our finances.	2	1	1

		Yes	No	Don't Collect Data

The performance data that this organization collects:

		Yes	No	Don't Collect Data
153.	are tracked over time.	2	1	1
154.	are compared with goals, standards, or objectives.	2	1	1
155.	are compared with other similar organizations.	2	1	1

	Yes	No	Don't Collect Data
The performance data that this organization collects:			
156. are evaluated at least quarterly.	2	1	1
157. are used to identify problems/ barriers.	2	1	1
158. are evaluated by a team or task force.	2	1	1
159. are used to identify opportunities for quality improvement.	2	1	1

	Yes	No	Not Sure
160. Organizational members are informed about how this work unit stands in relation to goals, objectives, or standards.	2	1	1

Top-performing managers at all levels in this organization:

	Yes	No	Not Sure
161. can expect a monetary bonus or award.	2	1	1
162. can expect an award.	2	1	1
163. can expect to be recognized by leaders at the top level.	2	1	1
164. can expect to be told they are doing a great job.	2	1	1
165. can expect increased responsibility.	2	1	1

Top-performing organizational members:

	Yes	No	Not Sure
166. can expect a monetary bonus or award.	2	1	1

	Yes	No	Not Sure
167. can expect an award.	2	1	1
168. can expect to be recognized by leaders at the top level.	2	1	1
169. can expect to be told they are doing a great job.	2	1	1
170. can expect increased responsibility.	2	1	1
171. The performance appraisals (non-Deming organizations) of managers at all levels include quality improvement criteria.	2	1	1
172. The performance appraisals (non-Deming organizations) of organizational members include quality improvement criteria.	2	1	1

MANAGEMENT TOOLS ASSESSMENT

	Yes	No	Not Sure
This organization has:			
173. used surveys to assess employee opinion about the organization's practices or policies.	2	1	1
174. used surveys to gather information about what in the organization needs improving.	2	1	1
175. used surveys to assess the outcomes of its work.	2	1	1

	Yes	No	Not Sure
176. used surveys to assess the quality of its work.	2	1	1
177. used surveys to assess employee opinions about the goals/objectives they are working toward.	2	1	1
178. called groups of individuals together to define or clarify the organization's mission and/or work.	2	1	1
179. called groups of individuals together to define long-term organizational-level goals and/or long-term work unit-level goals.	2	1	1
180. called groups of individuals together to define short-term organizational objectives and/or short-term work unit objectives.	2	1	1
181. called groups of individuals together to identify obstacles to goal/objective accomplishment.	2	1	1
182. called groups of individuals together to define performance measures to track progress toward goal attainment.	2	1	1
183. The organization uses statistical process-control charts or graphs to track data over time.	2	1	1
184. This organization uses diagrams or flow charts to highlight potential causes of problems.	2	1	1

	Yes	No	Not Sure
185. This organization has evaluated its office and work space design.	2	1	1
186. This organization has a high-quality information resource library.	2	1	1
187. This organization has arranged workshops to promote quality awareness among its members.	2	1	1
188. This organization has published newsletters containing quality improvement information.	2	1	1
189. This organization has posted information on bulletin boards about quality improvement.	2	1	1
190. This organization has held contests to reward the "most improved" work units.	2	1	1
191. This organization has attempted to inform and involve everyone in quality improvement.	2	1	1
192. This organization has used team building (techniques to improve group member relationships).	2	1	1
193. This organization has established improvement teams (groups of individuals who come together to solve quality-related problems).	2	1	1

ORGANIZATIONAL ASSESSMENT

	Strongly Disagree				*Strongly Agree*	
194. Work delays are uncommon in this organization.	1	2	3	4	5	6
195. Once a job or project gets started, it's usually finished without undue delay.	1	2	3	4	5	6
196. There is little wastage of materials and supplies.	1	2	3	4	5	6
197. People make efforts to reuse or salvage excess materials and supplies whenever possible.	1	2	3	4	5	6
198. Tools and/or equipment are maintained and operated at peak efficiency.	1	2	3	4	5	6
199. Our tools and/or equipment rarely require repair.	1	2	3	4	5	6
200. This organization has sufficient personnel to accomplish its mission.	1	2	3	4	5	6
201. The personnel turnover rate is low.	1	2	3	4	5	6
202. Working conditions (noise, heat, light, dirt) in this organization are excellent.	1	2	3	4	5	6
203. Work facilities (bathrooms, cafeterias, conference rooms, etc.) are excellent.	1	2	3	4	5	6

Legend: (1) strongly disagree, (2) disagree, (3) somewhat disagree, (4) somewhat agree, (5) agree, and (6) strongly agree.

	Strongly Disagree				Strongly Agree	
204. Organizational members are well trained.	1	2	3	4	5	6
205. Organizational members receive the guidance and assistance they need to accomplish their work.	1	2	3	4	5	6
206. This organization's materials and supplies are well accounted for without unexplained losses.	1	2	3	4	5	6
207. This organization's materials and supplies meet quality specifications.	1	2	3	4	5	6

Organizational members rarely need to:

208. shift work priorities in order to get jobs done.	1	2	3	4	5	6
209. rework a job or task.	1	2	3	4	5	6

The organization's customers:

210. are satisfied with the quality of our work.	1	2	3	4	5	6
211. seldom complain.	1	2	3	4	5	6

The organization's customers:

212. are satisfied with the quantity of our work.	1	2	3	4	5	6
213. are satisfied with the timeliness of our work.	1	2	3	4	5	6

Legend: (1) strongly disagree, (2) disagree, (3) somewhat disagree, (4) somewhat agree, (5) agree, and (6) strongly agree.

	Strongly Disagree				*Strongly Agree*	

The organization's customers:

214. find minimal errors in our work.   1 2 3 4 5 6

215. find our work consistent.   1 2 3 4 5 6

Legend: (1) strongly disagree, (2) disagree, (3) somewhat disagree, (4) somewhat agree, (5) agree, and (6) strongly agree.

SCORING SELF-ASSESSMENT

The following scoring worksheets provide a way to evaluate your self-assessment. Transfer the value of your responses to the questions or sets of questions, as indicated by the worksheet groupings, then divide the number shown on the form. Carry out the division to two decimal points. For example, say you responded "6," "5," "4," "3," "2," and "1" to Climate questions 1 through 6, respectively. On the Climate Scoring Worksheet you would write "21" in the blank for Awareness of Strategic Challenge, divide 21 by 6 (the value indicated), then write "3.50" in the blank in the Your Score column. A scoring summary table, which shows the target score for each category, follows each worksheet. Transfer the worksheet scores to the corresponding category in the table. In our example, you would write "3.50" in the Your Score column next to the Awareness of Strategic Challenge category.

By comparing your scores with the target scores, you can evaluate how you and your organization perceive quality. If your score is equal to or lower than a target score, you need to improve your approach to quality in that area. Review the "Quality First" principles and practices described in Chapter 7 to discover ways you can significantly improve your quality.

Climate Scoring Worksheet

Your Score

Awareness of Strategic Challenge	Add response numbers from questions 1–6 and place total in space at right.	___ ÷ 6 = ___
Vision for the Future	Add response numbers from questions 7–11 and place total in space at right.	___ ÷ 5 = ___
Innovation	Add response numbers from questions 12–13 and place total in space at right.	___ ÷ 2 = ___
Quality Policy/ Philosophy	Add response numbers from questions 14–18 and place total in space at right.	___ ÷ 5 = ___
Value Systems/ Ethics	Add response numbers from questions 19–21 and place total in space at right.	___ ÷ 3 = ___
Strategic Focus =	Total of scores (questions 1–21)	___ ÷ 21 = ___
Top Management Involvement	Add response numbers from questions 22–25 and place total in space at right.	___ ÷ 4 = ___
Visible Commitment to Goals	Add response numbers from questions 26–28 and place total in space at right.	___ ÷ 3 = ___

Your Score

Role in Quality Improvement Process	Add response numbers from questions 29–31 and place total in space at right.	___ ÷ 3 = ___
Concern for Improvement	Add response numbers from questions 32–33 and place total in spaces at right.	___ ÷ 2 = ___
Systems/ Structure for Quality Improvement	Add response numbers from questions 34–35 and place total in space at right.	___ ÷ 2 = ___
Leadership and Management =	Total of scores (questions 22–35)	___ ÷ 14 = ___

Awareness of Quality Issues	Add response numbers from questions 36–37 and place total in space at right.	___ ÷ 2 = ___
Attitudes/ Morale	Add response numbers from questions 38–41 and place total in space at right.	___ ÷ 4 = ___
Cooperation	Add response numbers from questions 42–45 and place total in space at right.	___ ÷ 4 = ___
Involvement	Add response numbers from questions 46–47 and place total in space at right.	___ ÷ 2 = ___

Your Score

Perceptions of Work Environment	Add response numbers from questions 48–50 and place total in space at right.	___ ÷ 3 = ___
Social Interactions	Add response numbers from questions 51–52 and place total in space at right.	___ ÷ 2 = ___
Task Characteristics	Add response numbers from questions 53–57 and place total in space at right.	___ ÷ 5 = ___
Consequential Constraints	Add response numbers from questions 58–64 and place total in space at right.	___ ÷ 7 = ___
Work Force =	Total of scores (questions 36–64)	___ ÷ 29 = ___
Customer Orientation	Add response numbers from questions 65–66 and place total in space at right.	___ ÷ 2 = ___
Communi- cations	Add response numbers from questions 67–70 and place total in space at right.	___ ÷ 4 = ___

Copy the result for each category to the corresponding space in Table 6–1, 6–2, 6–3 or 6–4, respectively. If any score is *lower* than the target score it means that some practices typically considered helpful for quality may be absent in your organization.

TABLE 6–1
Summary of Climate Scores

Category	Your Score*	Target Score
Awareness of Strategic Challenge	_____	3.50
Vision for the Future	_____	3.50
Innovation	_____	3.50
Quality Policy/Philosophy	_____	3.50
Value System/Ethics	_____	3.50
Top Management Involvement	_____	3.50
Visible Commitment to Goals	_____	3.50
Role in Quality Improvement Process	_____	3.50
Concern for Improvement	_____	3.50
Systems/Structure for Quality Improvement	_____	3.50
Awareness of Productivity/Quality Issues	_____	3.50
Attitudes/Morale	_____	3.50
Cooperation	_____	3.50
Involvement	_____	3.50
Perceptions of Work Environment	_____	3.50
Social Interactions	_____	3.50
Task Characteristics	_____	3.50
Consequential Constraints	_____	3.50
Customer Orientation	_____	3.50
Communications	_____	3.50
	═══════	═══════
TOTAL (average your score by adding the values in this column and dividing by 20)	_____	3.50

* From the Climate Scoring Worksheet

Process Scoring Worksheet

Your Score

Job Analysis   Add response numbers   ___ ÷ 7 = ___
from questions 71–77
and place total in space
at right.

Your Score

Higher Authority	Add response numbers from questions 78–82 and place total in space at right.	___ ÷ 5 = ___
Quality Emphasis	Add response numbers from questions 83–87 and place total in space at right.	___ ÷ 5 = ___
Top Management Leadership	Add response numbers from questions 88–96 and place total in space at right.	___ ÷ 9 = ___
Customer/ Service Activities	Add response numbers from questions 97–100 and place total in space at right.	___ ÷ 4 = ___
Define Improvement	Add response numbers from questions 101–104 and place total in space at right.	___ ÷ 4 = ___
Unit Goals	Add response numbers from questions 105–108 and place total in space at right.	___ ÷ 4 = ___
Organization Goals	Add response numbers from questions 109–112 and place total in space at right.	___ ÷ 4 = ___
Quality Planning	Add response numbers from questions 113–118 and place total in space at right.	___ ÷ 6 = ___

Your Score

Planning Strategy	Add response numbers from questions 119–123 and place total in space at right.	___ ÷ 5 = ___
Organizational Streamlining	Add response numbers from questions 124–125 and place total in space at right.	___ ÷ 2 = ___
Investment/ Appropriate Technology	Add response numbers from questions 126–128 and place total in space at right.	___ ÷ 3 = ___
Methods/ Process Improvement	Add response numbers from questions 129–131 and place total in space at right.	___ ÷ 3 = ___
New Ideas	Add response numbers from questions 132–134 and place total in space at right.	___ ÷ 3 = ___
People- Oriented Input	Add response numbers from questions 135–137 and place total in space at right.	___ ÷ 3 = ___
Track Progress	Add response numbers from questions 138–144 and place total in space at right.	___ ÷ 7 = ___
Measurement	Add response numbers from questions 145–152 and place total in space at right.	___ ÷ 8 = ___

Your Score

Feedback   Add response numbers   ___ ÷ 3 = ___
                 from questions 153–155
                 and place total in space
                 at right.

Evaluation   Add response numbers   ___ ÷ 4 = ___
                 from questions 156–159
                 and place total in space
                 at right.

Results   Place response number   ___ = ___
                 from question 160 in
                 space at right.

Awards   Add response numbers   ___ ÷ 10 = ___
                 from questions 161–170
                 and place total in space
                 at right.

Personnel   Add response numbers   ___ ÷ 2 = ___
Evaluations   from questions 171–172
                 and place total in space
                 at right.

Copy the result for each process category to the corresponding space in Table 6–2. After you have placed your scores in the appropriate spaces, please refer to the adjacent column for score interpretation. Next to each category, if your score is *lower* than or equal to the target score, you need to review your quality program.

Management Tools Scoring Worksheet

Your Score

Assessments   Add response numbers   ___ ÷ 5 = ___
                 from questions 173–177
                 and place total in space
                 at right.

TABLE 6–2
Summary of Process Scores

Category	Your Score*	Target Score
Job Analysis	_____	1.50
Higher Authority	_____	1.50
Quality Emphasis	_____	1.70
Top Management Leadership	_____	1.55
Customer/Service Activities	_____	1.60
Define Improvement	_____	1.60
Unit Goals	_____	3.50
Organization Goals	_____	3.50
Quality Planning	_____	1.50
Planning Strategy	_____	1.50
Organizational Streamlining	_____	3.50
Investment/Appropriate Technology	_____	3.50
Methods/Process Improvement	_____	3.50
New Ideas	_____	3.50
People-Oriented Input	_____	1.40
Track Progress	_____	3.50
Measurement	_____	1.50
Feedback	_____	1.40
Evaluation	_____	1.50
Results	_____	1.00
Awards	_____	1.50
Personnel Evaluations	_____	1.50
	═══	═══
TOTAL (average your score by adding the values in this column and dividing by 22)	_____	2.12

*From the Process Scoring Worksheet

			Your Score
Definition of Tools	Add response numbers from questions 178–182 and place total in space at right.		___ ÷ 5 = ___

Your Score

Measurement/   Add response numbers   ___ ÷ 3 = ___
Process   from questions 183–185
Analysis   and place total in space
                 at right.

Awareness/   Add response numbers   ___ ÷ 5 = ___
Communi-   from questions 186–190
cation   and place total in space
                 at right.

Organizational   Add response numbers   ___ ÷ 3 = ___
Development   from questions 191–193
                 and place total in space
                 at right.

Copy the result for each management tools category to the corresponding space in Table 6–3. After you have placed your scores in the appropriate spaces, please refer to the adjacent column for score interpretation. Next to each category, if your score is *lower* than or equal to the target score, you may want to review your quality program.

TABLE 6–3
Summary of Management Tools Scores

Category	Your Score*	Target Score
Assessments	_____	1.30
Definition of Tools	_____	1.50
Measurement/Process Analysis	_____	1.50
Awareness/Communication	_____	1.50
Organizational Development	_____	1.50
	======	======
TOTAL (average your score by adding the values in this column and dividing by 5)	_____	1.46

*From the Management Tools Scoring Worksheet

Organizational Outcomes Scoring Worksheet

Your Score

Work Flow/
Delays
Add response numbers
from questions 194–195
and place total in space
at right.
___ ÷ 2 = ___

Waste
Add response numbers
from questions 196–197
and place total in space
at right.
___ ÷ 2 = ___

Tools/
Equipment
Add response numbers
from questions 198–199
and place total in space
at right.
___ ÷ 2 = ___

Staffing
Add response numbers
from questions 200–201
and place total in space
at right.
___ ÷ 2 = ___

Facilities
Add response numbers
from questions 202–203
and place total in space
at right.
___ ÷ 2 = ___

Training
Add response numbers
from questions 204–205
and place total in space
at right.
___ ÷ 2 = ___

Supplies/Parts
Add response numbers
from questions 206–207
and place total in space
at right.
___ ÷ 2 = ___

Organization/
Group
Structure
Add response numbers
from questions 208–209
and place total in space
at right.
___ ÷ 2 = ___

Your Score

Customer   Add response numbers   ___ ÷ 2 = ___
Quality   from questions 210–211
Survey   and place total in space
             at right.

Quantity   Add response numbers   ___ ÷ 2 = ___
             from questions 212–213
             and place total in space
             at right.

Reliability Add response numbers   ___ ÷ 2 = ___
             from questions 214–215
             and place total in space
             at right.

Copy the result for each organizational outcome category to the corresponding space in Table 6–4. If any score is *lower* than or equal to 3.50; you need to review your quality approach.

COMPUTERIZED ANALYSIS

This chapter is an edited version of the "Quality and Productivity Self-Assessment Guide." If you want to have more members of your company conduct this type of self-examination and compare your impressions of your perceived level of quality, consider purchasing an automated version of the analysis, available for use on IBM PC-compatible equipment. The software can be obtained from DPPO, Two Skyline Place, Room 1404, 5203 Leesburg Pike, Falls Church, Virginia 22041, (703) 756-3246. Contact Jack Denslow for the price and availability of the latest version of the software.

ASSESSMENT LEADS TO ACTION

This chapter has presented an "arm-chair" approach for self-assessment of your organization's perceived level of quality. It has provided a scoring methodology that alerts you to the

TABLE 6–4
Summary of Organization Outcomes Scores

Category	Your Score*	Target Score
Work Flow/Delays	_____	3.50
Waste	_____	3.50
Tools/Equipment	_____	3.50
Staffing	_____	3.50
Facilities	_____	3.50
Training	_____	3.50
Supplies/Parts	_____	3.50
Organzation/Group Structure	_____	3.50
Customer Quality Survey	_____	3.50
Quantity	_____	3.50
Reliability	_____	3.50
TOTAL (average your score by adding the values in this column and dividing by 11)	_____	3.50

* From the Organizational Outcomes Scoring Worksheet

strengths and weaknesses in your quality efforts. The total scores are really not important. But how you responded to each category and the impression you now have about the potential to improve your quality, your service, and your profitability is very important.

The next chapter provides the key "Quality First" principles and practices that you can apply to your business to significantly improve your quality.

## Chapter Seven

How to Significantly Improve Your Quality

"A journey of a thousand miles must begin with a single step."

The Way of Lao Tzu

ADOPT "QUALITY FIRST" STRATEGY

"Quality First" means that you are meeting your customer requirements by doing the right things right the first time. To provide high-quality products and services, management must believe that an obsession for quality and excellence must pervade all facets of a business, from customer input to product design and engineering, production, service support, and human resource management. The driving force behind "Quality First" is customer satisfaction.

"Quality First" begins with a strategic decision—a decision that must be made and fully supported by top management. That decision, simply put, is the decision to compete as a world-class company. "Quality First" concentrates on quality performance—in every facet of a business—as the primary strategy to achieve and maintain competitive advantage. It requires taking a systematic view of an organization and looking at how each part interrelates to the whole process. In addition, it demands continuous improvement as a way of life.

183

The "Quality First" methodology is built on four imperatives. These imperatives simply state that an organization must
have quality management systems; quality products, services,
and technology; quality people; and that the combined energies of its management, products, and people must be focused
on customer satisfaction.

"Quality First" provides a framework for your application of
its concepts, principles, and practices in terms of your specific
needs. "Quality First" is the integration and synergy of leading
quality initiatives developed by Crosby, Deming, and Juran,
which have also been presented in the Total Quality Management programs promoted by the U.S. government.

"QUALITY FIRST" CONCEPTS AND PRINCIPLES

Getting started with improvement would be easy if you didn't
have so much work to do! But you have so much work to do
precisely because you have not recognized the importance of
"Quality First" and the benefits of continuously improving every system and process. You must get your systems under control and eliminate the sources of unnecessary and unproductive work.

Getting started and sustaining the early quality-improvement initiative is the most difficult task in "Quality First." It requires you to make time in your already tight schedule to do
something that you perceive to be an additional task. You must
modify many of your long-held notions about what good management is all about in exchange for the promise of improvement. It is surprising that anyone is willing to take these first
steps; however, many have already done so and are being
richly rewarded. By ultimately gaining real control over your
work processes instead of permitting them to control you, you
will make large gains.

Those who have blazed the trail toward continuous improvement have left a legacy of many lessons learned. Many have
had false starts, traveled down dead-end roads, and had to
start over. If there is one consistent lesson from those who have
led this effort, it is that there is no universal strategy for suc-

cess. The road to continuous improvement is and must be an appropriately tailored, optimized, and personal one. A general behavior and set of actions, however, characterize most successful efforts. That behavior and those actions are presented here as a suggested general strategy for starting your "Quality First" journey.

While this section speaks directly to you, most behavior and many actions apply equally to your organization as a whole. The elements of this general strategy are listed roughly in order of recommended implementation. The experience of many organizations is that focused application of specific improvement techniques and tools promotes continuous improvement. In this chapter, the earlier elements provide a foundation that is essential to making successful process-improvement efforts and to creating a culture of continuous improvement that will have long-term success and ultimately be self-sustaining. Some elements are necessary only during the initial phases, but most are periodic or continuous activities that should become routine, ongoing behavior by the organization or individual.

The basic elements of "Quality First" fall into 12 areas of activity: (1) demonstrate leadership, (2) build awareness, (3) improve communication, (4) continue to present your vision, (5) focus on the customer, (6) demonstrate success, (7) develop teamwork, (8) provide support, training, and education, (9) build trust and respect, (10) create a "Quality First" environment in which continuous improvement is a way of life, (11) continuously improve all processes, and (12) apply your quality improvement process to your suppliers. Each of these areas encompasses a number of actions.

Demonstrate Leadership

"Quality First" depends on people more than anything else, and people lead or are led—they are not managed. "Quality First" depends on effective leadership, and you must provide that leadership. By taking the initiative, providing an example, and showing the way, you can lead your subordinates and inspire your peers to follow your example. Top leadership is essential, but "Quality First" leaders are needed at all organizational levels. Effective "Quality First" leadership does not necessarily depend on your place in the organization but rather on your enthusiasm and your visible commitment to the process of continuous improvement.

Build Awareness

Building awareness—understanding what "Quality First" is and why it is important to you and your organization—is one of the first and perhaps most important steps in implementing "Quality First." Every person in the organization must become aware of the need to improve, of the promise offered by "Quality First," of the various "Quality First" methodologies, and of the tools and techniques available for improvement efforts. Awareness is the key that opens the door to the potential of "Quality First."

Improve Communication

As you work on building awareness throughout your organization, begin to establish lines of communication both horizontally and vertically. Honest, open communication is probably the single most important factor in successfully creating a "Quality First" environment. It will take time, but it can lead to trust and mutual respect, and can sometimes be the only thing that keeps the effort alive. If people keep talking to one another, they can work through problems, overcome barriers, and find encouragement and support from others involved in quality efforts.

Continue to Present Your Vision

Constancy of purpose establishes a common direction for all organizational elements and ensures that efforts at all levels contribute to achieving broad objectives relevant to the entire organization. Communicating your vision of the organization's goals and objectives throughout the organization is essential to focusing improvement efforts for the common benefit. Your behavior and attitudes must reinforce this constancy of purpose, and you must be conscious of the unspoken signals you send to your subordinates.

Focus on the Customer

Every process in your organization has a customer, and without a customer a process has no purpose. The customer is the recipient of the process's products or services and defines the quality of those products and services. It is only through focusing on your customers that you can truly optimize your processes, because it is only through your customers that you may effectively define your goals and objectives for improvement. You must focus on both your organization's external customers and your internal customers, who are other members of your organization that depend on your products or services for their own processes.

Demonstrate Success

The success or failure of your initial "Quality First" efforts and projects can greatly affect how easily you can get your organization to adopt "Quality First" ideas. It pays to choose these early efforts carefully, looking for opportunities that (1) have a good chance of success, (2) are visible throughout the company, and preferably, to important external customers, and (3) can significantly improve the lives of workers and managers alike. The trick is to find something that is neither so large that you are doomed to failure nor so small that no one will notice if improvements are made.

Develop Teamwork

Teamwork is the engine that drives many improvement efforts. Creating teams allows you to apply diverse skills and experience to your processes and problem solving. Teams provide an underlying basis of experience and history for your improvement effort and are a vehicle through which you allow all individuals to participate in that effort. Not only must individuals cooperate within teams, the teams must cooperate together throughout the organization. An atmosphere of team-work should permeate your organization, affecting not only formal team efforts but also each individual's interaction in the organization.

Often, encouraging teamwork involves teaching people who already work together to consciously act as a team. These nat-ural work groups exist as permanent teams whose objective is the continuous improvement of the processes they own.

Provide Support, Training, and Education

If you expect to implement "Quality First" yourself and expect your subordinates to follow suit, you must ensure adequate time and training resources are available to support your effort. "Quality First" does not depend on additional people or money; rather, it relies on the availability of time for individuals and groups to pursue improvement efforts, and on the avail-ability of training and education to develop needed skills and experience in "Quality First" improvement tools and tech-niques. You must make those time and training resources avail-able for yourself and your people; doing so is one way for you to demonstrate your commitment to the improvement effort.

While awareness is the way you get your "Quality First" ef-fort moving, education and training help accelerate it dramati-cally. Provided in the right place at the right time, education and training allow you and your subordinates to develop skills and experience in the techniques necessary to implement "Quality First." That experience is the first step to making "Quality First" a part of your day-to-day work life. And, of course, technical training and education are essential to im-proving each employee's specific job skills. Education and training are comprehensive, intensive, and unending. Quality improvement efforts begin and continue with lifelong educa-tion and training.

Build Trust and Respect

Employees who trust their managers and who are trusted and respected in turn can provide the edge that organizations need to provide superior services or products. Workers have the best, most up-to-date knowledge about how well processes are working, what problems have arisen, and how things could be better. If their opinions are respected, they will share their knowledge and creativity with management—the only way to ensure continuous improvement.

Trust and respect are essential for individual participation. Without such an atmosphere, people will not take actions or make recommendations they perceive to be risky to themselves. "Quality First" is a process that depends on every person being unafraid to take chances and not worried about risking self-esteem. You must be open and honest with your people and establish channels of communication that are reliable and accessible to everyone in the organization. If people broach ideas, they should be praised; if they identify problems in the process or system, they should be thanked; when they contribute, they should be recognized; when they fail, they should be supported; and when they succeed, they should be rewarded. As their leader, you are responsible for creating an atmosphere of trust and support, and you are responsible for maintaining each individual's sense of self-worth and self-esteem.

Create a "Quality First" Environment in Which Continuous Improvement Is a Way of Life

By making continuous improvement a part of your daily routine, you will integrate it into all aspects of your work. Continuous improvement only approaches maturity when it is applied routinely to all of your organization's work. Routine application entails using the process-improvement cycle in all areas, collecting data and using those data to assess process suitability, removing roadblocks to your improvement efforts and those of others, and continuously improving your knowledge and expertise in process improvement. Ideally, continuous improvement should be your normal approach to doing your work; it must become your way of life.

Continuously Improve All Processes

Continuous process improvement, as the basis of "Quality First," is a never-ending effort. Perfection is an ultimate, unattainable goal, but its ideal is the basis for continuous improvement efforts. You must view everything your organization does in terms of interrelated processes. Process improvement should become your organization's way of life. Goals and objectives are realized through process improvement. Your own focus should be to improve all the processes you own and remove all those barriers under your control that hinder others from improving their own processes. The only true measure of your performance over time is the degree of process improvement you effect.

Process standardization is a means of defining a process and ensuring that everyone understands and employs it in a consistent manner. It is difficult to improve something that is not well-defined. Process standards communicate the current, best-known way of performing a process and ensure consistent process performance by a variety of individuals. With a standard, people have a way to know that they are doing their jobs correctly and you have a means of assessing their performance objectively. Process standards provide the baseline from which to continuously improve the process. The people doing the work should maintain and update standards as they improve their processes so that the standards always reflect the current, best-known means of doing the work.

Apply Your Quality Improvement Process to Your Suppliers

Your organization's ability to improve its processes depends in part on the inputs to those processes. To the extent that you procure materials and services from other organizations, your continuous improvement effort depends on those suppliers. Expanding your improvement culture to all your suppliers will help ensure that the quality of your process inputs is sufficient to meet your own improvement objectives. You can expand your culture of continuous improvement by working more closely with your suppliers, helping them get their own improvement efforts underway, building mutual trust and respect, and generally by becoming a better customer yourself.

QUALITY IS NOT ENOUGH

A firm's competitiveness with the company down the street, down the coast or on the other side of the world, is a composite of many factors. The quality of a firm's products or services is but one of these factors. Nonetheless there is a tendency, when trying to stress a point—such as quality—to focus one's attention on a limited number of factors. During the 1980s this is exactly what happened when the nation rediscovered quality. Business leaders tended to forget about the rest of the competitiveness equation.

Most business analysts, for example, have concentrated their attention in recent years on the benefits accruing to the American firms that adopted quality management methods in the early and mid-1980s. In particular, areas that have most benefited—quality control, delivery, and inventory turnover— were widely covered in the trade journals.

At least one major and ongoing study, however, has sounded an alarm as well. Boston University's "Beyond the Quality Revolution"* acknowledges that quality is a very important component of competitiveness in the 1990s. But, the report also raises fears that the excessive attention being given to advances in organizational and infrastructure processes in quality-managed firms may be distracting executives away from other equally important, but largely neglected, components of the competitiveness equation. These areas include teamwork, cost reduction, product development speed, and the integration of business and manufacturing strategies.

As American firms concentrate on quality, however, they are setting a low priority on other factors. These areas of neglect, if not given sufficient top-management attention, could result in self-inflicted competitive disadvantages in the future. If, while boosting our ability to compete worldwide in terms of quality we allow our standing in other areas—such as research and development—to wither, we will not have advanced our over-

*"Beyond the Quality Revolution," Jeffrey G. Miller and Jay S. Kim, Boston University, School of Management, Manufacturing Rountable, 1990.

all competitive standing in the coming years. Trading one weakness for another is hardly the way to go.

IMPROVE YOUR QUALITY

This chapter has described the concepts and principles involved in implementing the "Quality First" methodology. By tailoring these concepts and principles to your unique operation, you can significantly improve your quality, increase productivity, improve your world-class competitive position, and make more money than by doing business as usual.

The following two chapters provide an elementary road map for the planning and implementation of a "Quality First" program.

Chapter Eight
"Quality First" Planning

"Every great president in our history had a policy of his own, which eventually won the people's support."

Harry S. Truman
Memoirs—Years of Trial and Hope

TEN STEPS TO IMPLEMENTATION

A merican companies all too often have jumped to implement "hot" new solutions to their problems. They tend to spend too little time, thought, and energy on developing the corporate policy and planning needs to implement their actions. The Japanese, for example, spend two-thirds of their effort on building consensus, developing understanding of the clients' needs, and reviewing options for implementation. Then they think through all the steps needed to implement this change or process. In America companies tend to spend one-third of their efforts on planning, then jump into the implementation phase and continue to "fight fires" to resolve the errors and inconsistencies that with proper planning they could have avoided. The concept of doing things right the first time depends on realistic, thorough planning.

This chapter on planning, and Chapter 9 on implementation of your "Quality First" effort, form a unit. Described in these two chapters are a total of 17 planning and implementation steps for your review, modification, and adoption in your own unique "Quality First" program.

This chapter describes the 10 planning steps (see Figure 8–1) needed to help you identify your policy and plans for implementing a "Quality First" program in your company.

Step 1.   Top Management Commitment to "Quality First"

Simply put, "Quality First" is a new way for companies to do business. Since the methods by which a company conducts its business are clearly the prerogative of top management, it is, therefore, top management that must be convinced of the merits of "Quality First." Top management's recognition of the need for improvement and its willingness to learn more are the first steps toward implementation.

It is probably not possible to overstate the importance of the role of top management. Leadership is essential during every phase in the development of your company's "Quality First" program, and is particularly vital at the initial stages of planning. In fact, indifference and lack of involvement by top management are frequently cited as the principal reasons for the failure of quality improvement efforts.

To be successfully implemented, "Quality First" requires not only the vision, planning, and active, involved leadership of top management, it also requires such practical support as providing the resources for implementation—the time, money, and personnel needed. Delegation and rhetoric are insufficient.

John A. Betti, former Ford Motor Co. executive and former Under Secretary of Defense for Acquisition, said "commitment to quality must start at the top. But as we at Ford learned, commitment in itself is not enough. Along with commitment must be dedication and involvement. Actions, not words, produce results."

To obtain top management commitment, you need to begin to educate senior managers regarding the impact of global quality-

FIGURE 8–1
"Quality First" Planning Steps

Step 1	Top management commitment to "Quality First"
Step 2	Create a vision and philosophy
Step 3	Establish a quality council
Step 4	Identify customer needs
Step 5	Develop your own "Quality First" strategy
Step 6	Select organization(s) to implement "Quality First"
Step 7	Conduct training needs analysis
Step 8	Determine resources for implementation
Step 9	Conduct training
Step 10	Identify performance measures
	Implement "Quality First"

driven competitiveness; you need to encourage them to learn the basic philosophy, principles, and practices (Chapters 1, 2, and 3) involved in making your company policy "Quality First."

You may wish to host a command-performance presentation describing how "Quality First" has been successfully implemented in other organizations (see Chapter 5).

The bottom line is that top management must enthusiastically participate in changing your corporate culture. Table 8–1 identifies some of the cultural changes that your top management needs to understand and address to achieve improved quality.

Without top management's active participation as the champions of "Quality First" your organization will not obtain the full scope of benefits possible.

Step 2.   Create a Vision and Philosophy

A key step in the "Quality First" process is the creation of a common understanding among top managers about what they want the company to look like in the future and what principles will guide the actions they take to achieve the desired future. These agreements will become the basis for formal statements of the company's vision and values.

The vision is a clear, positive, forceful statement of what the organization wants to be in five, and even 10 years. It is expressed in simple, specific terms. The vision allows the company to stretch and aim for a high target. The vision must be powerful enough to excite people and show them the way things can be. A well-crafted vision statement supported by action can be a powerful tool for focusing the company toward a common goal.

Whatever form the vision and guiding principles take, it is important that they be communicated throughout the company frequently and with conviction. The timing and method of communication provide an opportunity for creativity by top management. It is important that the vision be followed soon by a concrete plan of action to avoid its being dismissed as a hollow slogan.

TABLE 8–1
Examples of "Quality First" Cultural Changes

Category	Previous State	New Culture
Mission	Maximum return on investment/management by objectives (ROI/MBO)	Ethical behavior and customer satisfaction; climate for continuous improvement; ROI a performance measure
Customer Requirements	Incomplete or ambiguous understanding of customer requirements	Use of a systematic approach to seek out, understand, and satisfy both internal and external customer requirements
Suppliers	Unidirectional relationship	Partnership
Objectives	Orientation to short-term objectives and actions with limited long-term perspective	Deliberate balance of long-term goals with successive short-term objectives
Improvement	Acceptance of process variability and subsequent corrective action assigning blame as the norm	Understanding and continually improving the process
Problem Solving	Unstructured individualistic problem solving and decision making	Predominantly participative and interdisciplinary problem solving and decision making based on substantive data
Jobs and People	Functional, narrow scope; management-controlled	Management and employee involvement; work teams; integrated functions
Management Style	Management style with uncertain objectives, which instills fear of failure	Open style with clear and consistent objectives, which encourages group-derived continuous improvement
Role of Manager	Plan, organize, assign, control, and enforce	Communicate, consult, delegate, coach, mentor, remove barriers, and establish trust
Rewards and Recognition	Pay by job; few team incentives	Individual and group recognition and rewards, negotiated criteria
Measurement	Orientation toward data-gathering for problem identification	Data used to understand and continuously improve processes

Source: Department of Defense

Step 3.   Establish Quality Council

Developing an organizational structure that will institute, sustain, and facilitate expansion of your "Quality First" improvement effort is an essential element for success. The structure is the vehicle for focusing the energy and resources of the company toward one common goal—continuous improvement of the products and services it provides to your customer. Successful companies tailor the structure so that it maximizes strong points and accommodates their unique mission, culture, and approach for improving quality. This accounts for some of the differences in the way organizational charts are drawn and for variations in the nomenclature used to describe the "Quality First" organization. In spite of these differences, several common practices emerge and merit examination.

Virtually every company that has successfully introduced the "Quality First" approach has formed a quality council of top managers during the early stages of implementation. This team is also sometimes called the Executive Steering Committee (ESC), Executive Steering Group (ESG), or Executive Quality Council (EQC).

By establishing your Quality Council, top management provides identity, structure, and legitimacy to the "Quality First" improvement effort. It is the first concrete indication that top management has recognized the need to improve and has begun to change the way the organization conducts business. The direction this change will take becomes clear when the council publishes its vision, guiding principles, and mission statement.

The council is chaired by the organization head or deputy and includes membership of the top management team. The council is responsible for launching, coordinating, and overseeing the "Quality First" improvement effort.

The "AT&T Quality Improvement Process Guidebook" describes a typical Quality Council Structure, shown in Figure 8–2, that consists of:

- A Leadership Structure of Linked Councils
  The leadership structure is comprised of an Executive Quality Council, Vice President Quality Councils, and

FIGURE 8–2
Quality Council Structure

Source: Based on *AT&T*, *Quality Improvement Process Guidebook*, February 1988.

Quality Councils within each Vice President's unit.
These interlocking councils perform the overall
"Quality First" planning and management function.
They direct and set policy, create an environment in
which quality improvement will flourish, and identify
strategic quality-improvement projects for which
Quality Improvement Teams are needed.

- Quality Improvement Teams
  These teams work both on the quality improvement
  projects they create, and on those defined by the
  councils. The teams define the roles of their team
  members and make quality improvement goals a
  reality.

- The Quality Support Structure
  This group is comprised of a Quality Planning Director
  and staff, Vice Presidents, District Quality Managers,
  and quality consultants. These individuals are
  responsible for supporting the implementation of the
  Quality Improvement Process.

The Quality Leadership structure includes:

- Executive Quality Council
  The Quality Leadership Structure is headed by the
  Executive Quality Council, which includes the
  president, direct-reporting vice presidents, and other
  members appointed by the president. Its charter
  includes developing policy to create, foster, and
  contribute to all aspects of the quality program.

- Vice President Quality Council
  The members of each Vice President Quality Council
  include the vice president, the direct-reporting
  managers, and other members appointed by the vice
  president. Their charter includes ensuring the
  application of the "Quality First" principles
  throughout the vice president's area of responsibility.

- Quality Councils
  The members of the Quality Councils for organizations within a vice president's unit include the formal head of the organization (e.g., executive director, director, division, district manager), the direct-reporting managers/supervisors, and other members appointed by the organization head. Their charter includes implementing a "Quality First" concept throughout the organization and creating an environment in which quality improvement can flourish.

- All Councils are charged with establishing an environment in which quality will be improved and sustained, providing the leadership and personal involvement to guide quality management in its organization, and developing its own Quality Improvement Plan that will enable it to carry out its specific charge.

Quality Councils also can be used to link your "Quality First" company together. Vertical linkage is accomplished by having a member of a top-level Quality Council serve as chairperson of a lower-level (second tier) council. A member of that council, in turn, chairs a lower-level (third tier) council or leads a subordinate-level team. Horizontal linkage is accomplished by having members of different functional departments (e.g., manufacturing, personnel, administration, service, finance) serve together on cross-functional teams. These teams are sometimes called Quality Management Boards.

This type of Quality Council structural linkage offers a number of benefits to your company:

- It helps the organization stay focused on pursuing the same goals rather than having functional departments working at cross purposes.

- It fosters better teamwork and less internal competition.

- It improves communication throughout the

organization and better understanding of how all the pieces fit together.

- It improves the ability to replicate ideas and standardize solutions that have applicability to processes in other departments of the organization.

Step 4. Identify Customer Needs

"Quality First" means that your company is meeting your customers' expectations. Customers can be co-workers (internal customers) or end users (external customers) of your products or services.

Expectations are your customers' needs and wants. Meeting customer expectations through application of "Quality First" principles is the key to your competitive future.

The Customer/Supplier Model described in Chapter 10 is an excellent technique for determining what your customers want, need, or expect. Only by interaction between the supplier (you) and the customer can this be answered.

The Customer/Supplier Model, which was designed to analyze and help improve your customer needs analysis, involves four key steps:

- Define your process or task.
- Define your value-added contribution to that process.
- Define your customer's expectations—i.e., negotiate specific requirements and define appropriate feedback of measurements.
- Communicate with your supplier and negotiate your requirements and feedback mechanisms just as you did with your customer.

To define "requirements" and "feedback," consider:

- Requirements are the most critical key characteristics of your output as defined by your customer.
- Feedback from your customer communicates the

degree to which your output conforms to the
requirements negotiated with your customer.

Taking these simple steps will significantly improve the quality of your work as it is defined by the most important person in
the process: your customer.

Step 5. Develop Your Own "Quality First" Strategy

There is no *one* right way to implement "Quality First" successfully in your company, no guaranteed recipe for success. The
process proposed in this book is a synthesis of approaches used
successfully by companies in manufacturing and service businesses. It is offered only as a guide in developing strategies and
associated plans to carry out these strategies. The intent of a flexible approach is to capitalize on a company's strong points to
allow energy to be focused on key improvement opportunities.

Because the missions, cultures, and management styles of
companies vary so greatly, it would be inadvisable to attempt
to develop one "ideal" plan or organizational structure for implementing "Quality First." Furthermore, it would be useless
to graft the experience of one organization wholesale onto another, without tailoring it to meet the unique needs of that second organization.

The best plans are those that result in action—action that improves the processes of the company and results in better services and products for the customer. A simple plan that generates action and gets results is better than an elaborate plan that
collects dust. Some initial "Quality First" strategic actions
might consist of specific projects designed to address system-
wide problems—projects that have potential for expanding to
other processes of the company; or, there might be efforts to
implement "Quality First" in one organization or across the
board. Examples of such efforts might include:

- Creating a team to review the "Quality First" concept
  and define a unique strategy for your company.

- Conducting customer surveys and feedback efforts to
  be reflected in quality indicators.

- Creating quality teams to address specific known operating problems.
- Defining your own quality problem-solving process.
- Defining your own "Quality First" Improvement Plan.

It is a good idea for your company to have at least begun in some key areas the process of identifying customers and their requirements, and reviewing quality indicators for products and services. This might occur in organizational components where "Quality First" will be implemented initially, or on a more wide-scale basis in anticipation of future "Quality First" implementation.

Step 6.   Select Organization(s) to Implement "Quality First"

At the outset of the quality improvement effort, organizations usually choose to implement "Quality First" either organization-wide or with one or more pilots. It is also possible to tailor a combination of the two approaches to fit particular circumstances. In any case, the decision is one that each company must make after realistically assessing a number of factors, including:

- The size and complexity of the company.
- The resources (time, money, and people) that can be allocated to introduce and sustain the effort.
- The amount of resistance that can be anticipated.
- The level and intensity of support for "Quality First" throughout the organization.

Implementing "Quality First" on a broad scale across a large organization is a major undertaking. It requires significant allocations of time, money, and people, and for most companies, requires substantive operational and cultural changes. The larger the company, the more massive the change.

Some advantages to broad-scale implementation are as follows:

- It promotes consistent implementation. Each organizational element uses the same "Quality First" philosophy, language, and training, and is guided by the same vision and core principles.

- The decision to implement "Quality First" company-wide demonstrates strong commitment at the very top level of the organization. This can facilitate the removal of barriers *between* organizations.

- The "Quality First" organization structure can be cascaded throughout a company, providing linkage between the corporate headquarters and operating units for improved communications.

- It provides for economies of scale (such as when procuring consultant services, or developing in-house training support). For example, a large training contract is generally less expensive per person than a series of smaller contracts.

- It allows the company to capitalize on its staff offices to support implementation. For example, statistical specialists located at the corporate level can be used to provide technical assistance to operating units.

You would be well advised to study closely your peers' efforts (refer to Chapter 5) before undertaking a similar venture.

Some companies have found advantages to starting pilot efforts including:

- Initial expenditures of resources are less.

- Development of wholly new product/service/venture allows company to start from "green field" and create new quality culture from the start. An excellent major example is GM (General Motors Corp.) in the development, production, and marketing of their Saturn car.

- Resistance is minimized by targeting locations where local "champions" reside. Alternatively, the effort can be engineered for success by targeting locations that have demonstrated adaptability to change by participating successfully in previous pilot efforts.

- Early successes can be used to galvanize support in other parts of the organization. Skeptics can be converted by seeing that it can work in their organization.

- Early failures can be turned into lessons learned, without major disruptions throughout the parent company.

- The pilot effort can be used as a model for broad-scale implementation.

- Pilot efforts are consistent with the Plan-Do-Check-Act (PDCA) approach to improvement.

- Develop unique plan of attack for adoption of quality initiative and showcase success.

Step 7. Conduct Training Needs Analysis

Chapter 6 provides a self-assessment methodology that encourages the analysis of your perceptions of your company's quality status. This self-assessment provides a baseline analysis that can be used to identify when and where you need additional quality training.

If you examined the Malcolm Baldrige Quality Award criteria (Chapter 4) either through in-depth self-assessment or application for the award, the ongoing learning about your company's needs will also be an extremely valuable tool in improving your training.

Step 8. Determine Resources for Implementation

Your "Quality First" plan must disclose how the effort will be funded, where the required time will come from and how it is to be accounted for, who will provide what personnel, and what facilities will be used for "Quality First." Obviously, these resource decisions must be coordinated with all those affected by the decisions. This part of the plan may be the hardest to develop because "Quality First" will now be competing with other requirements for corporate resources. One must keep in mind that "Quality First" is to become a way of life in the organization, in fact, the new way of managing. In reality, "Quality First" is not competing for mission resources because it will be an integral part of the future corporate mission. This part of the plan may be the first big test of management's commitment to "Quality First." Milestones for providing the identified resources should also be included in the plan.

Step 9.   Conduct Training

Training is essential to the success of your "Quality First" initiative. It is important to note that during the early stages of implementation of your "Quality First" effort, attention should be given to developing a detailed plan for training.

Ted Cocheu, writing in the January 1989 issue of *Training and Development Journal*, says:

> Quality experts . . . all agree that a comprehensive training curriculum is critical to providing everyone in the organization with the knowledge and skills to fulfill his or her quality-improvement responsibilities. Training must include:
>
> • Explaining the need for improvement as well as its individual and collective benefits.
>
> • Communicating the organization's quality goals.
>
> • Developing a common language to talk about quality-related issues.
>
> • Defining the structure and process through which quality improvement will take place.
>
> • Clarifying everyone's responsibilities.
>
> • Providing people with tools and techniques to manage the quality of their work.

In addition to specific "Quality First" principles and practices such as statistical quality control, continuous process improvement, benchmarking, use of data, and process analysis, most companies will also find it advisable to conduct training in such related areas as participative management, group dynamics and team development. The ideal training program will target the specific needs of each group—top management, middle managers, supervisors, and employees in various team groups—and will deliver training just at the time it is needed for smooth transition to the next step in your "Quality First" program.

All employees must understand their jobs and their roles in the company, and how their jobs will change. Such understanding goes beyond the instruction given in manuals or job descriptions. Employees need to know where their work fits into the larger context: how their work is influenced by workers who precede them and how their work influences workers who follow.

The organization's training plan should be an outgrowth of your unique "Quality First" implementation strategy, and should be directed to the organizational units or projects where top management has focused the implementation effort in the first year.

To prevent surprises and delays in implementation, the training plan must include reasonably accurate estimates of the schedule and required resources.

Step 10.   Identifying Performance Measures

Earlier this book discussed measuring the success of your quality improvement efforts operationally—in terms of how your customers view you, employee satisfaction, and profitability. These measure the success of your business.

These key business-performance indicators are also critical to measuring the success of all "Quality First" activities. They are measurements that reflect the success of the quality improvement process. The objective of every "Quality First" program must be to identify performance measures for your business, then continue to improve the key measures of success.

It is also important to measure the success of the "Quality

First" process itself, and of the progress and implementation of each organization's "Quality First" Improvement Plan.

DOCUMENT YOUR "QUALITY FIRST" PLAN

Document your plan for "Quality First" adoption in your company. Create a living plan that reflects the continuous improvement of your operations and "Quality First" management efforts. Make this plan available to your managers and personnel to assure that your goals and approach are communicated throughout your company.

Chapter 9, Implementation of Quality, describes the process for implementing "Quality First" in your company.

Chapter Nine

Implementation of "Quality First"

"Practice is the best of all instructors."

Publilus Syrus
Maxim 439

IMPLEMENT YOUR "QUALITY FIRST" PLAN

This chapter delineates the seven steps to improve your quality by implementing a "Quality First" program in your company. To begin the process, the initial decision to change your emphasis to one of "Quality First" must be made and the initial planning completed as described in Chapter 8. Then, as depicted in Figure 9–1, you need to understand how your products and/or services compare with your competitors. Step 12 describes the Xerox Corporation's approach to benchmarking. Then your company must embed the continuous improvement concepts (Step 13) throughout your company. This is a major change in how your company will operate in the 1990s. Step 14 describes the need to monitor and evaluate your progress in improving your quality performance. Tell the world of your success, but more importantly let your people know

FIGURE 9–1
"Quality First" Implementation Steps

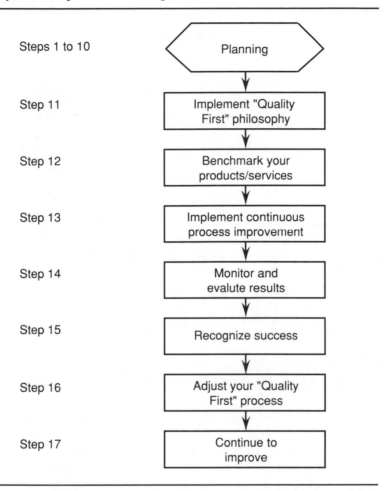

Steps 1 to 10	Planning
Step 11	Implement "Quality First" philosophy
Step 12	Benchmark your products/services
Step 13	Implement continuous process improvement
Step 14	Monitor and evelute results
Step 15	Recognize success
Step 16	Adjust your "Quality First" process
Step 17	Continue to improve

how they have contributed (Step 15) to the improved operation of your company. Recognize success! As you begin to demonstrate success and convince the doubters, you must continue to learn from feedback as to how you can do better. You must revise or adjust your "Quality First" program to meet the changing needs of your company as noted in Step 16. And finally, you must continue to improve.

FIGURE 9–2
A "Quality First" Improvement Cycle

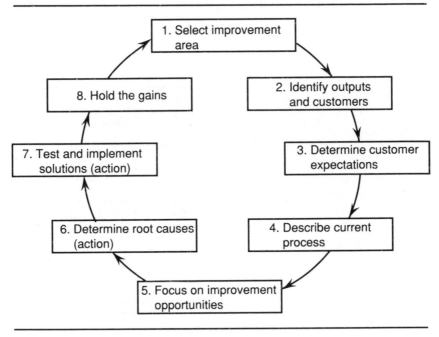

Step 11. Implement "Quality First" Philosophy

To help you implement "Quality First" in your company, an approach based on the Plan-Do-Check-Act cycle should be applied to each area of your quality improvement areas. A structured and systematic approach to identify quality improvement opportunities and resolve business-process problems is shown in Figure 9–2.

The "Quality First" Improvement Cycle offers a common language and a problem-solving methodology for use throughout your organization. It facilitates communication about work underway among groups with similar interests. It also supports the basic quality value of "managing by fact" by offering individuals and teams a disciplined, problem-solving approach. Finally, the "Quality First" Improvement Cycle increases the credibility of solutions that are developed in one part of the organization, allowing them to be readily replicated in other areas of your business.

This cycle embodies several basic quality-management theories and principles. These linkages to quality theory further assure that "managing by fact" is accomplished through the use of the cycle.

The cycle is also important as a tool for managers who are responsible for quality improvement efforts in their organizations. It provides a framework for reviewing the status of quality improvement projects underway and for preparing presentations on completed projects. Finally, it can assist in tracking the effectiveness of solutions in permanently eliminating root causes of quality problems.

The objectives of each step of the "Quality First" Improvement Cycle and recommended tools and techniques are shown in Table 9–1, and the key activities to achieve each step are outlined for use as a reference by individuals and teams as you proceed in your "Quality First" improvement efforts.

Step 12.   Benchmark Your Products/Services

In 1979, Xerox initiated a process called competitive benchmarking. At first, only a few of the operating units used this process, but by 1981 it was adopted as a corporation-wide effort. Today, benchmarking practices are used throughout Xerox. Other companies look to Xerox as a benchmarking model.

In fact, Xerox's recent strong performance in regaining its competitive edge in the marketplace can be attributed largely to its benchmarking program. According to a 1987 *DataQuest* research newsletter quoted in *A Guide to Benchmarking in Xerox*:

> "Xerox's benchmarking program deserves the lion's share of the credit for the company's turnaround in recent years. A whole new way of doing business was inaugurated with the start of this program. Every group, product, and system was dissected as Xerox searched for ways to become more competitive. Although this discussion has focused on Xerox's product development system, other organizations and systems at Xerox have also been dramatically changed."

TABLE 9–1
"Quality First" Use of Tools and Techniques

Objectives	Key Activities	Tools and Techniques	Outputs
Identify a problem area and the reason for working on it.	• List possible problem areas. • Collect data. • Select problem area for improvement. • Schedule activities.	Brainstorming Multivoting Interviewing Checksheet, Graph Problem Selection Matrix	• Problem area and rationale • Team project planning schedule
Identify outputs and customers.	• Identify outputs. • Identify customers.	Customer/Supplier Model	• List of outputs • List of customers
Understand customer requirements and degree of satisfaction.	• Identify characteristics, customer requirements, and priorities. • Establish measures and collect data. • Assess conformance to requirements and describe the gap.	Customer Needs Analysis, Survey Checksheet Graph	• Description of the gap • Customer requirements and satisfaction level
Understand how things actually work and the performance necessary to meet customer requirements.	• Identify inputs and suppliers. • Flow chart the process. • Collect data. • Assess process performance and establish targets.	Customer/Supplier Model Flow Chart Checksheet Graph	• List of inputs and suppliers • Flowchart of process in question • Targets for overall process performance and outputs
Select opportunities to pursue.	• Identify contributing factors. • Select opportunities to pursue. • Write the problem statement.	Pareto Diagram Multivoting Problem Selection Matrix Problem Statement Matrix	• Prioritized list of potential problem areas • Clear, concise problem statement • Clear, concise objective statement

TABLE 9–1 (*continued*)

Objectives	Key Activities	Tools and Techniques	Outputs
Identify root causes of the problem.	• Perform cause-and-effect analysis on the problem to the level of root cause. • Select actionable root causes. • Support potential root causes with data. • Select root causes with greatest probable impact.	Fishbone Diagram Checksheet Pareto Diagram Histogram Graph	• List of root causes to be addressed
Develop, test, evaluate, and implement solutions.	• Develop and select potential solutions. • Develop an action plan. • Test, evaluate, and revise solutions. • Implement and monitor solutions.	Barriers and Aids Solutions Selection Matrix Action Plan Cost Estimation	• Implemented solution and data on impact
Sustain improvement, consider replication, evaluate implementation, and plan future actions.	• Recommend required education and revised methods and procedures. • Establish tracking system to monitor results. • Recommend areas for replication. • Plan further actions, if necessary. • Evaluate implementation.	Graph Control Chart Action Plan	• Control at new performance level • Replication recommendations • Celebration • Plans for next project

One of the first and most successful steps Xerox took to regain its competitive edge was to institute a benchmarking program. After studying the Japanese product-development system (with the help of Xerox's partner, Fuji Xerox), Xerox began to completely revamp the way its products were designed. Xerox has established benchmarks for each class of copier and for some functional business areas as well. For example, L.L. Bean served as a benchmark for shipping operations and Sears, Roebuck and Co. provided a model for management of field distribution.

In this book we have defined "benchmark" as a standard of excellence or achievement against which other similar things must be measured or judged.

Simply speaking, benchmarking is the process of:

- Figuring out what to benchmark.

- Finding out what the benchmark is.

- Determining how it's achieved.

- Deciding to make changes or improvements in one's own business practices to meet or exceed the benchmark.

These four questions—while sounding fairly simple—require thinking and analysis. They require that you know your own business processes and practices down to the smallest detail.

The Xerox benchmarking template, shown in Figure 9–3, is a guide, a mold, or a pattern for accomplishing the various analyses required for benchmarking. Unlike a process model, the template is not strictly "sequence-sensitive," nor does it focus on "actions to take." Rather, it poses four questions that might be answered in different sequences (even though the four quadrants are numbered for reference).

Notice the two vertical axes of the template—"Us and Them." The two quadrants to the left pose questions about your results or processes (US); the two quadrants to the right refer to whom or to what you are making the comparisons (THEM). The "them" may represent an outside company or another division within your company.

FIGURE 9–3
Xerox Benchmarking Template

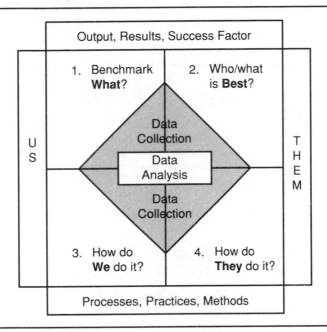

In the first comparison (tier one), when you cut the template in half horizontally (see Figure 9–4), the top two quadrants suggest comparing outputs or results. To begin a comparison, you must answer the questions, "Benchmark what?" and "Who or what is best?" In other words, what will you choose to compare yourself against? We will refer to this first comparison as the "upper tier" comparison.

At the heart of the template are data collection and analysis. "Data" is just another name for information. You will need to have a plan for collecting information both about yourself and about the object of your benchmark study. Naturally, you will need the information to be in a form that allows comparison. So, much of what you find in Chapter 10 will guide you through the process of collecting good, usable information, and some basic discussions about how to analyze and display your information.

FIGURE 9–4
Upper Tier Comparison

If you went no further than the top two quadrants, you would have accomplished a competitive analysis. You would know what the benchmark is (today) and how you measured against it.

The "lower tier" comparison is the comparison of the bottom two quadrants (see Figure 9–5) that constitutes true benchmarking—understanding the reasons for the differences and understanding what changes in processes, practices, or methods must be undertaken to meet or exceed the benchmark.

For example, assume that your training department averages a 3.6 (out of a possible 5.0) participant satisfaction rating on a particular course. You ask other divisions or departments that offer the same course for their participant satisfaction rating and find that one division achieves a 4.2. You have completed the upper tier study—establishing the benchmark and who has achieved it. Moreover, the gap between you and the benchmark is 0.6.

But only the lower tier study results will allow you to make changes toward improvement. Lower tier questions—"*Why* are their results better than ours?" and "*How* do they achieve that better score?"—are the questions that lead to change or improvement.

The objective of benchmarking is change leading to improvement. Without change in processes, practices, and ultimately,

FIGURE 9–5
Lower Tier Comparison

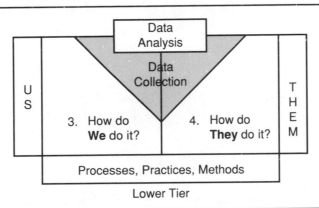

results, benchmarking is an incomplete, academic exercise. You must increase your rating by 0.6 or more in order to achieve the benchmark status prescribed above.

If your work processes are documented and measured, you will find benchmarking to be an extremely valuable (and not terribly difficult) activity. On the other hand, if you wander into a benchmark project without understanding your own process, you will find your lack of knowledge to be a barrier to your successful benchmarking attempts.

Determined to proceed anyway? Then be prepared for some hard work in the two "Us" quadrants of the template.

Competitive benchmarking helps formulate real-world guides as to whether or not you are meeting your customers' needs. If the results of a competitive benchmarking activity show that some other company is meeting customer requirements better than yours—then change in your quality efforts is clearly called for. In other words, competitive benchmarking tells you how you have met customer requirements.

Competitive benchmarking is the continuous process of measuring your products, services, and practices against your toughest competitors or those companies renowned as industry leaders. The process provides a better awareness of what competitors are doing, how they are doing it, and how well it is working.

I would encourage you to learn more about benchmarking. Xerox, as part of its technology transfer commitment under the Malcolm Baldrige Award Program, has made available to the public its corporate bible on benchmarking. The report is called "Leadership Through Quality Training Programs: A Guide to Benchmarking in Xerox." It is available through a partnership with the U.S. Department of Commerce, National Technical Information Services, in Springfield, Virginia. The NTIS document number is PB91-780106. (See Appendix C.)

Step 13. Implement Continuous Improvement Process

Continuous process improvement addresses the creation of positive change in the way work is done. It includes the definition of work flows, strengthening of supplier-customer relationships, elimination of non-value-added effort, reduction of variation, and control of processes.

The continuous process-improvement model shown in Figure 9–6 is a seven-step process that begins with the activities needed to create an environment conducive to "Quality First." It then continues through selecting and improving a process to finally assessing the level of performance improvement, where the model cycles turn around to focus on the next process-improvement effort. Even this chapter of the "Quality First" book is modeled after the process.

1. Set the stage for process improvement.

At the organizational level, setting the stage for process improvement involves everything the company does to become aware of the need for improvement and to establish a commitment to the continuous improvement process. It includes basic education and training, goal setting, barrier reduction, and leadership. Setting the stage means the company must create an environment in which continuous process improvement is encouraged and nourished. Management must have a clear vision of what it wants to accomplish and where it wants to go, and it must lay in place support systems to help the improvement effort.

FIGURE 9–6
Flow Chart of Continuous Improvement Strategy

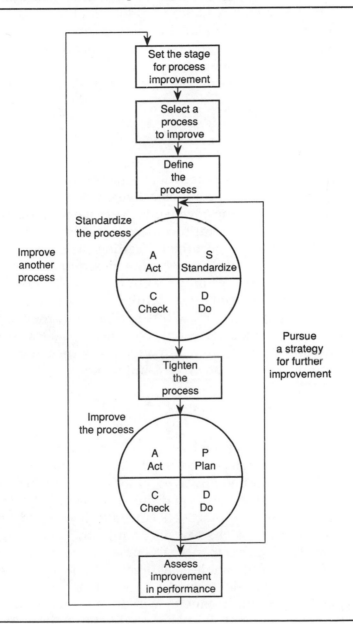

Source: ITT Reliability Analysis Center Report, SOAR-7, 1990.

At the team and individual levels, setting the stage involves selecting and educating the team or the individuals and training them in the specific concepts, tools, and techniques they will need for the contemplated improvement effort. The team or individual should determine how to function in the overall organizational environment and should ensure that all individuals involved are determined to accomplish their perceived mission.

2. Select a process to improve.

A team must identify potential processes and, in conjunction with organizational and team objectives, select one process on which it will focus its improvement effort on each pass through the cycle. Selecting the improvement target involves identifying all the potential opportunities, setting their priorities, and choosing the process that presents the most serious problem or offers the greatest opportunity for improvement. Once the process is selected, the team must identify its major problems and isolate their root causes. From this background, the team may modify its plan for improvement according to the team's objectives. Identifying measurement points is also necessary before beginning the continuous process-improvement effort.

3. Define the process.

Once a process has been targeted for improvement, the team should define that process as clearly and completely as possible. Process definition involves determining the customers (both internal and external) and the suppliers of the process, documenting how the process is currently performed (usually through using a flow chart or diagram), and identifying measures of process performance. Documentation should be formal and consistent among all organizational processes. A sound process definition provides a consistent base from which to begin process improvement; without knowing where you are at a given moment, it is hard to determine how to get to your destination.

4. Standardize the process.

By standardizing a process, the team institutionalizes the current best way to perform that process. Standardization creates a means for instructing people in their jobs within a consistent performance definition, provides a means for evaluating performance consistently, and provides a basis for evaluating the success of the improvement efforts. The team accomplishes all this by following the Standardize-Do-Check-Act cycle, which initially requires the team to bring its measurement system under control, to identify and document the current method of performing the process (which becomes the process standard), and to communicate and promote use of the standard. Management ensures that individuals are trained to the standard, and facilitates and enforces that standard's use. Once the standard is in force, teams measure all process performance against that standard and respond appropriately to deviations from it. Reducing performance variation by assessing the causes of deviation and eliminating those causes allows the teams to prevent recurrent deviation. The standard should always reflect the best current way of performing the process.

5. Tighten the process.

Once a team has defined a process standard, it should tighten the process before actually attempting to improve it. Tightening is the maintenance work that makes process-improvement efforts as effective as possible. This means ensuring that the process meets its stated and perceived requirements; cleaning and straightening the process work areas; eliminating unnecessary equipment; instituting total productive maintenance; and establishing reliable, adequate data-collection systems.

6. Improve the process.

Efforts to improve the process should follow the classic Plan-Do-Check-Act (PDCA) cycle in which an improvement plan is available and teams implement solutions, check for improvement, and act to institutionalize the improvements. The team's effort involves developing solutions that address stated requirements and conform to theories on problem causes. Data collection and measurement methodologies must support the envisioned solution. The team must be trained in the techniques necessary to carry out the plan. After it carries out its planned improvement, it should assess the data to determine how well actual performance matches planned improvements. Successful improvement should be institutionalized; less-than-successful efforts require another pass through the improvement cycle.

   7. Assess improvement performance.

   After an improvement has been implemented, a team should document the improved performance and the successful improvement effort thoroughly. That documentation allows others to benefit from the lessons the team has learned and brings recognition for the team's efforts. It also provides a road map for replicating successful improvement techniques. Documenting the improved process also requires the team to update its process definition and flow diagrams, and requires that process standards be rewritten to reflect the new standard of performance. Teams should set in place a means of continuously measuring performance level if this system does not already exist. Recommending follow-up actions or subsequent improvement efforts is also appropriate.
   The principles at the heart of the continuous improvement process include:

- A constancy of purpose that provides a steady and consistent vision of where your organization is going.

- A commitment to quality that drives productive change in all the products and services you produce.

- A customer focus and customer involvement that ensures your improvement efforts are driven by meaningful purposes.

- Process orientation that addresses the means of work accomplishment and not just the outcomes.

- Continuous improvement that ensures dynamic and adaptive processes over time.

- System-centered management that ensures improvement of the whole and not just the parts.

- Investment in knowledge that leverages the effectiveness of the improvement process.

- Teamwork that leverages the knowledge and provides essential synergy.

- Conservation of human resources that preserves your organization's most valuable assets.

- Total involvement that brings the entire intellectual power of your organization to bear on improvement.

- Perpetual commitment that precludes giving up when the road gets a little rough.

You apply these principles together in a logical and holistic manner to give substance and vitality to the continuously improving organizational culture. A number of the suggested readings at the end of this book examine in depth these principles and their supporting practices.

No single correct formula can be used to achieve continuous improvement in all situations or all organizations. A core set of ingredients, however, is evident in most successful continuous improvement efforts and can be applied to your own effort.

Your "Quality First" effort will be unique in its details, but in general it should move your organization toward satisfying the six criteria listed below:

- Exceeding your customer's requirements and expectations and being a high-quality supplier.

- Believing in people, working to eliminate barriers that prevent people from taking joy and pride in their work, and involving everyone.

- Tapping the power of individuals, multiplying that

power through training and teamwork, and focusing on understanding and process improvement.

- Recognizing that most problems are in your systems and are not due to particular individuals or circumstances, and providing leadership to continuously improve the systems.

- Making decisions based on data rather than on opinions or emotions; stimulating creative thinking; and seeking innovation in products, processes, and services.

- Focusing more on defect prevention than on defect detection.

Step 14.   Monitor and Evaluate Results

As part of their strategy for improvement, many organizations that have introduced "Quality First" have conducted more in-depth assessments aimed at identifying the existing culture and management style of the organization. An assessment helps to identify those vital processes to be targeted for change and provides a baseline measurement for judging progress. Assessments can take a variety of forms and frequently involve identifying and surveying the organization's internal and external customers, managers, and employees. The following key considerations are often probed:

- What is the mission of the company? What products and services are provided?

- Who are the internal and external customers?

- What measurement systems are presently in place?

- Does the company measure its success in terms of meeting customer requirements and expectations?

- How well does the company communicate with its customers and its suppliers?

- How much emphasis is placed on planning as opposed to fire fighting?

- How does the company generate ideas for improvement? Improvement in general or quality improvement specifically?
- What type of suggestion system is in place? How effective is it?
- What does the company reward? Improvement in general or quality improvement specifically?
- To what extent is teamwork used, encouraged, and recognized?
- What is the nature of management's relationship with employees' unions?
- How well do functional units cooperate? Are "turf" battles endemic?
- Does the executive leadership have credibility in the eyes of middle and line managers? Frontline workers?
- What type of management style is employed? Is it directive or participative?
- How much discretion do employees have in making decisions? Is authority delegated to the lowest levels possible?
- What is the attitude toward training?
- What is the attitude toward quality work? Is the focus on quality of the end product or quality of the process?
- Are the company values, goals, objectives, policies, and procedures clearly stated and widely known?
- Does the company have an abundance of priorities or have a vital few been identified and articulated?

Step 15.   Recognize Success

The success of "Quality First" is determined, in large part, by the degree of importance the organization places on it. Recognition is one of the most important ways to reinforce a proactive, positive change in behavior as it relates to quality improvement. Recognition is given for the successful application of the "Quality First" principles and practices.

Your goal is to create an environment in which change in the customer's interest is encouraged and then celebrated when it does occur.

Recognition is a means to demonstrate respect and appreciation for all employees and the value they add to your business.

Traditionally, business rewards have been based on the "most" numbers: most revenue brought in, most profitable new product. "Quality First" of course also rewards bottom-line numbers; profit is a significant reason why your company is in business. But since continuous quality improvement is a process, "Quality First" also provides for recognition and reward for those who demonstrate success with the processes and behaviors of quality—in measurable or nonmeasurable ways.

Recognition and reward are not the same things. Recognition means noticing (recognizing) a person or group doing a good job. A manager may notice the good job at any point along its progress—not only when it is completed. Recognition usually takes the form of praise, either spoken or written. It may be as simple as a word of approval about the way an employee ran a team meeting, or as formal as a letter of commendation with copies sent to his or her management.

Recognition provides both motivation and support for employees; people work better when they feel their efforts are valued. Research has shown that such reinforcement can have a real and measurable impact on productivity.

To provide effective reinforcement, recognition should:

- Be specific. If someone is told, "Good job on that report, Hunt!" Hunt is left not knowing which part of the report succeeded so well. Was it the succinct executive summary, the fact that it was turned in two days early, the thoroughness of the research, the potential value of the recommendations, or the nice printing job? Managers stand a better chance of having desirable actions repeated if the actions are clearly specified.

- Be directed at the right person. If the report came from a team, and Hunt has been out of town in Springfield while it was being written, Hunt is not the person to recognize even if he is the team leader. Who wrote the report?

- Be genuine.

- Be timely. Reinforcement is most effective when given as close to when "Quality First" behavior occurs as possible.

- Recognize process, not just results. The results will be unique to any given situation. The "Quality First" processes, on the other hand, are versatile enough to handle a wide variety of situations. It is the internalization of the processes you wish to encourage; therefore, that is what you should reinforce with praise.

Reward is given at the completion of a job. It is tangible: usually cash, mementos, or merchandise. Rewards range from a simple plaque to a profit-sharing program. Rewards say, "You deserve to share in the tangible assets of your work," and as such can be powerful motivators.

"Quality First" is bolstered by effective use of recognition and reward. All managers, at all levels, should continually identify those people doing a good job—and then devise ways to tell them so.

On a corporate level, your company should bestow rewards and sponsor many recognition events. Two examples used by Xerox Corporation include Teamwork Days and the Team Excellence Awards.

Teamwork Days are recognition events designed to honor the achievements of quality teams. Teamwork Days can be held on district, regional, or functional levels. In addition, the corporation can sponsor annual Teamwork Days, at which everyone in the corporation is welcome to celebrate progress.

A teamwork event is like a cross between a professional conference, a trade fair, and a revival meeting. Teams create display booths, often with much ingenuity and exuberance, which showcase their accomplishments. Speakers discuss company progress in becoming a "Quality First" company. People learn from each other, and the total "Quality First" transformation grows.

The Team Excellence Award is a cash award given to several teams each year as a reward for using "Quality First" tools to achieve outstanding results. There are always more excellent teams than it is possible to reward. Recipients are chosen by senior staff after successfully competing at regional and district levels within their function. All teams reaching the status of "excellent" are recognized by a certificate.

What makes an "excellent team"? There are three criteria:

- Teamwork. How well does the team work together? Team members on an excellent team (1) all understand their purpose as a team, (2) start with a clear problem statement and/or desired output, (3) organize for maximum effectiveness, and (4) use interactive skills well and consistently.

- Use of quality tools and processes. Effective teams (1) use applicable analytical tools, (2) identify several possible alternatives to solving their problem, and (3) evaluate the results of their actions.

- Results. The team project should (1) produce tangible business results, (2) impact the external customer or those who support the external customer, (3) demonstrate an innovative approach, and (4) effectively maximize the Cost of Quality opportunities.

Recognition and reward must be woven into the very fabric of "Quality First." People who assume responsibility for continuous growth in meeting customer requirements are in turn motivated to further growth by honest recognition of the large role their efforts play.

Step 16. Adjust Your "Quality First" Process

Your "Quality First" planning and implementation efforts must not be locked in concrete. As you learn more about your company strengths and weaknesses, change your "Quality First" efforts to reflect the feedback.

If the results are not as expected, then a new approach for improvement, based on what was learned, must be developed.

Step 17.   Continue to Improve

Don't stop now! Continue to improve (see Figure 9–7) every facet of your company's operation.

FIGURE 9–7
PDCA Cycle for "Quality First" Continuous Improvement

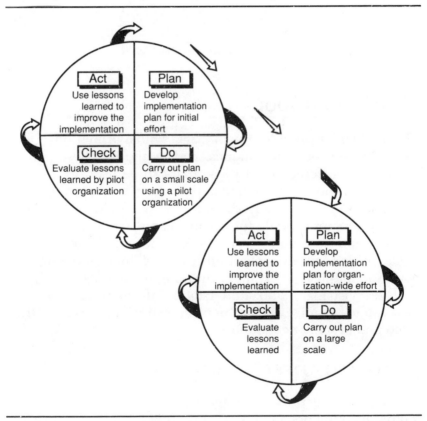

Chapter Ten

"Quality First" Tools and Techniques

"One picture is worth more than ten thousand words."

Anonymous Chinese Proverb

THE RIGHT TOOL

This chapter provides the manager with a primer on "Quality First" tools, techniques, and methods. These generic tools are representative of those that can be used to improve any process and are presented to provide an awareness of what they are, why they are used, and how to use them. Not all of the tools are appropriate for use in all applications.

Tools and techniques are essential for implementing the "Quality First" improvement process. *Tools* make it possible for you to accomplish work; make meaningful measurements; and analyze, visualize, and understand information. *Techniques* help you to organize and accomplish quality analysis in a structured and systematic manner.

"QUALITY FIRST" GRAPHIC TOOLS

As the Chinese proverb suggests, a picture is worth many words *and* numbers. Graphic displays allow you to create a logical storyboard that most people can understand at a glance.

A number of factors can lead to the decision for using a particular graphic tool, including the unique application and an individual's or team's experience and preferences. Most graphic tools are oriented toward a certain type of activity, and each tool has its strengths and weaknesses. This section summarizes some of the common graphic tools used to implement the "Quality First" methodology. Table 10–1 shows when you need to use particular graphic tools.

Each of these graphic tools is briefly described to enhance the manager's understanding of its use under the "Quality First" methodology.

TABLE 10–1
Use of Graphic Tools

Graphic Tool	Use when you need to . . .
Bar Chart	Compare quantity of data among different categories to help visualize differences.
Cause-and-Effect (Fishbone) Diagram	Systematically analyze cause-and-effect relationships and identify potential root causes of a problem.
Checksheet	Gather a variety of data in a systematic fashion for a clear and objective picture of the facts.
Control Chart	Monitor the performance of a process with frequent outputs to determine if its performance is meeting customer requirements or if it can be improved to meet or exceed them.
Flow Chart	Describe an existing process, develop modifications, or design an entirely new process.
Histogram	Display the dispersion or spread of the data under consideration.
Pareto Chart	Identify major factors in a subject being analyzed and highlight "the vital few" in contrast to "the trivial many."
Scatter Diagram	Show the relationship between two variables.
Time Line Chart	Visually display complex and quantifiable data; often shows changes in quantity over time.

Bar Chart

Bar charts show a comparison of quantities by the length of the bars that represent them (such as frequencies of events in different locations, cost of different types of breakdowns, and so on). Bars may be horizontal or vertical.

Along with time line charts, bar charts are among the most common types of data displays. There are two differences between them that are worth noting. The obvious difference is that a bar chart uses height columns, while the time line chart connects data points with a line. Visually, then, the bar chart emphasizes differences (or similarities) between and among the columns of various heights. The time line chart emphasizes the direction of change over time. The second difference is that the divisions along the horizontal line of the time line are time (quantitative) intervals. The divisions along the horizontal axis of the bar chart are nominal categories.

Figure 10–1 is an example of a bar chart. It shows the number of household appliances with some measured group (such as "within households with annual earnings of more than $50,000 per year"). Then we are led to conclude that TVs continue to be the item most frequently purchased, microwaves are increasing in popularity, but ranges and refrigerators are purchased relatively infrequently.

The bar chart (Figure 10–1) is really two bar charts superimposed: one for 1980 and one for 1990.

As with all graphic displays of data, the bar chart tells its story at a glance. The more data you have to analyze, the more important the use of graphics becomes. Bar charts make graphic comparisons of quantity easy to see.

To construct a bar chart proceed as follows:

- Collect the raw data on a checksheet, if necessary.

- List the categories (usually words rather than numbers) across the horizontal scale at the bottom. You may set them in any sequence, such as in descending order or any other way that makes sense. Label all categories.

- To set the vertical scale to the left, find both the

FIGURE 10–1
Example of Bar Chart

Sale of household appliances
1980 vs. 1990
(in millions)

Source: A Guide to Benchmarking in Xerox

largest and smallest value from the data and make sure the scale is broad enough to include both. Label both the scale and the intervals.

- Determine the quantity of each category and draw the bar accordingly. Generally speaking, bars should not touch or overlap.

- Bar charts can show and compare double or triple bars for different years or different populations (for example, households with earnings under $50,000).

- Give your bar chart a descriptive title. Include any legends that show what different patterns or colors represent.

Cause-and-Effect (Fishbone) Diagram

The cause-and-effect diagram (Figure 10–2) is a graphic representation of the relationships between an effect (problem) and

FIGURE 10–2
Example of Cause-and-Effect (Fishbone) Diagram

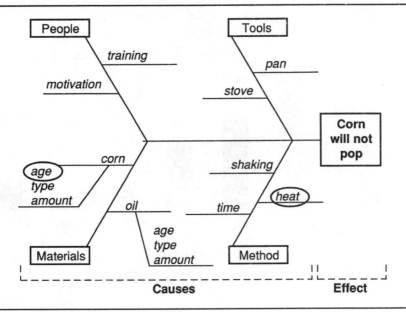

its potential causes. It is a useful tool in brainstorming, examining processes, and planning activities. The process of constructing a cause-and-effect diagram helps stimulate thinking about an issue, helps organize thoughts into a rational whole, and generates discussion and the airing of viewpoints. The cause-and-effect diagram documents the level of understanding about an issue and provides a framework from which to begin expanding that understanding.

Cause-and-effect diagrams can be used to explore a wide variety of topics, including the relationships between an existing problem and the factors that might bear on it; a desired future outcome and the factors that relate to it; or any event past, present, or future, and its causal factors.

Cause-and-effect diagrams go by several names: fishbone diagram, which describes how it looks; and Ishikawa diagram, for its inventor, Kaoru Ishikawa, a Japanese quality leader.

The problem—or effect—appears in a box to the right (the

head of the fish) as shown in Figure 10–2. To the left are the "bones" of the fish on which causes are organized and displayed as categories. The entries are words or nominal data.

In this example, the problem or effect is that the corn will not pop. The four factors that may be causing this are people, tools for popping corn, materials, and the method or process used. These are the four main bones for this example, but a different problem would suggest different major bones. For example, if our problem were "poor sales of the X3 portable," we might select salespeople, product, price, promotion, and/or environment as the major bones of the diagram.

The fishbone diagram ensures that quality analysis groups thoroughly examine all possible causes or categories. More importantly, it provides a process for groups to follow. And because the fishbone is a graphic display, it serves to focus the attention of the group on something more concrete that everyone sees and interprets in a more or less consistent manner.

To develop a cause-and-effect diagram:

- Define the effect or current situation as clearly as possible. You can always go back and refine it later as you collect new data. Write the effect in the "head of the fish."

- Many groups prefer to begin by brainstorming causes, and listing them on a flip chart in no particular order. When the group runs dry of ideas, they look for categories and similarities suggested by the list. These major categories or themes become the big bones.

- To encourage lots of ideas, ask, "Why? Why? Why?" When the answers begin to sound silly, you can stop.

- Draw the major bones and label them. You may decides on three, four, or more major themes. Use generic branches (people, methods, materials, machines) if helpful.

- Place the causes from the brainstorm list as small bones under the appropriate big bone.

- The organization of the brainstormed causes will no

doubt stimulate other ideas for causes. The group should be encouraged to add as many potential causes as they can think of. For each cause identified, ask, "What caused this?"

- The group can then highlight the cause(s) it believes to be contributing to the effect. In the popcorn example (Figure 10–2), the group has circled "age of corn" and "amount of heat" as the most likely causes.

- To verify causes, you will need to collect information to either accept or reject the cause(s).

- Work on most important causes (e.g., use design of experiments).

- Desensitize, eliminate, or control causes.

Checksheet

A checksheet provides a list of checkoff items that permit data to be collected quickly and easily in a simple standardized format that lends itself to quantitative analysis. Checksheets are frequently used to collect data on numbers of defective items, defect locations, and defect causes. Figure 10–3 is a simple example of a checksheet.

Make a checksheet by laying out the categories of information and data about the items onto a standardized form or grid. Determine the categories by asking such fact-finding questions as:

- What happens?
- Who does it, receives it, is responsible for it?
- Where—place?
- When—time of day, month, how often?
- How does it happen, how much, how long, etc.?

Do not ask, "Why?" This will lead you to search for causes while still trying to determine if a problem exists. The checksheet should be designed to facilitate the collection of as many

FIGURE 10-3
Simple Example of a Checksheet

Product: TRC Receiver unit   Date: 9/09/91

Name: Hunt
Lot: 51

Total examined: 200

Defect type	Defect count	Subtotal
Chipped	ЦНТ ННТ ЦНТ	15
Off-color	ЦНТ ЖП ЦНТ ННТ II	22
Bent	ННТ	5
	Grand total: 42	

---

different kinds of data as are useful. The team can brainstorm items and then refine the list through multivoting. It is also helpful to gather a little data before designing your checksheet. You may determine the appropriate categories from this smaller sample. The checksheet should also clearly indicate who collected the data and where, when, and how the data was collected. In a sample, the total population from which the data were gathered should also be indicated.

Control Chart

A control chart is used to monitor the performance of a process with frequent outputs. It provides a pictorial representation of an ongoing process and is based on four concepts:

- All processes fluctuate with time.
- Individual points are unpredictable.

- A stable process fluctuates randomly, and groups of points from a stable process tend to fall within predictable bounds.

- An unstable process does not fluctuate randomly, and these fluctuations are generally out of the range of normal operations.

The control chart, shown in Figure 10–4, is a graph that displays data taken over time and also shows computed variations of those data. Control charts are used to show the variation on a variety of variables including average ($\overline{X}$) and range (R) and also the number of defects (PN), percent defective (P), defects per variable unit (U), and defects per fixed unit (C). *A Guide to Quality Control* by Ishikawa provides excellent guidance on using control charts. The control chart allows you to distinguish between measurements that are predictably within the inherent capability of the process (common causes of variation) and measurements that are unpredictable and produced by special causes.

The upper and lower control limits (UCL and LCL, respectively) must not be confused with specification limits. Control limits describe the natural variation of the process such that points within the limits are generally indicative of normal and expected variation. Points outside the limits signal that something has occurred that requires special attention because it is outside of the built-in systematic cause of variation in the process. Note that the circled point on the $\overline{X}$-bar chart, while outside the control limits, does not mean the process is out of control. A series of points outside control limits would be necessary for that determination. Each individual point out of the limits should be explained, however.

These charts help you understand the inherent capability of your processes, bring your processes under control by eliminating the special causes of variation, reduce tampering with processes that are under statistical control, and monitor the effects of process changes aimed at improvement.

To construct a control chart, follow these basic steps:

- Determine control limits to describe the expected variation of a process.

FIGURE 10–4
Example of Control Chart

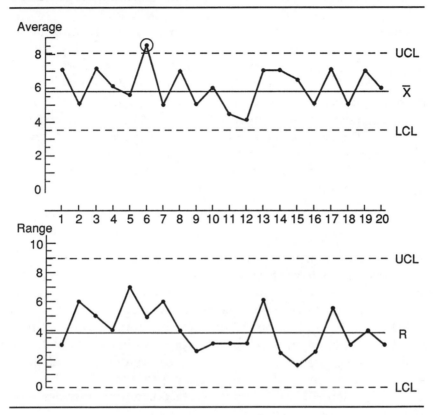

- Collect data.
- Plot data on the control chart to assess performance and identify points outside established control limits.
- Determine causes of points outside control limits.
- Identify ways to eliminate special causes, reduce normal variation, and improve the mean.

After constructing your control chart, examine it to see where the data points are located. If your process is fairly consistent and stable, most of the data points should fall within the established limits. Control charts illustrate fluctuations within the process that occur in a non-random pattern. Points that fall outside one of the control limits should be reported or investigated.

Once you've created your control chart, you can continue to use it to determine whether your operations are staying within the operating limits you've established. As you add points, examine the chart for favorable or unfavorable out-of-control points, and look for special or assignable causes.

There are many types of control charts. The one you use depends on the type of data collected. Since choosing and developing control charts are rather complex processes, it is suggested that your quality specialist be asked for assistance when a control chart is deemed necessary.

Flow Chart

A flow chart is a pictorial representation of the steps in a process. It is a useful tool for determining how a process really works. By examining how various steps in a process relate to one another, you can often uncover potential sources of trouble.

Flow charts can be applied to anything from the flow of materials to the steps in making a sale or servicing a product.

Flow charts permit you to examine and understand relationships in a process or project. They provide a step-by-step schema or picture that serves to create a common language, ensures common understanding about sequence, and focuses collective attention on shared concerns.

Several different types of flow charts are particularly useful in the continuous improvement process. Three frequently used charts are the top-down flow chart, the detailed flow chart, and the work-flow diagram. The top-down flow chart (Figure 10–5) presents only the major or most fundamental steps in a process or project. It helps you and your team to easily visualize the process in a single, simple flow diagram. Key value-added actions associated with each major activity are listed below their respective flow diagram steps. You can construct a top-down flow chart fairly quickly and easily. You generally do so before attempting to produce detailed flow charts for a process. By limiting the top-down flow chart to significant value-added ac-

FIGURE 10–5
Example of Top-Down Flow Chart

tivity, you reduce the likelihood of becoming bogged down in the detail.

The detailed flow chart (Figure 10–6) provides very specific information about process flow. At its most detailed level, every decision point, feedback loop, and process step is represented. Detailed flow charts should be used only when the level of detail provided by the top-down or other simpler flow charts is insufficient to support understanding, analysis, and improvement activity. The detailed flow chart may also be useful and appropriate for critical processes, where precisely following a specific procedure is essential. The work-flow diagram is a graphic representation or picture of how work actually flows through a physical space or facility. It is very useful for analyzing flow processes, illustrating flow inefficiency, and planning process-flow improvement.

Histogram

A histogram is a visual representation of the spread or dispersion of variable data (e.g., the number of defects per lot). In histograms of natural data, there is a tendency for many items to fall toward the center of the distribution (central tendency), with progressively fewer items as you move from the center.

This information is represented by a series of rectangles or bars proportional in height to the frequency of the group or class represented, as shown in Figure 10–7. Since class intervals

FIGURE 10–6
Sample Detailed Flow Chart

FIGURE 10–7
Example of a Histogram

(but not numbers) will be equal in size, the rectangles are of equal width. The heights of the rectangles relative to one another indicate the proportion of data points in each class.

A histogram helps to identify changes or shifts in processes as changes are made. It shows how variable measurements of a process or product can be, and it helps in the establishment of standards. Once standards have been set, measurements can be compared to these standards.

To construct a histogram proceed as follows:

• Collect the data you plan to chart and count the total number of data points.

- Determine the range of your data by subtracting the smallest data point from the largest.

- Keep the number of data bars in your graph between six and twelve. To determine the width of each class interval (bar), divide the range (above) by the desired number of bars.

- Place your class intervals (groupings of data) on the horizontal axis.

- Place your frequency or number scale on the vertical axis.

- Arrange the data points in ascending order.

- Draw the height of each bar to represent the number or frequency of its class interval using the scale on the vertical axis; each bar should be the same width with all data points included.

Pareto Chart

A Pareto chart is used when you need to discover or display the relative importance of data or variables (problems, causes, or conditions). It helps highlight the *vital few* in contrast to the *trivial many*. It may be used to examine the "how," "what," "when," "where," and "why" of a suspected problem cause. It also helps teams identify which problems, causes, or conditions are the most significant or frequent so they can work on these first.

Like most charts and graphs, the Pareto chart is an illustration of your data as of a specific time and date. Once your team has addressed the most significant problem, cause, or condition in your Pareto chart, you can redraw it with new data and pick another area to improve.

In the late 1800s, Vilfredo Pareto, an Italian economist, found that typically 80 percent of the wealth in a region was concentrated in less than 20 percent of the population. Later, Joseph Juran formulated what he called the Pareto Principle of problems: Only a vital few elements (20 percent) account for the majority (80 percent) of the problems. For example, only 20 percent of your equipment problems account for 80 percent of your

FIGURE 10–8
Example of a Pareto Chart

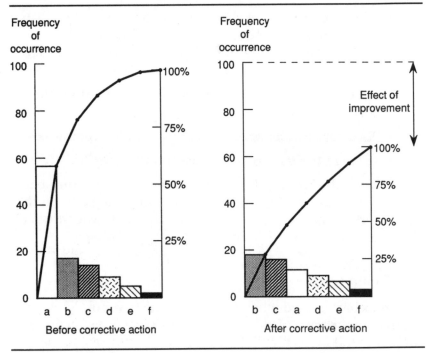

down time. Because this Pareto principle has proven to be valid in numerous situations, it is useful to examine your data carefully to identify the vital few items that most deserve attention.

The Pareto chart shown in Figure 10–8 is a bar chart in which the data are arranged in descending order of their importance, generally by magnitude of frequency, cost, time, or a similar parameter. The chart is really two charts in one. It's part bar chart and part pie chart. The bars are easy to see, but the ascending line that plots the cumulative height of the bars is really a pie chart "unrolled."

To create a Pareto chart proceed as follows:

- Select the most likely causes of a problem (from the cause/effect diagram).

- Collect the data on causes (using a checksheet, perhaps).

- Summarize the numbers of observations and calculate the percentages of each cause.
- The right vertical scale is always set from zero to 100 percent.
- The left vertical scale is the same height as the right scale; it begins with zero at the bottom and ends with the number of observations at the top, directly across from 100 percent.
- Draw the columns using the left scale.
- Plot the first point at the upper right corner of the first column.
- Calculate and add together the percentages of cause 1 and cause 2. Place the second point, corresponding to the sum, across from the right scale, directly over the second column or bar. For the third point, add the percentage of cause 3 to the total of 1 and 2 and plot accordingly. The total of all the columns added together should be 100 percent, and the last point will be at the 100 percent point.
- Join the dots with a line.

Scatter Diagram

Scatter diagrams (Figure 10–9) and their related correlation analysis permit you to examine two factors at one time and to determine the relationship that may exist between them. The graphic display can help lead you to the possible causes of problems, even when the linkage between the factors is surprising. The pattern or distribution of data points in a scatter diagram describes the strength of the relationship between the factors being examined. However, even a strong correlation does not imply a cause-and-effect relationship between the factors. Additional work may be required to uncover the nature of the indicated relationship.

The scatter diagram shows plotted points against two measures: one displayed on the vertical (y) axis, the other on the

FIGURE 10–9
Examples of Scatter Diagram Correlation

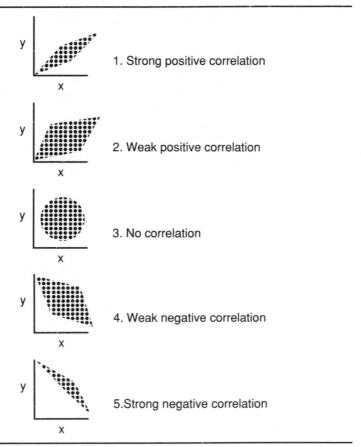

1. Strong positive correlation

2. Weak positive correlation

3. No correlation

4. Weak negative correlation

5. Strong negative correlation

horizontal (x) axis. The visual pattern of the plotted points gives quick information about the presence of a relationship or correlation.

If there is a correlation (either positive or negative) between two measures, you can assume that if you can change the incidence of one measure, the other will move as well. For example, if telephone call duration is positively correlated to customer satisfaction, then changing telephone call duration will produce a change in customer satisfaction.

To prepare a scatter diagram proceed as follows:

- Collect the two selected measures for each occurrence.

- Draw the horizontal and vertical scales of equal lengths.

- Assign the horizontal (x) axis to the dependent variable. The dependent variable is the one you can have an effect on, such as call duration. The independent variable is the other variable that depends on the first. The independent variable is assigned to the vertical (y) axis. Establish the interval scales for both and label.

- Plot each data point on the grid.

- To interpret the relationship, you can "eyeball" it, but a statistician can perform some quantitative tests on the data to give you a more accurate numeric indication of correlation.

Time Line Chart

The time line chart as shown in Figure 10–10 is a graphic display of changes over some period of time. The left scale is a quantity: percentages or simple counts of frequency. The horizontal line is divided into time intervals such as "days of the week," "months," or even an ordinal sequence such as "first job," "second job," and so on.

The line that joins the plot marks gives a visual "moving picture" of the fluctuations over time. Defect rates are reported on time lines in order to spot trends.

To prepare a time line chart proceed as follows:

- Collect the raw data on a checksheet, if necessary.

- Develop time intervals (usually hour, day, week, etc.) across the horizontal axis at the bottom. The intervals should be evenly spaced. Label each interval.

- Draw a line to connect the quantities observed on each successive interval.

- Connect the points with a line.

- Add horizontal and vertical grid lines if the points are difficult to read, as shown in the figure.
- Title the chart to define the period of time over which the data were collected.

Use of "Quality First" Tools

There are a number of factors that may lead to the decision to use a particular tool or set of tools, including an individual's or team's experience and preference. Table 10–2 summarizes some of the tools used in implementing "Quality First" practices.

"QUALITY FIRST" TECHNIQUES

This section summarizes some of the basic techniques used to implement the "Quality First" methodology. Table 10–3 shows when you need to use particular techniques.

FIGURE 10–10
Example of Time Line Chart

TABLE 10-2
Matrix of "Quality First" Tool Applications

Tools and Techniques (Listed without regard to priority)	1. Bounds and Prioritize Problems	2. Compile Information	3. Analysis	4. General Alternatives	5. Evaluate	6. Plan and Implement
			Problem-Solving Activities			
Benchmarking	✓	✓	✓		✓	
Cause-and-Effect Diagrams	✓	✓	✓			
Nominal Group Technique	✓	✓		✓	✓	✓
Quality Function Deployment	✓		✓		✓	
Pareto Charts	✓	✓	✓			
Statistical Process Control		✓	✓			
Histograms		✓	✓			
Checksheets		✓	✓			
Input/Output Analysis			✓			
Scatter Diagrams			✓			
Concurrent Engineering			✓	✓		
Design of Experiments			✓	✓	✓	
Cost of Quality			✓		✓	
Control Charts			✓		✓	
Work Flow Analysis Flow Charts			✓			✓
Team Building						✓
Time Management	✓					✓
Shewhart Cycle	✓	✓	✓	✓	✓	✓

TABLE 10–3
Use of "Quality First" Techniques

Technique	Use when you need to . . .
Action Plan	Explain implementation plans to management and workers, and ensure an organized, objective implementation.
Barriers and Aids	Analyze a situation and make use of available aids and/or overcome barriers that prevent implementation of a solution.
Benchmarking	Measure your processes/performance against your competitors.
Brainstorming	Generate, clarify, and evaluate a sizable list of ideas, problems, or issues.
Concurrent Engineering	Shorten the design-to-development life cycle of a product.
Cost Estimation	Determine the dollar impact when prioritizing and selecting improvement opportunities.
Cost of Quality	Understand the hidden costs of a product or service.
Customer Needs Analysis	Identify what customer expectations and requirements are, and what you have jointly agreed to provide.
Customer/Supplier Model	Identify the total customer/supplier relationship and analyze and/or improve your work process.
Customer/Supplier Questionnaire	Assess your relations with your customers and suppliers.
Deming/Shewhart Cycle	Implement a continuous improvement process.
Design of Experiments	Reduce costs, stabilize production processes, and desensitize production variables.
Interviewing	Broaden the team's foundation of knowledge and identify other people who are not on the team but who are sources of needed information.
Multivoting	Accomplish list reduction and prioritization quickly and with a high degree of group agreement.
Nominal Group Technique (NGT)	Reach consensus within a structured situation.
Problem Selection Matrix	Prioritize improvement opportunities.
Problem Statement Matrix	State specifically the improvement opportunity that the team is addressing.
Quality Function Deployment (QFD)	Transform customer wants and needs into quantitative terms.
Solutions Selection Matrix	Select those potential solutions that best address the root causes of the problem.
Statistical Process Control (SPC)	Improve process performance.

FIGURE 10–11
Typical Example of an Action Plan

NO.	TASK/PROJECT	PRIORITY/ DUE DATE	ASSIGNED TO	DATE ASSIGNED	STATUS/REMARKS

Prepared By _____ Date_____ Page ___ of ___

TASK ASSIGNMENT RECORD   Loc'n/Proj. _____ Period _____

Source: *AT&T Quality Improvement Process Guidebook*, Florida Power and Light.

Each of these techniques is briefly described to enhance the manager's understanding of their use under the "Quality First" methodology.

Action Plan

The "Quality First" team's action plan is a catalog of things that must be done to ensure a smooth and objective trial and implementation of the solution. Although the action plan may have different formats, it should answer who, what, when, where, and how, and consider the barriers and aids for success. Figure 10–11 is a typical example of an action plan.

To develop an action plan proceed as follows:

- Have the team analyze the proposed improvement or solution.

- Break it down into steps.

- Consider the materials and numbers of people involved at each level.

- Brainstorm, if necessary, for other items of possible significance.

- Add items to the list until you think the list is complete.

FIGURE 10–12

Example of Elements of a Barriers-and-Aids Analysis

Forces Pushing Against Quality Improvement	Forces Pushing For Quality Improvement
• Lack of dollars	• Team
• People shortage	• Personal commitment
• Vested interest/old attitude	• Management support
• Would the team stay together?	• Support of line manager
• Other priorities:	• Communications:
Time	Within team
Maintain work flow	Outside team
Complicated techniques	• New techniques
	• Increasing cost of failure
	• Good planning
	• Specific goals

Barriers and Aids

Barriers-and-aids analysis is a technique for pinpointing and analyzing elements that resist change (barriers) or push for change (aids). This focused brainstorming technique helps a team to meet its objectives by planning to overcome barriers and making maximum use of available aids. Factors to consider are:

- people.
- environment.
- hardware.
- dollars.

Figure 10–12 is an example of a barriers-and-aids analysis. To construct a barriers-and-aids analysis proceed as follows:*

- Identify the solution, task, change, or concern.
- Brainstorm a list of barriers (forces pushing against change).

---

*It is not necessary to come up with an aid for every barrier.

FIGURE 10–13
Illustration of Comparative Benchmarking

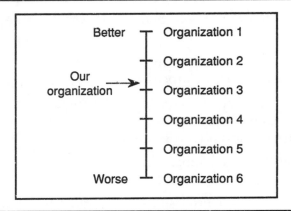

- Brainstorm a list of aids (forces pushing for change).
- Rank listed items by level of significance: high, medium, or low.
- Match aids that balance or overcome barriers.
- List matching barriers and aids on a chart.
- List nonmatching barriers and aids and brainstorm any offsetting factors.
- Using your rankings, identify items needing team action.
- Develop an action plan.

Benchmarking

Benchmarking, as described in greater detail in Chapter 8, is a principal element of the "Quality First" methodology. Benchmarking (Figure 10–13) provides a method of measuring your processes against those of recognized leaders. It helps you to establish priorities and targets leading to process improvement. Benchmarking is conducted when you want to know where you stand with respect to your local competitors or other world-class competitors.

Refer to Chapter 8 for details on conducting benchmark evaluations. The basic elements of benchmarking include the following:

- Identify processes to benchmark and their key characteristics.

- Determine what to benchmark: companies, organizations, or processes.

- Determine benchmarks by collecting and analyzing data from direct contact, surveys, interviews, technical journals, and advertisements.

- From each benchmark item identified, determine the "best of class" target.

- Evaluate your process in terms of the benchmarks and set improvement goals.

Brainstorming

Brainstorming is a way of using a group of people to quickly generate, clarify, and evaluate a sizable list of ideas, problems, issues, and so on. In this case, the emphasis is on *quantity* of ideas, not quality. It can be an excellent technique for tapping the creative thinking of a team. There are three phases of brainstorming:

- During the *generation phase*, the leader reviews the rules for brainstorming and the team members generate a list of items.

- During the *clarification phase*, the team goes over the list to make sure that everyone understands all the items. Discussion will take place later.

- Finally, during the *evaluation phase*, the team reviews the list to eliminate duplications, irrelevancies, or issues that are off-limits.

To conduct a brainstorming session, proceed as follows:*

---

*Brainstorming is a subjective technique that must later be substantiated by data.

- State purpose clearly.
- Each person takes a turn in sequence, or ideas may be expressed spontaneously.
- Offer one thought at a time.
- Don't criticize ideas.
- Don't discuss ideas.
- Build on others' ideas.
- Record ideas where visible to team members.

Techniques such as multivoting or Nominal Group Techniques (NGT) will generally be used next to select those items that the team should pursue.

Simultaneous (Concurrent) Engineering

Simultaneous (concurrent) engineering is an approach where design alternatives, manufacturing process alternatives, and manufacturing technology alternatives are dealt with in parallel and interactively beginning with the initial design trade-off studies.

Traditionally, quality and producibility have been an after-the-fact review of designs to assess the impact of proposed design features on manufacturing cost and to identify alternatives for the major production cost drivers. With simultaneous (concurrent) engineering, the focus is on both product and process definition simultaneously.

This approach can be used to shorten the design-to-development life cycle and reduce costs by examining the interaction of functional disciplines from the perspective of a cross-functional process.

The basic elements involved in applying simultaneous (concurrent) engineering include the following:

- Use cross-functional teams, including design, quality, marketing, manufacturing, and support.

- Carefully select design parameters to identify and reduce variability in production and use.

- Extend traditional design approach to include such techniques as enterprise integration, design for assembly, robust design, computer-aided design, design for manufacture, group technology, electronic data interchange, and value analysis.

- See also the description of the following tools: design of experiments; quality function deployment (QFD); and team building.

Cost Estimation

Cost estimation aids in selecting improvement opportunities. "Quality First" teams can determine problems with the largest dollar impact by estimating costs using the bottom-up approach and top-down approach. Use these two approaches as follows:

Bottom-Up Approach

- Estimate how many times the problem occurs per unit (example: three times per week).

- Estimate time and cost per unit to fix (example: two people × three hours × $17 per hour equals $102).

- Calculate annual cost (without overhead expenses) by multiplying above factors by weeks worked (example: three people per week × $102 × 50 weeks per year equals $15,300 per year).

Top-Down Approach

- Estimate percent of total labor or other expenditure.

- Multiply estimate by budgeted annual cost to calculate amount spent on the problem (example: 13 percent × $18,000 per year budgeted equals $2,340 per year).

Cost of Quality

Cost of quality consists of all the costs associated with maintaining acceptable quality plus the costs incurred as a result of

FIGURE 10–14
Example of Cost of Quality Impact on Nonconformance

failure to achieve this quality. The cost of quality technique provides managers with cost details often hidden from them. Cost of quality analysis should be performed to highlight costs savings by doing the job right the first time.

To conduct a cost of quality review proceed as follows:

- Identify quality costs. These are cost of nonconformance and cost of conformance, as shown in Figure 10–14.
- Develop a method for collecting data and reporting on cost of quality.
- Identify the most significant costs.
- Identify the cause of these major costs.
- Identify the solutions to reduce or eliminate causes.
- Implement solutions.

Customer Needs Analysis

Customer needs analysis is a technique for determining the key measurable characteristics that are important to your customer. Customer needs analysis is a "Quality First" team effort between you and your customers to answer the following questions:

- What are the *major outputs* of your process?

- Who are the *customers* (both immediate and downstream) for each of these outputs?
- What do your customers say are the *key quality characteristics* that they need in your outputs?
- How can you *measure* your performance on these key characteristics?
- What *goal* would your customers like to see you achieve on these measures?

Possible key quality characteristics are:

- accuracy
- timeliness
- relevance
- completeness
- uniformity
- consistency
- flexibility
- understandability
- reliability

Potential measurements are:

- physical parameters
- time
- cost
- customer satisfaction
- defects and rework
- work output

Customer/Supplier Model

The customer/supplier model is a representation of the customer/supplier relationship depicted by three triangles, shown

FIGURE 10–15
Illlustration of Customer/Supplier Model

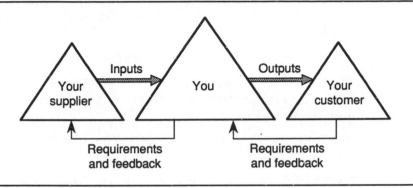

in Figure 10–15, in which the center triangle represents the work you do (i.e., your value-added tasks).

The left triangle represents your supplier(s)—the people or organizations who provide you with the input(s) you need to perform your job.

The right triangle represents your customer(s)—the people or organization(s) who receive your output or the result of your work.

Additional components of the customer/supplier model are requirements and feedback. Requirements are the most critical characteristics of your outputs as defined by your customer. Feedback from your customers communicates the degree to which your output conforms to the negotiated requirements.

Analysis of your organization's customer/supplier model is an effective technique to appraise the total impact of quality.

Customer/Supplier Questionnaire

Use this questionnaire as a technique to assess your relations with your customers and suppliers.

The following are questions you need to ask about your relationship with your customers:

- What are your primary outputs as a supplier: information, products, and/or services?

- Who are your customers—the primary, direct users or recipients of your outputs?

- What are your customers' requirements for your outputs?

- How do you determine their requirements?

- What are the characteristics of your outputs that can be measured to determine whether your customers' requirements are met?

- What are the major quality problems that prevent you from meeting your customers' requirements?

- What obstacles stand in your way of resolving these problems?

- What would it take to resolve these problems?

These are questions you need to ask about your relationship with your suppliers:

- Who are your suppliers? Who do you depend on for input—information, products, and/or services—to fulfill your requirements as one who adds value to their inputs?

- What primary inputs do you receive from them?

- What are your requirements for those inputs?

- How do you communicate your requirements to your suppliers?

- How do you provide feedback to suppliers regarding how they are performing?

Deming/Shewhart (PDCA) Cycle

The Shewhart Cycle [also known as the Deming or Plan-Do-Check-Act (PDCA) cycle] shown in Figure 10–16, represents a cyclic continuous-improvement process for planning and testing improvement activities. When an improvement idea is identified, it is often wise to validate its benefit by testing it on

FIGURE 10–16
Illustration of PDCA Shewhart Cycle

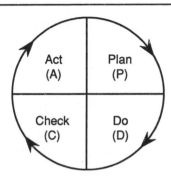

a small scale prior to full implementation. Additionally, by introducing a change on a small scale, employees have time to accept it and are more likely to support it.

The basic elements of the Deming/Shewhart cycle are the Plan (P), Do (D), Check (C), and Act (A) steps often referred to as the PDCA cycle. To implement this technique, proceed as noted below:

- Plan (P) a change or test.
- Do (D) the change or test, preferably on a small scale.
- Check (C) the effects of the change or test.
- Act (A) on what was learned.
- Repeat the Plan step, with new knowledge.
- Repeat the Do step, and continue onward with continuous process improvement.

Design of Experiments

Design-of-experiments analysis is a technique where the analyst chooses factors for study, deliberately varies those factors in a predetermined way, and then studies the effect of these actions.

Design of experiments improves the design-to-production

transition by quickly optimizing product and process design, reduces costs, stabilizes production processes, and desensitizes production variables.

The following are among the many applications for the design-of-experiments analysis:

- Compare two machines or methods.
- Study the relative effects of various process variables.
- Determine the optimal values for process variables.
- Evaluate measurement system error.
- Determine design tolerances.

To implement the design-of-experiments technique:

- Identify the important variables, whether they are product or process parameters, material or components from suppliers, or environmental or measuring equipment factors.
- Separate these important variables—generally no more than one to four.
- Reduce the variation on the important variables (including the tight control of interaction effects) through redesign, close tolerancing design, supplier process improvement, etc.
- Open up the tolerances on the unimportant variables to reduce costs.

Interviewing

Interviewing is a data-gathering process to help "Quality First" teams gain the benefit of others' experience and specialized knowledge.

Things to do:

Before the Interview

- Gather background information on topic and interviewee.

- Outline areas to be covered and major questions to be asked.
- Tell interviewee the purpose and proposed length of the interview.
- Meet in a comfortable setting.

During the Interview

- Help interviewee feel comfortable.
- Remain analytical and objective.
- Take notes.
- Ask open-ended questions to encourage ideas.
- Ask who, what, where, when, why, and how.
- Summarize what you learned.

After the Interview

- Thank the interviewee.
- Review and interpret data as soon as possible (while still fresh in your mind).

Multivoting

Multivoting is a structured series of votes by a "Quality First" team used to help reduce and prioritize a list containing a large number of items to a manageable few (usually three to five).

Multivoting may be used throughout the process after a team discusses the various items on a brainstorm list that is too lengthy for the items to be addressed at once.

Multivoting steps are as follows:

- First vote: Each person votes for as many items as desired, but only once per item. Circle the items receiving a relatively higher number of votes than the other items. (Example: For a team with 10 members, items receiving five or more votes are circled.)

- Second and subsequent votes: Each person votes the number of times equal to one-half the number of circled items. (Example: If six items received five or more votes during the first vote, then each person gets to vote three times during the second vote.)

- Continue multivoting until the list is reduced to three to five items, which can be further analyzed. Never multivote down to only one.

Nominal Group Technique (NGT)

(Nominal Group Technique NGT) is another method used for reaching consensus. It is a group decision-making process used when priority or rank order must be established. NGT is similar to brainstorming; however, it is a structured approach to generate ideas and survey the opinions of a small (10 to fifteen persons) group. NGT is very effective in producing many new ideas/solutions in a short time. It is structured to focus on problems, not people; to open lines of communication; to ensure participation; and to tolerate conflicting ideas. NGT helps build consensus and commitment to the final result.

The basic steps in using NGT are noted below:

- Present issue, instructions.

- Generate ideas during five to 10 minutes of quiet time (no discussion).

- Gather ideas round-robin, one idea at a time, written on a flip chart without discussing them.

- Process/clarify ideas by eliminating duplicates and combining like ideas. Discuss the ideas as a group, but only to clarify their meaning, not to argue about them.

- Set priorities silently.

- Vote to establish the priority or rank of each item.

- Tabulate votes.

- Develop an action plan.

FIGURE 10–17
Example of a Problem Selection Matrix

Problem Areas	Impact On Customer	Can Team Implement	Overall
Are those 3 or 4 remaining after the team has multivoted. Teams should only consider problem areas within their responsibility and control.	A rating based on the team present knowledge and judgement of the direct effect this problem area has on consumer satisfaction. Higher ratings are given to problem areas which have a more direct effect on customers.	A rating based on the team present knowledge and judgement of the difference between the present performance and what is needed to meet the customer's requirements. Higher ratings are given to problem areas with greater need to improve.	The product of impact on customers X need to improve. The problem area receiving the highest ranking should be investigated setting an indicator and actually measuring the present level and comparing it to the requirements. If there is a difference then the team should proceed. If not they should investigate the next.

Scale: 1 None   2 Somewhat   3 Moderate   4 Very   5 Extreme

Source: *AT&T Quality Improvement Process Guidebook,* Florida Power and Light.

Problem Selection Matrix

The problem selection matrix helps the "Quality First" team to select a problem area on which to begin gathering data. If a problem area can be shown to impact both the customer and business objectives, then the analysis should proceed.

Figure 10–17 is an example of a Problem Selection Matrix. The analysis team may come up with more categories to aid in the selection of a problem than are shown in the figure. For example, each column may be "rated" using a five-point scale and, thus, the problem areas are "rank ordered."

Problem Statement Matrix

A good problem statement is one of the keys to using the "Quality First" methodology. A well-stated problem is half solved. A good problem statement describes what is wrong in concrete terms, avoids hidden solutions, and meets the following requirements:

- Specific: State where and when the problem is occurring. It should locate the "pain" of the problem.

- Declarative: Clearly and definitively state the problem. It should not be a question or an incomplete statement.

- Quantified: State the difference between "what is" and "what should be." If the problem statement cannot be stated in quantified (measurable) terms, then it is not a good problem statement. While some problems may be more difficult to quantify than others, it is possible to quantify any problem. If it is not possible to quantify the problem, it is not possible to state the problem in measurable terms. The "problem" then should be reexamined.

- Should not imply cause or solution: Do not imply a solution or assume a cause. Any problem statement using "lack of" or "due to" (or similar phasing) is implying a cause or solution.

The problem statement matrix, shown in Figure 10–18, is a tool for "Quality First" teams to use in developing a good problem statement.

Quality Function Deployment (QFD)

Quality Function Deployment (QFD) is a conceptual map that provides the means for cross-functional planning and communications. It is a method for transforming customer wants and needs into quantitative terms.

Quality Function Deployment, developed in Japan, is a process for ensuring that quality is designed into products and services in an efficient and effective manner. QFD helps organizations design more competitive, higher-quality, lower-cost products more easily and quickly and is aimed primarily at the development of new products. It starts early in new product design efforts and translates customer requirements into design and product characteristics, communicating them in a

FIGURE 10–18
Example of a Problem Statement Matrix

Problem Statement (Who, What When, Where– But Not Why)	States the Effects, Not the Cause	Focuses on the Gap Between "What Is And "What Should Be"	Is It Measurable	Is It Specific (Avoids Broad Categories)	Is It Positive (Avoids "Lack Of" Statements)	Does It Focus on the Pain (How Things Are Affected)
# 1						
# 2						
# 3						

Source: *AT&T Quality Improvement Process Guidebook,* Florida Power and Light.

structured way to influence upstream design decisions and actions. Traditional design organizations have focused more on meeting specifications or technical requirements than on satisfying customer expectations. QFD links customer expectations to the technical considerations of the designer and manufacturer, and to the concept of value in a manner that connections and relationships can be understood and addressed.

Quality Function Deployment helps ensure quality products and processes by detecting and solving problems early. Downstream problems may occur and product quality may suffer when those who work on components and parts have little knowledge of customer requirements or the specifics of the final product and manufacturing processes. The QFD process forces management to analyze broad customer needs and expectations (such as ease of use or comfort) and relate them directly to product characteristics such as weight, strength, speed, and temperature. Those characteristics in turn are related to the processes involved in achieving the technical requirements. Specific techniques and tools are employed in the course of quality function deployment. One of the principal quality-function deployment tools is the "house of quality" matrix shown in Figure 10–19.

FIGURE 10–19
House of Quality Matrix

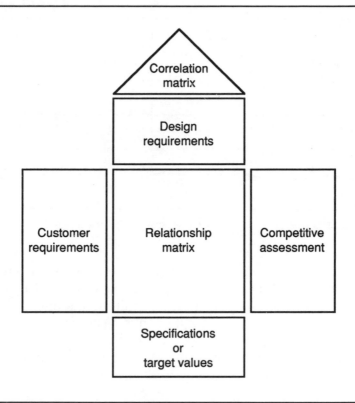

The matrix identifies specific customer-required characteristics, assigns priorities to them, and converts them to product attributes and design characteristics through cross-functional team activity. The matrix relates customer needs and expectations to specific product characteristics and links those characteristics to the product-related functional area processes. It communicates product-specific requirements, standards, and specifications in a coordinated and consistent way across all the functions that have responsibilities affecting the product. The generation and distribution of quality matrixes force early identification of conflicting objectives and potential bottlenecks. Early cross-functional communication should be centered on quality, resolving many potential problems before major investments of time and money have been made.

Products should be designed to meet customer wants and needs so that customers will buy products and services and continue to buy them. Marketing people, design engineers, manufacturing engineers, and procurement specialists work closely together from the time a product/service is first conceived to be able to meet customer requirements. Quality Function Deployment provides a framework within which the cross-functional teams can work.

To begin the QFD process, ask these questions:

- What do customers want (attributes)?

- Are all preferences equally important?

- Will responding to perceived needs yield a competitive advantage?

- What are the characteristics that match customers' attributes?

- How does each characteristic affect each customer attribute?

- How does one change affect other characteristics?

Solutions Selection Matrix

A solutions selection matrix is an illustration of factors affecting possible improvement actions or problem solutions. To help choose the best solution, the matrix could use headings similar to those in Figure 10–20 or you can develop your own headings. Be creative. Develop a matrix suitable to your situation. It is a proven technique for organizing information. It aids in comparing possible solutions and identifying voids in known information.

This matrix can help the "Quality First" team members to analyze the most significant factors affecting the solution. They can do this through analyzing the data collected during their investigation and choosing the factors of greatest significance. The team can also brainstorm to discover other, as yet hidden,

FIGURE 10–20
Example of Solutions Selection Matrix

Possible Solution	Dollar Cost to Implement	Are Involved Departments/ Areas Committed	Percentage of Problem Solved	Can Team Implement	Other
# 1					
# 2					
# 3					

Source: *AT&T Quality Improvement Process Guidebook* and Florida Power and Light.

factors. These should be reduced to a usable number of significant categories (usually five to seven) and entered in the matrix.

Then simply fill in the matrix according to data collected or data-based estimations. Remember: we want to speak with facts. Guesses and opinions are permissible but they must be educated ones—and immediately researched.

Statistical Process Control (SPC)

Statistical Process Control (SPC) is an effective tool for improving performance of any process. It helps identify problems quickly and accurately. It also provides quantifiable data for analysis, provides a reference baseline, and promotes participation and decision making by people doing the job.

Statistical Process Control is an excellent technique for determining the cause of variation based on a statistical analysis of the problem. SPC uses probability theory to control and improve processes.

Statistical Process Control is a major technique used to implement the "Quality First" methodology. Refer to one of the fundamental statistical publications noted in Appendix A—Executive Reading for substantial "how-to" information. The basic steps involved in SPC include:

- Identify problems or performance improvement areas. Identify common and special causes. Common causes are random in nature, often minor. Special causes result from an abnormality in the system that prevents the process from becoming stable.

- Do a cause-and-effect analysis.

- Collect data.

- Apply statistical techniques (may need a quality statistical specialist).

- Analyze variations.

- Take corrective action.

THE OPTIONS

This chapter has briefly described the "Quality First" tools and techniques that you may use to improve your quality. It has provided a basic vocabulary and delineation of the application options for each of the "Quality First" tools and techniques.

The past several chapters have described the principles, practices, tools, and techniques that can help you begin your "Quality First" improvement program. It's up to you to act now!

Chapter Eleven
Act Now!

"It is time for a new generation of leadership, to cope with new problems and new opportunities. For there is a new world to be won."

John Fitzgerald Kennedy
July 4, 1960

LEAD YOUR "QUALITY FIRST" TEAM

Whoever you are, it is often easy to fall into the trap of thinking that your company is too big to be affected by your individual actions. That perception is common and frustrating, and fortunately, it is a false one. Only through the collective efforts of their individual members do companies change; companies are incapable of changing themselves.

Whatever your position in your company, your efforts to perform a job and to improve that performance directly affect the influence you will have in the organization, the control you will have over your personal situation, and your ability to manage and lead. Combined with the efforts of others, your effectiveness directly influences the company's overall ability to meet its mission and ultimately affects our performance as a nation. Furthermore, how we perform today will also affect future generations.

"Quality First" is a means for improving personal effectiveness and performance and for aligning and focusing all individual quality efforts throughout your company. It provides a framework within which you may continuously improve everything you do and affect. It is a way of leveraging your individual effort and extending its effect and its importance throughout your organization and beyond.

MAKE THE DECISION TODAY

You have examined in this book the need to adopt the "Quality First" strategy to improve your competitiveness. A guide to the costs and benefits has been presented, showing that you can't afford *not* to act now in improving your level of quality performance. You have read about the different philosophies of quality improvement from Crosby, Deming, and Juran, and found that an amalgam of these principles and practices needs to be created to meet your specific needs. The Malcolm Baldrige National Quality Award has set the scene for self-assessment; and the companies that have won the award have described their experiences and the lessons they have learned in improving the quality of their products or services. A series of approximately 200 questions were raised for you to perform an armchair assessment of how your company/organization is doing in terms of quality. The "Quality First" methodology has laid out the basic planning and implementation steps needed for you to aggressively and continuously improve your operations. And the tools and techniques you and your staff need to use to understand your level of quality and show areas for improvement have also been presented.

Table 11–1 provides the basic "Quality First" action items you need to implement to improve your quality.

It is now up to you. Do it!

TABLE 11–1
"Quality First" Action Items

Planning

Step 1   Top Management Commitment to "Quality First"
- Bring executive team up to speed on quality principles.
  - Recognize importance of management commitment.
  - Review "Quality First" principles.
  - Review your competitive position.
  - Take team approach to quality improvement.

Step 2   Create a Vision and Philosophy
- Formulate your vision and philosophy to implement "Quality First," which will guide the company's quality efforts.
- Issue policy statement on the principles of quality.

Step 3   Establish Quality Council
- Include executives from headquarters office and field offices.
- Include the head of the company as an active member of the Quality Council.

Step 4   Identify Customer Needs
- Identify customers.
- Determine customer needs.
- Determine level of customer satisfaction.
- Translate needs into requirements.

Step 5   Develop Your Own "Quality First" Strategy
- Determine approach to enhance quality in the company.
- Incorporate "Quality First" activities into the strategic and business planning process.
- Establish a system for each unit to set quality improvement goals.
- Encourage early participation by the employee union in implementation of "Quality First."
- Use existing management systems, wherever appropriate, in implementing "Quality First."

Step 6   Select Organization to Implement "Quality First"
- Determine readiness of the organization.
- Decide on the scope of implementation (across the company or within a unit).

TABLE 11–1 *(continued)*

Step 7   Conduct Training Needs Analysis
- Analyze training needs of executives, managers, and employees.
- Determine what types of courses need to be developed (awareness, problem-solving, group dynamics, statistics, etc.) for each group.

Step 8   Determine Resources for Implementation
- Determine time frames and costs for developing and conducting training.
- Identify the sources of funding for training and award systems.
- Determine whether in-house staff can develop and conduct training.

Step 9   Conduct Training
- Identify individual(s) with quality expertise to help train staff.
- Identify suppliers of training.
- Develop and conduct training.

Step 10   Identify Performance Measures
- Ensure that organizational units develop standards for measuring whether products and services meet customer requirements.
- Adjust existing measurement and management systems to measure whether customer requirements are being met.

Implementation

Step 11   Implement "Quality First" Philosophy
- Implement continuous process-improvement principles.
- Implement systems for training, involving, rewarding, and recognizing employees.
- Implement strategies, goal-setting, and measurement of improvements in quality.
- Implement process analysis and structured problem-solving approaches.

TABLE 11–1 *(continued)*

Step 12   Benchmark Your Products and Services
    • Identify worldwide competitor products/services.
    • Assess who is the "best of class."
    • Develop product/services improvement goals.

Step 13   Implement Continuous Improvement Process
    • Set the stage for process improvement.
    • Select a process to improve.
    • Define the process.
    • Standardize the process.
    • Tighten the process.
    • Improve the process.
    • Assess improved performance.

Step 14   Monitor and Evaluate Results
    • Monitor the progress of teams on quality improvement
      projects.
    • Track quality improvements against goals.

Step 15   Recognize Success
    • Publicize successes.
    • Reward and recognize quality improvement.
    • Promote "Quality First" throughout the company.

Step 16   Adjust Your "Quality First" Process
    • Use feedback to modify and improve the process.
    • Expand to other segments of the company.

Step 17   Continue to Improve
    • Select new processes to improve.
    • Continue to improve all processes to remove defects.
    • Don't stop.

Appendix A
Executive Reading

INTRODUCTORY MATERIALS

Crosby, Philip B. *Quality is Free: The Art of Making Quality Certain*. New York: McGraw-Hill, 1979.

Ishikawa, Kaoru. *What Is Total Quality Control? The Japanese Way*. Englewood Cliffs, N.J.: Prentice-Hall, 1985.

Juran, Joseph M. *Juran on Leadership for Quality: An Executive Handbook*. New York: Free Press, 1989.

Scherkenbach, William W. *The Deming Route to Quality and Productivity*. Rockville, Md.: Mercury Press, 1988.

Walton, Mary. *Deming Management at Work*. New York: Putnam, 1990.

ADDITIONAL READINGS

Albrecht, Karl. *At America's Service: How Corporations Can Revolutionize the Way They Treat Their Customers*. Homewood, Ill.: Dow Jones-Irwin, 1988.

Albrecht, Karl, and Ron Zemke. *Service America: Doing Business in the New Economy*. Homewood, Ill.: Dow Jones-Irwin, 1985.

Aubrey II, Charles A., and Patricia K. Felkins. *Teamwork: Involving People in Quality and Productivity Improvement*. Milwaukee, Wis.: Quality Press, 1988.

Bennis, Warren, and Burt Nanus. *Leaders: The Strategies for Taking Charge*. New York: Harper & Row, 1985.

Crosby, Philip B. *Quality Without Tears: The Art of Hassle-Free Management*. New York: McGraw-Hill, 1984.

Deming, W. Edwards. *Out of the Crisis*. Cambridge, Mass.: MIT Center for Advanced Engineering Study, 1982.

Ealey, Lance A. *Quality By Design: Taguchi Methods and U.S. Industry*. Dearborn, Mich.: ASI Press, 1988.

Ernst & Young Quality Improvement Consulting Group. *Total Quality: An Executive's Guide for the 1990's*. Homewood, Ill.: The Dow Jones-Irwin/APICS Series in Production Management, 1990.

Garvin, David A. *Managing Quality: The Strategic and Competitive Edge*. New York: Free Press, 1988.

Harrington, H. James. *Excellence – The IBM Way*. Milwaukee, Wis.: Publisher's Quality Press, 1988.

Harrington, H. James. *The Improvement Process – How America's Leading Companies Improve Quality*. New York: McGraw-Hill, 1987.

Hickman, Craig R., and Michael A. Silva. *Creating Excellence*. New York: New American Library, 1984.

Imai, Masaki. *Kaizen: The Key to Japan's Competitive Success*. New York: Random House, 1986.

Ishikawa, Kaoru. *Guide to Quality Control*. White Plains, N.Y.: Kraus International Publications, 1982.

Juran, Joseph M. *Juran on Planning for Quality*. New York: Free Press, 1988.

Juran, Joseph M. *Juran's Quality Control Handbook*. New York: McGraw-Hill, 1988.

McGregor, Douglas. *The Human Side of Enterprise*. New York: McGraw-Hill, 1985.

Michalak, Donald F., and Edwin G. Yager. *Making the Training Process Work*. New York: Harper & Row, 1979.

Peters, Tom. *Thriving on Chaos*. New York: Alfred A. Knopf, 1987.

Scholtes, Peter R., et. al. *The Team Handbook – How to Use Teams to Improve Quality*. Madison, Wis.: Joiner Associates Inc., 1988.

Zemke, Ron, and Dick Schaaf. *The Service Edge: 101 Companies that Profit from Customer Care*. New York: New American Library, 1989.

Walton, Mary. *The Deming Management Method*. New York: Dodd, Mead, 1986.

Appendix B
Definitions

appraisal costs The costs associated with inspecting the product to ensure that it meets the customer's (either internal or external) needs and requirements.

best of class When overall performance, in terms of effectiveness, efficiency, and adaptability, is superior to all comparables.

brainstorming A technique used by a group of people for thought generation. The aim is to elicit as many ideas as possible within a given time frame.

cause An established reason for the existence of a defect.

common cause A source of variation in the process output that is inherent to the process and will affect all the individual results or values of process output.

control The set of activities employed to detect and correct deviation in order to maintain or restore a desired state. A historically oriented approach to quality management.

correction The totality of actions to minimize or remove variations and their causes.

cost of quality The sum of the cost of prevention, appraisal, and failure. The key financial measurement tool that ties process control and process optimization into a total process-management effort. It can be used both as an indicator and a signal for variation (more often, for patterns of variation), as well as a measure of productivity and efficiency.

corrective action   The implementation of effective solutions that result in the elimination of identified product, service, and process problems.

cross-functional teams   Teams similar to quality teams but whose members are from several work units that interface with one another. These teams are particularly useful when work units are dependent upon one another for materials, information, etc.

culture   A prevailing pattern of activities, interactions, norms, sentiments, beliefs, attitudes, values, and products in an organization.

customer   The recipient or beneficiary of the outputs of your work efforts or the purchaser of your products and services. May be either internal or external to the organization, and must be satisfied with the output of your work efforts.

data   Information or a set of facts presented in descriptive form. There are two basic kinds of data: measured (also known as variable data) and counted (also known as attribute data).

defect   Any state of nonconformance to requirements.

Deming Prize   In 1950, W. Edwards Deming was invited to Japan by the Union of Japanese Scientists and Engineers (JUSE) to lecture on the applicability of using quality control in manufacturing companies. The impact of Deming's teaching was widespread and swift to take root. In 1951, JUSE instituted the Deming Prize to honor Deming for his friendship and achievements in industrial quality control. Today, Japanese companies wishing to improve the level of quality within their organization compete for the Deming Prize, not only to achieve the honor and prestige of winning, but also for the improvements that come from implementing his quality principles.

effectiveness   How closely an organization's output meets its goal and/or meets the customer's requirement.

efficiency   Production of required output at a perceived minimum cost. It is measured by the ratio of the quantity of resources expected or planned to be consumed in meeting customer requirements to the resources actually consumed.

external failure costs   The costs incurred when an external customer receives a defective product.

fishbone diagrams   A diagram that depicts the characteristics of a problem or process and the factors or root causes that contribute to them.

force field analysis A technique involving the identification of forces "for" and "against" a certain course of action. The nominal group technique could be used in conjunction with force field analysis. The group might prioritize the forces for and against by assessing their magnitude and probability of occurrence. The group might then develop an action plan to minimize the forces against and maximize the forces for.

frequency distribution Of a discrete variable is the count of the number of occurrences of individual values over a given range.

Of a continuous variable is the count of cases that lie between certain predetermined limits over the range of values the variable may assume.

functional administrative control technique A tool designed to improve performance through a process combining time management and value engineering. The process involves breaking activities down into functions and establishing action teams to target and solve problems in each function.

functional organization An organization responsible for one of the major organizational functions such as marketing, sales, design, manufacturing, and distribution.

gainsharing A reward system that shares productivity gains between owners and employees. Gainsharing is generally used to provide incentive for group efforts toward improvement.

goal A statement of attainment/achievement that one proposes to accomplish or attain with an implication of sustained effort and energy directed to it over a long term.

guideline A suggested practice that is not mandatory in programs intended to comply with a standard.

hypothesis An assertion made about the value of some parameter of a population.

input Materials, energy, or information required to complete the activities necessary to produce a specified output (work product).

internal failure costs The costs generated by defects found within the enterprise prior to the product reaching the external customer.

mean time between failures (MTBF) The average time between successive failures of a given product.

measurement   The act or process of measuring to compare results to requirements. A quantitative estimate of performance.

need   A lack of something requisite, desired, or useful; a condition requiring provision or relief. Usually expressed by users or customers.

nominal group technique   A tool for idea generation, problem solving, mission, and key result area definition, performance measure definition, goals/objectives definition.

normative performance measurement technique   Incorporates structured group processes so that work groups can design measurement systems suited for their own needs. This approach considers behavioral consequences of measurement to foster acceptance of measurement effort.

objective   A statement of the desired result to be achieved within a specified time. By definition, an objective always has an associated schedule.

output   The specified end result. Required by the recipient.

outputs   Materials or information provided to others (internal or external customers).

Pareto charts   Are used to classify problems or causes by priority. It helps highlight the vital few as opposed to the trivial many. It also helps to identify which cause or problem is the most significant.

performance   A term used both as an attribute of the work product itself and as a general process characteristic. The broad performance characteristics that are of interest to management are quality (effectiveness), cost (efficiency), and schedule. Performance is the highly effective common measurement that links the quality of the work product to efficiency and productivity.

plan   A specified course of action designed to attain a stated objective.

policy   A statement of principles and beliefs, or a settled course, adopted to guide the overall management of affairs in support of a stated aim or goal. It is mostly related to fundamental conduct and usually defines a general framework within which other business and management actions are carried out.

population   A large collection of items (product observations, data) about certain characteristics of which conclusions and decisions are to be made for purposes of process assessment and quality improvement.

prevention   A future-oriented approach to quality management that achieves quality improvement through curative action on the process.

prevention costs The costs associated with actions taken to plan the product or process to ensure that defects do not occur.

problem A question or situation proposed for solution. The result of not conforming to requirements, which can create a potential task resulting from the existence of defects.

process A system in operation to produce an output of higher value than that of the sum of its inputs. A process is also defined as the logical organization of people, materials, energy, equipment, and procedures into work activities designed to produce a specified end result (work product).

process capability Long-term performance level after the process has been brought under control.

process control The set of activities employed to detect and remove special causes of variation in order to maintain or restore stability (statistical control).

process flow analysis A technique for identification and analysis of key processes, and for areas and methods of possible improvement. It is particularly useful for roadblock removal.

process improvement The set of activities employed to detect and remove common causes of variation in order to improve process capability. Process improvement leads to quality improvement.

process management Management approach comprising quality management and process optimization.

process optimization The major aspect of process management that concerns itself with the efficiency and productivity of the process; that is, with economic factors.

process owner A designated person within the process, who has authority to manage the process and responsibility for its overall performance.

process performance A measure of how effectively and efficiently a process satisfies customer requirements.

process review An objective assessment of how well the methodology has been applied to your process. Emphasizes the potential for long-term process results rather than the actual results achieved.

productivity Ratio of outputs produced (or service transactions) to inputs required for production/completion. Productivity is an expected outcome of quality and a necessary companion to improving service.

quality The extent to which products and services produced conform to customer requirements. Customers can be internal as well as external to the organizational system (e.g., products or services may flow to the person at the next desk or work area rather than to people outside of the immediate organization). The Federal Quality Institute defines quality as meeting the customer requirements the first time and every time. The Department of Defense (DoD) defines quality as conformance to a set of customer requirements that, if met, result in a product that is fit for its intended use.

quality circles A group of workers and their supervisors who voluntarily meet to identify and solve job-related problems. Structured processes are used by the group to accomplish their task.

quality function deployment (QFD) A disciplined approach to solving quality problems before the design phase of a product. The foundation of QFD is the belief that products should be designed to reflect customer desires; therefore, marketers, design engineers, and manufacturing personnel must work closely together from the beginning to ensure a successful product. The approach involves finding out what features are important to customers, ranking them in importance, identifying conflicts, and translating them into engineering specifications.

quality of working life The extent to which the organizational culture provides employees with information, knowledge, authority, and rewards to enable them to perform safely and effectively, be compensated equitably, and maintain a sense of human dignity.

quality teams Also referred to as Performance Action Teams or Quality Improvement Teams. They might be composed of volunteers who meet regularly to review progress toward goal attainment, plan for changes, decide upon corrective actions, etc. Members are usually from the same work unit.

range The difference between the maximum and the minimum value of data in a sample.

reliability The probability that a product entity will perform its specified function under specified conditions, without failure, for a specified period of time.

requirement A formal statement of a need, and the expected manner in which it is to be met.

requirements What is expected in providing a product or service. The "it" in "do it right the first time." Specific and measurable customer needs with an associated performance standard.

roadblock identification analysis A tool that focuses upon identifying roadblocks to performance improvement and/or problems that are causing the group to be less productive than it could be. This tool utilizes the nominal group technique to identify and prioritize performance roadblocks. Action teams are formed to analyze barriers and develop proposals to remove roadblocks. The proposals are implemented, tracked, and evaluated.

root cause analysis The bottom line of a problem. Often, problems present themselves only as symptoms. Symptoms do not explain problems, they point to them. A root cause is the reason for the problem or symptom. Root cause analysis, then, is a method used to identify potential root causes of problems, narrow those down to the most significant causes, and analyze them using other "Quality First" tools.

sample A finite number of items taken from a population.

Scanlon committees Committees comprised of managers, supervisors, and employees who work together to implement a philosophy of management/labor cooperation that is believed to enhance productivity. There are a number of principles and techniques involved, with employee participation being a major component.

simulation The technique of observing and manipulating an artificial mechanism (model) that represents a real world process that, for technical or economical reasons, is not suitable or available for direct experimentation.

special cause A source of variation in the process output that is unpredictable, unstable, or intermittent. Also called assignable cause.

specification A document containing a detailed description or enumeration of particulars. Formal description of a work product and the intended manner of providing it (the provider's view of the work product).

standard deviation A parameter describing the spread of the process output, denoted by the Greek letter sigma, σ. The positive square root of the variance.

statistic   Any parameter that can be determined on the basis of the quantitative characteristics of a sample.

A descriptive statistic is a computed measure of some property of a set of values, making possible a definitive statement about the meaning of the collected data.

An inferential statistic indicates the confidence that can be placed in any statement regarding its expected accuracy, the range of its applicability, and the probability of its being true. Consequently, decisions can be based on inferential statistics.

statistics   The branch of applied mathematics that describes and analyzes empirical observations for the purpose of predicting certain events in order to make decisions in the face of uncertainty. Statistics, in turn, are based on the theory of probability. The two together provide the abstraction for the mathematical model underlying the study of problems involving uncertainty.

statistical control   The status of a process from which all special causes of variation have been removed and only common causes remain. Such a process is also said to be stable.

statistical estimation   The analysis of a sample parameter in order to predict the values of the corresponding population parameter.

statistical methods   The application of the theory of probability to problems of variation. There are two groups of statistical methods.

Basic statistical methods are relatively simple problem-solving tools and techniques, such as control charts, capability analysis, data summarization and analysis, and statistical inference.

Advanced statistical methods are more sophisticated specialized techniques of statistical analysis, such as the design of experiments, regression and correlation analysis, and the analyses of variance.

statistical process control   A disciplined way of identifying and solving problems in order to improve performance. It involves use of fishbone diagrams to identify causes and effects of problems. Data are then collected and organized in various ways (graphs, fishbone diagrams, Pareto charts, and/or histograms) to further examine problems. The data may be tracked over time (control charts) to determine variation in the process. The process is then changed in some way and new data are collected and analyzed to determine whether the process has been improved.

strategy   A broad course of action, chosen from a number of alternatives, to accomplish a stated goal in the face of uncertainty.

subprocesses   The internal processes that make up a process.

suppliers   Individuals, organizations, or firms that provide inputs to you. Suppliers can be internal or external to a company, firm, or organization.

team building   A process of developing and maintaining a group of people who are working toward a common goal. Team building usually focuses on one or more of the following objectives:

(1) clarifying role expectations and obligations of team members, (2) improving superior-subordinate or peer relationships, (3) improving problem solving, decision making, resource utilization, or planning activities, (4) reducing conflict, and (5) improving organizational climate.

timeliness   The promptness with which quality products and services are delivered, relative to customer expectations.

transactional analysis   A process that helps people change to be more effective on the job and can also help organizations to change. The process involves several exercises that help identify organizational scripts and games that people may be playing. The results help point the way toward change.

variable   A data item that takes on values within some range with a certain frequency or pattern. Variables may be discrete, that is, limited in value to integer quantities (for example, the number of bolts produced in a manufacturing process). Discrete variables relate to attribute data. Variables may also be continuous, that is, measured to any desired degree of accuracy (for example, the diameter of a shaft). Continuous variables relate to variables data.

variance   In quality management terminology, any nonconformance to specifications. In statistics, it is the square of the standard deviation.

Appendix C
Information Resources

NATIONAL ASSOCIATIONS AND CENTERS

American Production and Inventory Control Society
500 W. Annandale Road
Falls Church, VA 22046
(703) 237-8344

Focus on just-in-time, capacity management, materials requirements, production activity, and master planning. Annual conference, seminars/workshops, exhibitions, *Production Inventory Management Journal*, technical publications, professional certification, local chapters.

Quality and Productivity Management Association
300 Martingale Road
Schaumburg, IL 60173
(708) 619-2909

Network of North American quality and productivity coordinators, operating managers, and staff managers. Conferences, workshops, journal, newsletter, resources guide, local chapters.

American Productivity & Quality Center
123 North Post Oak Lane
Houston, TX 77024
(713) 681-4020

Educational advisory services to organizations in the private and public sectors. Courses, research publications, case studies, the *Letter* newsletter, resource guide, library, consulting.

American Society for Quality Control
310 West Wisconsin Avenue
Milwaukee, WI 53203
(414) 272-8575
The nation's largest professional society that is dedicated to the advancement of quality. Conferences, educational courses, seminars, *The Quality Review* magazine, journal, book service, professional certification, technical divisions and committees, local chapters.

American Society for Training and Development
1630 Duke Street
Alexandria, VA 22313
(703) 683-8100
Leader in the development of training programs.

Association for Quality and Participation
801-B West 8th Street
Suite 501
Cincinnati, OH 45023
(513) 381-1959
Focus on quality circles, self-managing teams, union-management committees, sociotechnical analysis, and other aspects of employee involvement. Conferences, library and research service, *Quality and Participation* journal, newsletter, resource guide, local chapters.

Work in America Institute
700 White Plains Road
Scarsdale, NY 10583
(914) 472-9600
Research and member advisory services focusing on productivity and quality through employee involvement, labor-management relations, and quality of working life. Member forum and seminars, site visits, policy studies, *Work in America* newsletter, library, research service, technical publications, speakers, and consultants bureau.

REGIONAL AND UNIVERSITY-BASED CENTERS

Linked through the National Productivity Network, the following centers provide a variety of productivity related services, including technical assistance, planning studies, technology transfer, continuing education, productivity audits, management development, contractual assistance, publications, seminars/workshops, and research and development.

Community Quality Coalition
c/o Transformation of America Industry Project
Jackson Community College
2111 Emmons Road
Jackson, MI 49201
(517) 789-1627

Georgia Productivity Center
Georgia Institute of Technology
219 O'Keeffe Building
Atlanta, GA 30332
(404) 894-6101

Manufacturing Productivity Center
10 West 35th Street
Chicago, IL 60616
(312) 567-4800

Center for Quality and Productivity
University of Maryland
College Park, MD 20742-7215
(301) 403-4535

Center for the Productive Use of Technology
George Mason University
Metro Campus
3401 North Fairfax, #322
Arlington, VA 22201
(703) 841-2675

Pennsylvania Technical Assistance Program (PENNTAP)
Pennsylvania State University
University Park, PA 16802
(814) 865-0427

University of Wisconsin-Madison
Center for Quality and Productivity Improvement
620 Walnut Street
Madison, WI 53705
(608) 263-2520

OTHER ORGANIZATIONAL RESOURCES

American Center for the Quality of Work Life
37 Tip Top Way
Berkeley Heights, NJ 07922
(201) 464-4609

Information, training, and consulting focused on creating and implementing organizational change and renewal.

American Supplier Institute
6 Parklane Boulevard, Suite 411
Dearborn, MI 48126
(313) 336-8877

Focus on Taguchi methods, quality function deployment, total quality management. Training, consulting, special conferences, books, videotapes, journal.

Canadian Supplier Institute
Skyline Complex
644 Dixon Road
Rexdale, Ontario M9W 1J4
(416) 235-1777

Focus on Taguchi methods, quality function deployment, total quality management. Training, consulting, books and videotapes, special conferences.

QCI International
P.O. Box 1503
Red Bluff, CA 96080
(916) 527-6970

Focus on employee involvement, total quality, and statistical process control. Seminars, in-house training, books, videotapes, *Quality Digest* magazine.

QUALITY CONSULTANTS

American Productivity & Quality Center
123 North Post Oak Lane
Houston, TX 77024
Contact: Jackie Comola
(713) 681-4020

American Supplier Institute
15041 Commerce Drive, South
Dearborn, MI 48126
Contact: John McHugh
(313) 336-8877

Coopers & Lybrand
1525 Wilson Boulevard, Suite 800
Arlington, VA 22209
Contact: Ian Littman
(703) 875-2102

Philip Crosby Associates, Inc.
807 West Morse Boulevard
P.O. Box 2369
Winter Park, FL 32790
(305) 645-1733

Dr. W. Edwards Deming
4924 Butterworth Place
Washington, DC 20016
(202) 363-8552

Ernst & Young
1225 Connecticut Avenue Northwest
Washington, DC 20036
Contact: Renee Jakubiak
(202) 862-6000

General Systems Company, Inc.
Berkshire Common, South Street
Pittsfield, MA 01201
Contact: Armand Fiegenbaum
(413) 499-2880

Goal/QPC
13 Branch Street
Methuen, MA 01844
Contact: Stan Marsh
(508) 685-3900

IIT Research Institute
Beeches Technical Campus
Route 26 North
Rome, NY 13440-8200
Contact: Steve Flint
(315) 337-0900

Juran Institute, Inc.
88 Danbury Road
Wilton, CT 06897
(203) 834-1700

Technology Research Corporation
5716 Jonathan Mitchell Road
Fairfax Station, VA 22039
(703) 451-8830 and (703) 250-5136
Contact: V. Daniel Hunt

FEDERAL GOVERNMENT

Federal Quality Institute
441 F Street Northwest
Washington, DC 20001
Contacts: John Franke, Director
(202) 376-3747
Jeff Manthos, Information Network Office
(202) 376-3753

The Federal Quality Institute (FQI) provides a start-up service in Total Quality Management for top-level federal government management teams. The FQI serves as a government-wide focal point for information about Total Quality Management through the FQI Information Network, which lends to the "federal" sector materials such as videotapes, books, and case studies at no cost.

Navy Personnel Research and Development Center
Quality Support Center
San Diego, CA 92152-6800
(619) 553-7956   (619) 553-7956 (AV)

U.S. Army Management Engineering College
Rock Island, IL 61299-7040
(309) 782-0470   (309) 793-0470 (AV)

QUALITY AWARDS

Deming Prize
Information concerning the Deming Prize application can be
obtained by contacting:
Junji Noguchi
Executive Director
Union of Japanese Scientists and Engineers
5-10-11 Sendagaya
Shibuya-Ku
Tokyo 151, Japan
FAX: 9-011-813-225-1813

Malcolm Baldrige National Quality Award
Malcolm Baldrige National Quality Award
National Institute of Standards and Technology
Route 270 and Quince Orchard Road
Administration Building, Room A537
Gaithersburg, MD 20899
(301) 975-2036
FAX: (301) 948-3716

MAGAZINES AND NEWSLETTERS

PRIDE Publications
P.O. Box 695
Arlington Heights, IL 60004
(708) 398-0430

Commitment-Plus newsletter, monthly, $95/yr.

American Productivity & Quality Center
123 North Post Oak Lane
Houston, TX 77024
(713) 681-4020

The **Letter** newsletter, monthly, $125/yr.

Manufacturing Productivity Center, IIT Center
10 West 35th Street
Chicago, IL 60616
(312) 567-4808

Manufacturing Competitiveness Frontiers magazine, monthly, $100/yr.

Society of Manufacturing Engineers
P.O. Box 930
Dearborn, MI 48121
(313) 271-1500

Manufacturing Engineering magazine, monthly, $60/yr.

American Production and Inventory Control Society
500 West Annandale Road
Falls Church, VA 22046
(703) 237-8344

Production Inventory Management Journal, quarterly, $110/yr.

Productivity, Inc.
101 Merritt 7
Norwalk, CT 06851
(203) 846-3777

Productivity newsletter, monthly, $167/yr.

Hitchcock Publishing Co.
191 South Gary Avenue
Carol Stream, IL 60188
(708) 665-1000

Quality magazine, monthly, $65/yr.

QCI International
P.O. Box 882
Red Bluff, CA 96080

Quality Digest magazine, monthly, $75/yr.

Association for Quality and Participation
801-B West 8th Street
Cincinnati, OH 45023
(513) 381-1959

Quality and Participation journal, quarterly, $35/yr.

American Society for Quality Control (ASQC)
310 West Wisconsin Avenue
Milwaukee, WI 53203
(414) 272-8575

Quality Progress, 12 issues/$40, monthly publication

American Society for Quality Control
310 West Wisconsin Avenue
Milwaukee, WI 53203
(414) 272-8575

Journal of Quality Technology, 12 issues/$13, monthly publication

American Society for Quality Control
310 West Wisconsin Avenue
Milwaukee, WI 53203
(414) 272-8575

The Quality Review magazine, quarterly, $36/yr.

Buraff Publications
2445 M Street Northwest, Suite 275
Washington, DC 20037
(202) 452-7889

Work in America newsletter, monthly, $247/yr.

VIDEOTAPES

The Deming Library (16 videotapes). Contact Joyce Leon, at Films, Inc., 5547 Ravenswood Avenue, Chicago, Illinois 60640-1199, (800) 323-4222, extension 381. No preview fee for government agencies. Videotapes may be purchased for $595 each, two or more at $495 each, or the complete set of 16 volumes for $7,920. The Deming Library is a video training seminar that covers all aspects of W. Edwards Deming's philosophy.

> Volume 1: The New Economic Age (33 minutes)
>
> Volume 2: The 14 Points (40 minutes, two parts)
>
> Volume 3: Corporate Leadership (25 minutes)
>
> Volume 4: Adoption of the New Philosophy (21 minutes)
>
> Volume 5: Communication of the New Philosophy (22 minutes)
>
> Volume 6: Application of the New Philosophy (24 minutes)

Britannica Films
780 Lapeer Road
Lake Orion, MI 48035
(800) 554-6970
(313) 693-4232

The Change Masters and Change Master Companies, with Rosabeth Moss Kanter

AMA Film/Video
9 Galen Street
Watertown, MA 02172
(800) 225-3215
(617) 926-4600

Customer Service, Innovation, and Productivity Through People, with Robert Waterman

    If Japan Can, Why Can't We? 77 minutes, NBC White Paper

    Japan vs. U.S.A.—High Tech Shootout, 52 minutes, Films Incorporated for NBC Reports

    Journey to the Future, Joel Arthur Barker, Chart House Learning Corp.

    Juran On Quality Improvement, 16-tape series including workbook and leader's manual, and visual aids, Juran Institute

    Juran On Quality Planning, 15-tape series including workbook, leader's manual, and visual aids, Juran Institute

    Managing the Journey, Ken Blanchard, Films Inc.

    Nashua Corporation Seminar—William Conway, 160 minutes, Nashua Corp. (Process Control)

    On the Line, 37 minutes, King Arthur Productions for National Semiconductor (Productivity Improvement)

    The Power of Vision, Joel Arthur Barker, Chart House Learning Corp.

    Quality is Free, 23 minutes, Phil Crosby

    Type Z: An Alternative Management Style, 105 minutes (film), Professor William Ouchi

Index